DIMENSION
A Reader of German Literature Since 1968

Edited by
A. Leslie Willson

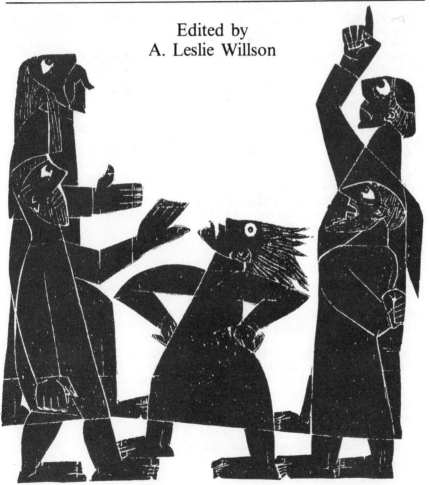

CONTINUUM · NEW YORK

ACKNOWLEDGMENTS

Many selections in this volume appeared in print in German for the first time in various issues of DIMENSION. The editor wishes to express his deep appreciation to those authors represented here who sent poems, prose, and radio plays for first-time publication in DIMENSION. The following acknowledgments refer to permissions for publication of texts that appeared previously in print in German; thanks for permission for reprinting are due to:

Akzente, and its editor Hans Bender, for Horst Bienek, "Die Zeit danach," *Akzente* 4 (1968);

Deutsche Verlags-Anstalt for W.E. Richartz, "The Sex Attractant," which appeared in *Jahresring 1974/75,* © 1974;

Eremiten-Presse for Guido Bachmann, *Wannsee,* © 1967; selections from Dieter Fringeli, *Neue Gedichte,* © 1975; Herbert Heckmann, *Ubuville—Die Stadt des großen Ei's,* © 1973; Christoph Meckel, *Hotel für Schlafwandler,* © 1958, 1971; Christa Reinig, selections from *Schwalbe von Olevano,* © 1969; Gabriele Wohmann, for "Slaughter" from *Sonntag bei den Kreisands,* © 1970;

Hanser Verlag for Wolf Wondratschek, "German Lesson" from *Früher begann der Tag mit einer Schußwunde,* © 1969;

Luchterhand Verlag for Helmut Heißenbüttel, "bremen whereyou" from *Das Textbuch,* © 1970; Ernst Jandl, "Biography" from *dingfest,* © 1973; Hugo Loetscher, "The Discovery of Switzerland" from *Der Immune,* © 1975; Wolfgang Weyrauch, "Sign Language" from *Geschichten zum Weitererzählen,* © 1969;

Friedrich Middlehauve Verlag for Hilde Domin, "Report from an Island" from *Dichter erzählen Kindern,* ed. Gertraude Middlehauve, © 1966;

Rowohlt Verlag for Rolf Dieter Brinkmann, "A Skunk" from *Westwärts 1 & 2,* © 1975; Hubert Fichte, excerpts from *Detlevs Imitationen "Grünspan",* © 1971;

Suhrkamp Verlag for H.C. Artmann, "landscapes," selections from *ein lilienweißer brief aus lincolnshire,* © 1969; Thomas Bernhard, "Is It a Comedy? Is It a Tragedy" from *Prosa,* © 1967; Max Frisch, "Fragment from a Story" from *Gesammelte Werke in zeitlicher Folge,* volume 6, © 1976; Wolfgang Hildesheimer, "I Find My Way" from *Lieblose Legenden,* © 1962;

Verlag der Nation for excerpts from Eberhard Hilscher, *Der Morgenstern,* © 1976; and

Klaus Wagenbach for Martin Walser, "Attempt to Understand a Feeling" from *Tintenfisch 8,* © 1975.

THE CONTINUUM PUBLISHING COMPANY
575 Lexington Avenue, New York, NY 10022.

Library of Congress Cataloging in Publication Data

Main entry under title: Dimension.
    1. German literature—20th century—Translations into English.   2. English literature—Translations from German.   I. Willson, Amos Leslie, 1923–
PT1113.D48   830'.8'00914   80-27708   ISBN 0-8264-0042-6 (pbk.)

CONTENTS

Foreword	A. LESLIE WILLSON	V
landscapes	H. C. ARTMANN	1
The Time Afterwards	HORST BIENEK	7
Grasping the Present	GERALD BISINGER	9
Armstrong, Aldrin, Collins	VOLKER BRAUN	11
Two Poems	ROLF DIETER BRINKMANN	14
Serifos	ERICH FITZBAUER	17
You	KARLHANS FRANK	19
New Poems	DIETER FRINGELI	20
The Gazelle and Other Poems	RICHARD GERLACH	22
Priapus	PETER HACKS	25
bremen whereyou	HELMUT HEISSENBÜTTEL	26
Two Poems	DIETER HOFFMANN	28
biography	ERNST JANDL	30
Stefan Lochner Painted Me	HERMANN KESTEN	32
Top Secret	HANS KROLICZAK	36
Twofold Monologue—Short-Circuited	GÜNTER KUNERT	38
Curriculum Vitae	ONDRA LYSOHORSKY	39
Hotel for Sleepwalkers	CHRISTOPH MECKEL	40
Laugarvatn Autumn and Other Poems	HELGA M. NOVAK	41
Were We Not What We Are . . .	FRITZ VON OPEL	45
Two Poems	ARNO REINFRANK	47
The Tree That Learned to Talk and Other Poems	CHRISTA REINIG	50
Buskins	RUDOLF HELMUT RESCHKE	52
Words Not Extinguished	JÜRGEN THEOBALDY	54
Who Can Say More?	FRED VIEBAHN	56
Attempt to Understand a Feeling	MARTIN WALSER	59
Flight 690 PAA	GABRIELE WOHMANN	63
My Language and I	ILSE AICHINGER	66
Wannsee	GUIDO BACHMANN	69
End of the Line	JUREK BECKER	77

Going Begging   HANS BENDER   81
Is It a Comedy? Is It a Tragedy?   THOMAS BERNHARD   85
Report from an Island   HILDE DOMIN   91
The Engagement   GISELA ELSNER   93
The Woman Behind   WOLFGANG H. FLEISCHER   105
Mishap   KARLHANS FRANK   108
Comments on a Cityscape   WALTER HELMUT FRITZ   110
Visit to an Exhibition   MARTIN GREGOR-DELLIN   116
*Ubu*ville—The City of the Grand Egg   HERBERT HECKMANN   120
Mozart's Letters   STEPHAN HERMLIN   136
I Find My Way   WOLFGANG HILDESHEIMER   140
The Blindfold   SIEGFRIED LENZ   146
The Discovery of Switzerland   HUGO LOETSCHER   151
Blekpoint   MAX MAETZ   161
in a rundown neighborhood   FRIEDERIKE MAYRÖCKER   165
Sojourns in Bormio   ANGELIKA MECHTEL   168
Struggle   LUTZ RATHENOW   177
The Sex Attractant   W.E. RICHARTZ   180
Grauff   GEROLD SPÄTH   186
Sign Language   WOLFGANG WEYRAUCH   191
Slaughter   GABRIELE WOHMANN   195
Change of Perspective   CHRISTA WOLF   198
German Lesson   WOLF WONDRATSCHEK   209
Detlev   HUBERT FICHTE   212
Fragment from a Story   MAX FRISCH   225
The Morning Star   EBERHARD HILSCHER   235
A Part of New York   UWE JOHNSON   247
The Sixth Day   KARLHANS FRANK   261
Affair of Honor   GÜNTER KUNERT   273
Afterword   HANS BENDER   300
Authors and Translators   303

FOREWORD

DIMENSION, A Reader of German Literature since 1968 IS THE RESULT OF the intense involvement of the editor with contemporary German writing since the late sixties, as observer, critic, and translator. Since 1967, the year before the premier issue of DIMENSION, I corresponded with an ever-increasing number of German, Austrian, and Swiss writers, editors, and publishers. Then in the spring of 1979, with a semester free from academic duties at The University of Texas at Austin for the first time in sixteen years, I made a three-month journey to Germany (East and West), Austria, and Switzerland. Prior to my departure from Texas I arranged visits with over seventy of the more than 300 authors I "knew." Many I had met personally in Texas, where they were either visiting lecturers in the Department of Germanic Languages or spent a few days in Austin on a reading tour of America.

Equipped with a Eurail pass, I set off at the end of January 1979, having been fortunate enough to rent a tiny studio apartment in the heart of Frankfurt am Main, courtesy of Burgel Zeeh, the efficient secretary of the ebullient Suhrkamp publisher Siegfried Unseld, and a helpful counterpart in the Deutsche Bank. I did *not* take along a tape recorder, for I had no intention of conducting interviews; I *did* take an instant camera, which proved to be an object of curiosity and elicited unfailing cooperation from authors. I managed to collect a gallery of authors in unguarded but collaborative moments. The advantage of the immediate picture was that the author could decide on the spot whether to let the photograph leave the precinct of studio, office, or home. Gisela Elsner, Siegfried Lenz, Wolf Wondratschek ("I don't like that one"), Christoph Meckel, and a number of others required more than one shot. I caught Jurek Becker in a small Berlin restaurant looking idiotic with his tongue protruding from his lips, as he demonstrated the pronunciation of the recalcitrant English *th*.

I arranged my travels so that I could spend a week or ten days in each of several metropolitan centers, visiting authors who lived in the vicinity. And I was visiting—getting acquainted—with authors who often were for me unknown quantities as human beings, names on title pages and signatures on letters. Since I visited each of them—with few exceptions—in their homes, they were relaxed and often dismayingly frank because they were on familiar territory.

None will I forget, but some especially impressed me with remarks, actions, or surroundings. The friendliness and consideration of Siegfried Lenz—the gracious hospitality I was extended in his home by him and his wife—was notable. I traveled from Zurich to Berzona at the invitation of Max Frisch, who met me in Locarno and then, in a sleek black Jaguar, drove honking up the winding mountain road to his old farmhouse, which to my amazement I saw was roofed with enormous blocks of granite.

In a Greek restaurant in Vienna I admired the solemn and black-haired beauty of Friederike Mayröcker and the incessant wit of Ernst Jandl. With Günter and Marianne Kunert and their seven fat cats—who have a doglike devotion to their master—I dined from a huge cauldron of stew in Berlin-Buch, long before their wrenching move to Itzehoe near Hamburg. After a filling meal with her in a restaurant in Darmstadt, I caught Gabriele Wohmann on film with a warm smile in her toy-cluttered, clipping-strewn home. I greeted Helmut Heissenbüttel on the occasion of the twenty-fifth anniversary of the literary magazine *Akzente* in Cologne.

Walking along a sidewalk in Berlin with Christoph Meckel I watched in fascination when he interrupted a game of hopscotch played by two small boys and, with their chalk, drew a sketch of a cat to their excited giggles, a sketch that washed away in the rainfall that night. In Munich I located Wolf Wondratschek's hotel hideaway, where he was writing nonstop on a filmplay revision, and we went out to dinner just around the corner from his temporarily abandoned apartment.

South of Frankfurt W.E. Richartz proudly displayed his many framed pictures and small-edition books at dinner; he was bright and friendly and betrayed nothing of the melancholy that would bring him to take his own life just a year later. I chatted with Dieter Hoffman at a meeting of the Mainz Akademie and photographed him as he sat regally in an appropriate chair. Hans Bender in his book-lined apartment in Cologne was a frequent source of comraderie and easy enjoyment, even though the phone rang every five minutes with a call from one or another author.

In the three months of my visit I traveled by plane, taxi, bus, streetcar, subway, and train, collecting impressions and photographs. I brought back to Texas and to the DIMENSION office mementos in my mind: Christa Reinig sitting before a TV set covered with miniature lions; Angelika Mechtel in the livingroom-stable of her old farmhouse near Munich; the renovation shambles of the Literary Colloquium Berlin on the Wannsee, with the shade of Heinrich von Kleist in the dusky evening outside and a friendly guided tour by Gerald Bisinger on the inside; confidences about Wagner and Thomas Mann by Martin Gregor-Dellin in Munich; the graphics-filled apartment of Erich Fitzbauer in Perchtoldsdorf just south of Vienna; the owl-like gaze and the youth of Wolfgang Weyrauch, who died much too young at seventy-three in the fall of 1980. I remember the irrepressible pixy-face of Herbert Heckmann; the bearish hug and nervous driving of Karlhans Frank; the suave presence of the Cologne homicide detective Hans Kroliczak, in the sleek and now vanished literary hangout in Cologne, Campi's; the grin on the face of Martin Walser in an office strewn with mementos of Texas at the Suhrkamp Verlag.

I trudged through the snow in Salzburg but could not find H.C. Artmann, who was rumored to be in the city. And I remember that I failed to locate Hubert Fichte, who had disappeared from Hamburg into the jungles of Jamaica; I did not see Helga Novak, whom I once had met in Cincinnati; my path and that of Uwe Johnson did not cross, but I recalled his tour of Lake Travis near Austin and the memorial of that visit in the mouth of the incandescent child Marie in his novel *Anniversaries*; Wolfgang Hildesheimer and I failed to get together because of his lecture tours and my own reluctance to spend a weekend traveling to the far reaches of southeast Switzerland; Hermann Kesten was ill in New York, Thomas Bernhard absent from Vienna, and I missed Eberhard Hilscher and Lutz Rathenow in East Berlin because of Günter Kunert's dinner party in my honor (Christa Wolf could not come because of the illness of her husband).

But, all in all, the journey was a sentimental success, a revelation for me and perhaps for some of the authors, who found out that not all Texans wear boots and Stetsons. And I discovered—to my amazement and to my satisfaction—that the German-language authors of today are vital, anxious, gifted, and committed. Some of their voices are presented here. They deserve applause, understanding, a jubilant welcome, and appreciative grins.

A. LESLIE WILLSON
February 1981
Austin

landscapes
a selection

H. C. ARTMANN
translated by Ewald Osers

then turned i
westward towards tara
twas no distance
not one horse
among them reached
tara before me . .

(coillte mac rónáin)

landscape 6

on the air's beak a duck a piece of china a stone
an oval a grass-grown plain a riverbank butterflies above

parkland trees oak severed columns vertical stadia
horizontal torsos senator among men in the treetops quiet

and among the tombs of the mid-life the old the young
by the white entrance arch by the fleece of the sheep

and the swan's depluming or the wet ibis's that
plucks at the greenery and the frogs' quack-drumming after

a too-hot day when golddiggers rest when canisters speak
when small fires here lead the chorus echo on hard surfaces

repetition of sentences refrains of a spring-lid watch in
contemplative stillness hour of rest the archaeologist's laurels

after his labors drafting of terrestrial letters of space logs
the brushing of a broad-brimmed hat for instance if someone

returns from a hunt for birds little stones between
sock and shoe a hand brushes against the wall the ruins it

touches a conduit the senator proceeds at discretion he
rears up his shadow powerfully down to the gurgling stream

landscape 8

a hoped-for thunderstorm's settled between the cow's
horns it trots nearer the slow-moving cow is the

domestic animal of oaks through the shadows cast
ahead by a peaceful event this cow is parading

on its horns the storm seconds pass the express train it flashes
past every lightning still housed in the sleeves of brass

yoho the shepherd in his plaid is scratching his crotch there'll
be a storm I can feel it I've a lot to get finished

a youth flicks a cent into the fishpond it
winks like an eye the thunder's still drying

on Freya's line the man from the railway performs his
switching at half-darkened points he scratches his crotch

yoho there'll be a storm I can feel it I've a lot
to get finished a cow comes out of the oaks

sleeves of brass the leash a little leash from horn to
horn with the thunder drying in the fragrant west wind

which has woken in the oaks flapping Freya's purity a youth
scratches his crotch yoho there'll be a storm I can feel

it today I've nothing to do and I like that rain
is falling the lightning explodes the sleeves the thunder

slips from its brackets the cow becomes shy the oak
more inclined the youth towards it: with Freya's permission a kiss

landscape 11

in this sun there stands a powerful stove it makes hot summer
we spare no trouble grind the jasmine fragrant it dries

a cloud the size of a duck sailing west wild goes the clock in
the house we need rain roam about twice the light didn't once

pass through the glass dusty you dream a silken
grain we half open our lips thus encounter our clean teeth

smoothly the mouth wields its raspberry knife masters it effortlessly
gains rapid control blushes sighs reflects surmises seeks

guesses very silently sinks flesh into flesh hello dear duckie
I'm worried today the attendant knocks in the bath hey there

we open all windows and our shirts hours of bitter butter
dripping it's summer dear duckie clouds are blowing across

the line nettle groves green unsprinkled watch the elm winking it'll soon
be evening I say rye grows in the land oh how my duckie

rain-pregnant swells dear belly thus to stand in the window
full of drapes harebells ringing garden-deep in a shadow under

both eyes my fahrenheit my yesterday today tomorrow heaven
oh smooth the sheets stretch wind your arms breathe romp

landscape 15

a quiet evening in the forest lodge a rest in the cool who
has not known these but we see the smoke from nearby

clearings are they charcoal-burners or scouts Armin is crossing
the patches of sand emerging from the pines we watch this

from the veranda does he remember Helen the sorceress
by the copper beech in the Müritz forest yes people it's true

to that extent we resemble the lilies of the field the roses
on the table but in the dark underbrush hisseth

the viper the berry-guard the lady of the double thorn
and Helen encounters her the timid the fearful oh barefoot

in bed I beg you what is this but in the dusk of the
raspberry the swift ant asks its question and we on the forest's edge

can tell by the way Armin's wearing his hat askew on the
homeward journey by the line of his swaggering stick or

by the encounter with Helen's delicate vision in the grid
of the evening sun hundreds of luminous needles what does the skin

say how does the antenna of the snail react how does the
smooth viper's reflex operate here oh we hurry past raspberries

landscape 18

the nightingale's sweetness has pierced the forest it
enters my ear on waves of the evening it came whether

aimed at me who can tell but I take it like
a cup of rich milk I drink to the night it alone

clothes me in thief's garb when I am in love
searching in hollows on hills under a hidden tree

yes I breathe the nest yet unbuilt a forest moreover
in seeds suddenly sprouting and standing with shielding

shadow in which in her name I seize what can be
held like delightful power of breasts and slimness of body

oh and the attentive silence of hands when the moon
dreams in the closed blossoms of flowers you Dafydd

understand you have taught this language in lines of
prehistory as if I didn't now comprehend fearful of quarrel

of the snort of the cuckold ye just gods there is
a reflection of the forest in her eyes as if a breath

of greenness rippled two bright pools my walk is free and
upright who's going to stop me I ask not I take

THE TIME AFTERWARDS

HORST BIENEK

translated by Ruth and Matthew Mead

I
There is a time
    and the time afterwards
About which of these times do we want to talk

II
When the deer grazed beside the lion
when the apple ripened for the man who had dunged the tree
when he who caught the fish might eat the fish
that was a time
    a paradisical time
        which we were glad
to hear preached about

When we lay huddled together on wooden bunks
when darkness imprisoned our sweating bodies
when hunger shattered our sleep and our dream
that was a time
    a black time
        which we would not wish
on our enemies

When the guard's shout drove us out on to the parade ground
when we dug coal from the earth with blunt tools
when we sought in the black petrification for an answer
to why this time
    was as it was
        which we would have rather
read about in school

When we returned again to the cities without memory
when—unrecognised—we mingled with the inhabitants
when we broke into their houses and left suspicion behind
that was a time
        a painful time
                that we buried
with our sadness

III
We are on the way from the one time
to the other
        but wherever we go
        we do not arrive
        sometimes our knees give way
        and the rain cools our faces
we sing
      we are not heard
      (for fatigue welds our lips together)
our gestures are timid
      they are not understood
      (for despair tears our arms from our bodies)
we continue
on the way from the one time
           to the time afterwards

IV
Words are thrown
pityingly into our laps

GRASPING THE PRESENT

GERALD BISINGER
translated by Thomas I. Bacon

Grasp the present coming from Forte dei Marmi-
Querceta once again in the train mingling conception
of the future and experience past future
in between always the ego in the present which
withdraws this ego with the desire to gather
scattered thoughts from times and spaces to pile up on
this spot to unhinge the present the world seize
and live perceive no longer track con-
ception future experience awareness of know-how handed down

To overcome space in the train heading for Genoa and during this
time a few days back that shrivel in the imagination
with Gisela I walked through streets to
squares in Verona Vicenza the Teatro Olimpico I saw
again after twelve years and the arena with
Gisela this time who is now in Berlin must be
for the day before yesterday she departed for there I sit
in the train writing on the way to Turin I think
of Verona Vicenza the blazing sun there and the evening

Conversations with Gisela in the resturant in Vicenza in the
evening and in Verona the filled arena of Diocletian's
time mentioned by Goethe in seventeen hundred and eighty-six
who saw it empty we saw the arena full and
misused for an opera spectacle in the evening Verona
I am sitting in the train headed for Genoa thinking of Gisela whom
I miss of Goethe quoted so often by Sanguineti
and with pleasure in Vienna Joseph the Second was reigning when
Goethe toured Verona Vicenza and wrote about them

Franz Joseph the First was reigning in Vienna when Radetzky
lay in state in the Milan Cathedral a few
days ago I was climbing about with Gisela in the artificial stalag-
mite formations on the cathedral roof in Milan gleaming white

painful to the eyes for Gisela who is from Berlin
Radetzky means nothing Austria is only a word
Franz Joseph a name I think of the Spanish era
of Manzoni the path from Manzoni to Gadda national uni-
fication campaign then and today humanity regional

The path from Manzoni to Gadda would be worth
investigating the required unity language based on
literature and the sources of dialects concrete language as material for poetry in both cases the
train stops at the station at Genoa I read of the death
of Bert Brecht in '56 in the Sunday issue
of the Corriere and in Vicenza in my travel guide
Goethe is mentioned and that in his time he wrote with admiration about the Teatro Olimpico

I am sitting in the train for Turin and I am surprised
that this ornately charming illusionistic
structure in Vicenza requires Goethe's reference as
proof of its value or the arena too however in
Verona according to the travel guide its value as
a Roman structure protected from all doubt is quite
certain and Goethe's description and reflection
is not even mentioned I sit in the train for
Turin and still smoke cigarettes brought from Berlin

I am sitting in the train and sweating this sweat is
the present forgotten tomorrow or this evening
already in Turin preserved here as private
historical fact for later just as the
light itching on my back from the sunburn I
got on the beach of Forte dei Marmi next to Gisela
this train is the present now which is overcrowded
the compartments full and the corridor the present is
now the draft in the compartment I notice it

In the train between La Spezia
and Genoa, 16 August 1972

ARMSTRONG, ALDRIN, COLLINS

VOLKER BRAUN
translated by Rainer Schulte

Three of ours, blasted from
The old confines of earth, 1000 meters
Above the Sea of Tranquillity, alone
Without God and the world (signals
Rejoice without sound
In the transistors), righting the ship
Gangplank to Heaven! Man 1 m/s
Sublime metaphor, they navigate
Between the craters, the sensors
Groping for land, the feet of flesh

Drilled with practiced steps
By the administrators
Of the universe, white animals
Naked, in their cocoons, bent
On the cables
Praying, praying, praying
Before the optical altar: multi-staged
Columbus, programed like a German
Church choir

And they transmit their image
Down, where we recognize ourselves
By their divine calesthenics (*One small step*
For a man, one giant leap
for mankind), finish-man
Of the terrestrial relay, audaciously hurled
Out from the thousand-armed
Catapult
Of the collective!

And pursued by the masses
Of the suffering, who squint from the barracks
At the TV screen
With rumbling stomachs, dog food
In the throat (20% of the total mass), and the brutes
From Harlem, beaten by harder facts
In the countdown of crimes
And the pipe, smoking
In the mouthless skull

Pursued
Up the peaceful ramp by
The fighting, beautiful hordes
Upright among clubs and hooves

Happy in their defeat: *Turn your eyes*
Toward the earth! the long discovered
Dark.

While the larger
Collective of butchers, blinking
At the stars between their shots
Raze to the ground
Countries countries countries

Like the lunar surface. Where the superhumans
Start by themselves, igniting
Word! free from the earthly gravity
Of orders, Creators in the radio
Blackout: with a thrust
Of 1590 kg the engine snatches them
Away from the attraction of the coast (rate
Of climb 20 km/h
Into orbit at 6643 km/h)
After seven full minutes on the

Prescribed course. And downward
Faster and faster into the dependence
Of earth, from the clear skies
Into these contrasting
Systems, which dispense a bitter
Pill, or have to swallow it, drifting
Home into the closer circles
Where two times two is five
Or three for the poor, plunging
Into the troubled
Atmosphere. (Oh, free yourself

Last stage
Of the poem, from the burnt out
Sentences!) Falling sportively
On huge parachutes into the ocean
Called the peaceful
In their minds the blue planet
Celestially beautiful. *If men saw the earth*
From this angle, they would protect it.
And, amazed, we come
Closer to our own selves.

TWO POEMS

ROLF DIETER BRINKMANN
translated by Hartmut Schnell and A. Leslie Willson

A SKUNK

in the morning, dead, run over
on the already soft
asphalt, gives you the impression

that the morning itself
has been run over,
you hold your breath

and roll up the car window
where the land stretches endlessly
on both sides, Texas, fenced in,

the flat hide-out.
Who walks along the highway
in cowboy boots and cries about

the dead animals? Who curses
the air conditioning that
doesn't work? Who lives in the

trailer smoking the dream
weed, looking over the plain?
Who has eaten the bull's pizzle,

the mountain oyster? Who teaches
the children? The land and the
animals on it belong to somebody

you don't see. And the
strangest thing is that you
don't see the animals either,

although the drive lasts for
hours. A family is looking
out of a shack next to the

railroad tracks, no longer in service.
You ask yourself how they live.
They live, one after the other.

Next to the bushes, the yellow
Sunday-school bus is rusting away.
It looks abstract, awk

ward, without color, like a
child's drawing. Some years
later the town has vanished,

and you look over the bare frames
that have become incomprehensible,
you remember the dead

skunk on the highway one
morning, jostled by the bus,
the States, the town where I was

born no longer exists, the young
teacher tells the children, who
ask her: Where do you come from?

for Betsy Schnell   HS

LOVELY MORNING

Quarter past ten a.m.
a passenger plane low
over the parched grass
summer flies and cats

On the gravel path
a chaise, empty
in the white sunlight
a can of sardines

Three cats together
on a lawn chair
the cross-cut tree
beyond casts shadows

An empty shadow
quarter till eleven a.m. bright
on the gravel path
no one is to be seen.

                                                        ALW

SERIFOS

ERICH FITZBAUER
translated by Herman Salinger

Sometime or other in a windstill night,
when even the last sounds of surf have ebbed away,
and only the creatures of the constellations
still keep vigil,
you may perhaps hear
softly the echo of the scream of Polyphemus,
that broke forth from him,
when the fiery pole of Odysseus
bored through his single eye.

Perhaps then the long-lost myth will become for you:
dream-reality close as your breath,
whispering stories into your ear,
unrememberable the next morning,
though you still feel them with shudders in your blood.

And much later in the day
the reverberation of the terrible voice may shake your mind:
when you stand on the beach,
your hair tangled by the gusty wind,
looking up toward the *chora*
whose houses—frail and crouching—
clamber up the slope
till they stop at the peak,
discouraged
by higher, monotonously naked hills
circling round.

Then let your steps follow
your glance,
and somewhere up there in the heights
you will begin to surmise the cave in the cliff slope,
the cave out of which the few final spared ones
of those legions that had once set out,
trembling, clinging to the woolly fleece of the sheep,
escaped now into newly granted life.

Perhaps too the magic of the place will hold you, grasp you so mightily
that the wake of the peaceful liner down below
will frighten you,
because you are afraid that a final
piece of the cliff, hurled with the force of despair
by that blind monster thirsting for vengeance,
might yet, after all, reach the ship.

But your fear is not long-lived;
you know that the grim giant
with the flaming pain under his forehead
has missed his hastily-steered target
forever.

The crags that he threw
have long since burst on the ocean floor, disintegrated.
Homer's song
has better outlasted time.

YOU

KARLHANS FRANK
translated by A. Leslie Willson

Y O U

You
You are
You are not
You are not you

You are but I
          are only through me
          are what I feel through you

If you please me then you're good
If you hurt me then you're bad

I love you
          hate you whenever
I see you and
I don't know
          know you not as
You are

          If
you're not here then you're
nowhere
          I know you by what
You do to me as
You are to me as
You smell taste look at me

You are but
You through
                    Me

NEW POEMS

DIETER FRINGELI
translated by A. Leslie Willson

the hopes
awakened
are cradled again
in sleep

i can't help
myself:
i can't help
myself

high tension

today i survived
yesterday too:
there's tension aplenty

hoping

is a form
of forgetting

you

the only thing left
that speaks
for me

resignation

and now
i'll do nothing more:
i already shudder
at the memory
of what
i do
or don't do

you can count
on me
from 0 to ∞
and back

THE GAZELLE
AND OTHER POEMS

RICHARD GERLACH
translated by Frankie Suit

THE GAZELLE

Stars streaked
Into paired black pools.
From the depths of her eyes
Gazed the gazelle.
Scheherazade related
How the daughter of the vizier
Was transformed into the animal
By a magic spell.
Upon her white cheek
Still ran a trace of tears.
Above her head grew
Horns, firmly fluted
And like sickles,
As though forged with steel,
Were her slender pasterns,
And so she stood poised like a dancer
For the dash into the wilds,
Loveliest of forms,
No dream can overtake her now.

THE BAT

With tiny cries
The bat plumbs the echo,
Locates the luna moth,
Whirls around
And snaps him.
Then she circles the gable,
Darts in a zig-zag flurry,
Skids into an airpocket,
Pelts to the treetop.

ELEPHANTS

Coiled inward the trunks swing
Up to the gaping mouths.
Mauling molars
Crunch the hay lustily.
Skulls, craggy-gray, high-arched,
See-saw in light rhythm.
Smells of massive digestion
Steam about chomping giants
And a trumpet call,
In voracious exuberance,
Shrills over tusks and rounded ears.

GIRAFFE

The black eyes
Peer quizzically
From high above.
Sound is
Sought and felt
By funnel ears.
The long neck
Falls sloping
Toward the back's elongation.
The slender legs
Bear the torso lightly.
A widely meshed
White net stretches
Over the tobacco-brown coat
Tracing rhomboids
And acanthus leaves.
The tufted tail switches
And gives a warning signal.

PRIAPUS

PETER HACKS
translated by Edward Harris

PRIAPUS

You, who have of that by which a man's esteem
Is measured more than any other, and for that
Reason are more likely ridiculed than wooed,
Melancholy Gardener, what is it that you lack?
At the edge of the reaper's harvest feast,
Deep in sleep, lies the goddess, and you, with an
Offering that towers above her wildest dreams,
Take her between your knees. An ass bellows,
She starts, startled, spies your pruning hook, and does not
Spread lustily her compliant thighs, o no indeed,
Brays louder than the ass, twin clamor, hers and
His, of goddess and of ass, drives you from the place.
How sad for you, you inherited neither
Your mother's bewitching girdle, nor father's
Persuasive, heady brew. Your strength, strong one,
Suits you well, standing in full view for all to see.
But of this take note: Women are like the world. Their
Lust for lust is small. The happiness which they
Most need you must first plant glibly in their soul. Else
They always say: Go away, you'll hurt me.

bremen whereyou

HELMUT HEIßENBÜTTEL
translated by Sammy McLean

whereyou
what
whereyou
what
whereyouwere
where
youwere
inBremenofcourse
andhe
andwhat
washe
washewhat
washewithyou
inBremen
washewithyouinBremen
yeshewaswithmeinBremen
andshe
andwhat
wasshewithyou
shewaswithustoo
shewaswithustooinBremen
yesshewaswithustooinBremen

andso
andsowhat
andsoyouwerealltogether
inBremen
andsoyouwerealltogetherinBremen
yesofcourse
inBremen
yesofcoursewewerealltogetherinBremen
andthenyou
wewhat
didyoudoitthereImean
didwedoitthereyoumean
didyoudoitalltogetherImean
didwedoitalltogetheryoumean
didyoudoitalltogetherinBremen
welldontyouknow
dontIknowwhat
thatwe
thatyoudiditthere
yesthatwediditalltogether
alltogether
yeswediditalltogetherthere
inBremen
yeswediditalltogethertherinBremen

andthatsuchashorttimebeforeChristmas

TWO POEMS

DIETER HOFFMANN

translated by Stephen H. Wedgwood

DAMPIER

William Dampier—
a botanical-minded buccaneer—
landed on a foreign shore
to burn and rape and plunder,
when once at first he stayed his hand,
observing a single flower,
while his onward-storming henchmen
tore through the land,
trampling down his flora.

Where his bent for learning came from
is obscure.
All England read his travel journals,
adventures, and placid observations
on unfamiliar plants and animals.
The Admiralty was much impressed.

His notes and drawings, seeds from Australia
went down on a voyage home.
Just a few kernels
and forty pressed flowers and herbs
were rescued.
They lie now dry as dust
in the Oxford University Herbarium.

For Dampier was named
the splendid glory-flower,
Clianthus dampieri.
But this unparalleled monument
to a pirate
exists no more.
Other botanists changed its name.

GOETHE'S MAN-SERVANT

When Goethe drank wine,
his man-servant Stadelmann
imbibed cheap booze.
A dozen years
after Goethe's death
he, too, was called to Frankfurt
to be there for the unveiling
of the bronze memorial tablet.
He came
in a cast-off coat
and an old hat of his master.
Then he went home,
back to the poorhouse
where, it is said,
his alcoholism had brought him.
Got drunk,
sobered up,
hanged himself in shame.
On the very next day
as in fairy tales, lovely and cruel,
came the news: friends of Goethe had
set up a pension for him
out of love for Goethe.

biography

ERNST JANDL
translated by Paul Solyn

in memory of dietrich burkhard

he has talent
said the professor to my mother.
he has a lot of talent
said my mother to my father.
i have talent, the professor told my mother
said i to my friend.

my father had a long life.
my father had almost no white hair left.
my mother no longer plucked her white hairs, one by one.
women don't want to go bald.
i had very fair hair.
my father had almost no more hair.
my father had had so much time.
i shall not renew my acquaintance
with him.

i was named dietrich.
at fifteen i wrote a tango.
i played the tango for my professor
and the professor said: i shall
take care of your further education
and my mother told my father:
his further education is taken care of.

in 1926 i acquired a residence permit.
it said: 1926 until. . . .
19 already printed, 26 in green ink
until four printed dots;
the authorities are thinking of the twenty-first century.
the authorities think far ahead.

i was named dietrich.
i had talent for useless things.
in 1926 i acquired a residence permit.
at nine i finished grade school.
at fifteen i wrote a tango.
at seventeen i finished school.
since 1944 i've written on every form
the number 18 in the blank for age . . .

he has talent
said the professor to my mother.
he has a lot of talent
said my mother to my father.
he should apply for something
said my father.
but i didn't apply for anything.

then they measured me for a gray uniform
and sat at home and wrote picture postcards
and cut their nails every day.
his education is taken care of
said the sergeant to my mother
and took a blade of grass from his lips;
give this to his professor and tell him:
talent doesn't matter. only further education.

i was named dietrich.
from 1926 to 1944.
i no longer have a name.
from day to day i diminish
and the giant machines of death
that for some time
have shuddered over the earth again
hasten the process
of my further education.

STEFAN LOCHNER PAINTED ME

HERMANN KESTEN
translated by Hubert Heinen

A sultry wind
Drove the lovers
From the benches around the cathedral square
And the remnants of ancient Roman walls,
Reddened the sky in streaks
With distant fires' reflection,
Caused a white cloud to scud
As if afraid it would burn,
Caused a pair of MP's
To smile at the sight of some daughters of Germania
While they surveyed the other bank of the Rhine
As if they shared the homesickness for the Tiber of the Young Lictors
Who carried their fasces as ceremoniously
as the MP's do their rubber truncheons.
The wind induced me
To enter the cool cathedral—
Not in order to pray,
I'm not Catholic.
The massive cathedral columns,
Wavering in a storm wind of stone,
Underneath a sky of stone, resembled stonepines.
Chubby cherubs made music like Handel and Haydn.
Two girls were kneeling to the right and the left of the confessional.
Their sins smiled in their short dresses.
In the cathedral painting where the Three Holy Magi worship
And Mary in her blue cloak and with castdown eyes,
Which hide much,
Sits there and holds her child,
Who already is practicing the gesture of Judgment Day,
Saint Ursula stood in her red dress and cloak,
Among her twelve companions,
Twelve for twelve thousand.
Nodding my head I greeted all twelve,
Twelve thousand virgins.

One looked at me.
I liked her round forehead,
Under the elegant golden headband,
And her pretty hair,
The bridge of her coquettish little nose.
Her eyes smiled.
Eyes of one in love.
I waved to Saint Gereon, too.
For Christ he let himself be tortured, a Roman legionary.
Because he loved the Son of God, they beheaded him.
Fellow sufferers stood around him.
Martyrs like him.
Then I recognized myself.
In the midst of them
I was standing in a blue cloak,
The legionary from Jerusalem. There I was,
A Jew, made a martyr by mistake.
In the background of the picture I've stood, since around 1440,
Stefan Lochner painted me.
Then I and my blue cloak—
It is cool in the stone forest—
Watched centuries pass.
I conformed, from century to century,
Not in my costume, just in my expression, my view of the world,
A contemporary of many epochs.
Always, as I do today,
The living stared again and again
At me, their painted archetype.
Historical ghosts came,
Who were there long before him,
Agrippa, the son-in-law of Augustus,
Who transferred the Ubians in 38 B.C. from the right
To the left bank of the Rhine,
And Cologne was born.
In 27 B.C. Agrippa built
The Pantheon in Rome, that still stands there.
Petrarch and Joost van den Vondel came.
Later came my real observers,
The Boisserée brothers,
Sulpiz and Melchior, who promoted
Construction of the cathedral and discovered

The beauty of the old paintings, collected them,
Showed them to Goethe in his later years. He came in 1824.
In 1828 came the mother of the philosopher
Arthur Schopenhauer, she was called Johanna
And wrote novels like her daughter Adele,
And received Goethe in her literary salon in Weimar.
Coleridge, too, came to Cologne, saw the filth and asked:
What power divine
Shall henceforth wash the River Rhine?
In 1818 Friedrich Schlegel stood before me,
Ten years a convert,
Who lived with the Jewess Dorothea Veit
And loved Lucinde,
And called the cathedral painting in which I stand the most beautiful,
The most lovely,
The sweetest thing that was ever paynted on German soil. (Sic!)
Heinrich Heine came from Paris in 1844,
Accompanied by his hatchetman,
He hacked the Three Magi to pieces,
With the hatchet, upon a signal from Heine.
And I, painted on my picture,
Trembled at the hatchet of Heine's shade.
Later Karl Marx stepped before me, he was put off. I was put off.
In 1842 Victor Hugo came, in 1850 Eugène Delacroix
And William Makepeace Thackeray.
(Earlier Georg Forster had come
Disappointed by the French Revolution!)
In our century Ricarda Huch and Alfons Paquet came,
Heinrich Böll and Hans Bender,
And Joachim Ringelnatz, who said to me
My books were more drunk than I.
All of them stood before the Three Magi,
Gazed at the Child, at the Mother,
At all the saints, at the martyrs,
Did they look at me?
They overlooked me, otherwise they would have recognized me,
The victim of Christianity, the Jew from Jerusalem;
For he and I were always the same.
No one looked at me. I tilted my head
To the side. My curls fell
Onto my shoulder, I smiled,

Without regard to the torments,
And was all of them,
A mirror of twelve thousand, a Jew from Jerusalem,
Always he and I, Hermann Kesten.
For some five hundred years I've been in the cathedral,
Painted by the great master in Cologne,
Stefan Lochner.
When I left, it was already dark in the cathedral.
Then I hurriedly exchanged my cloak
For the cloak of the painted Jew
From Jerusalem.
Now I wear his blue cloak.
The next time, I told the man in the painting,
Who is now wearing my cloak,
We'll take each other's place.
I'll be the painted martyr
And enter the cathedral painting by Lochner,
One of the fellow sufferers of Saint Gereon.
And you fly
With Lufthansa
To Rome
And write my books.

Cologne, January 1974

TOP SECRET

HANS KROLICZAK
translated by A. Leslie Willson

At the funeral service
for Konrad Adenauer
in the Great Cathedral in Cologne
I took the post at the sacristy—
Above me Starfighters passed by.

At the pontifical requiem
for the first Federal chancellor
in the Great Cathedral in Cologne
I wore my wedding suit—
I like that outfit.

During the obsequies
for the multifold doctor
in the Great Cathedral in Cologne
I guarded the guests of honor:
de Gaulle, Johnson, Zarapkin—
The white telephone rang.

At the State ceremony
for the old Chief Mayor
in the Great Cathedral in Cologne
the congregation wore black—
Joseph Frings celebrated the mass
in vestments of cardinal red.

At the funeral mass
for the amateur rose gardener
in the Great Cathedral in Cologne
everybody shadowed everybody—
I seemed suspicious to myself.

At the ceremonial service
for the esteemed chieftain
in the Great Cathedral in Cologne
my laugh echoed at the catafalque—
The bigwigs shushed me.

I was so exuberant
in the Great Cathedral in Cologne
because of the Secret Service people
in glaring white trenchcoats—
Gleaming agents
in the Gothic nave.

They were the focus for me
in the Great Cathedral in Cologne.
The red round pin
sparkled on their lapels—
Top Secret—the trenchcoats—
That seemed suspicious to me.

TWOFOLD MONOLOGUE—SHORT-CIRCUITED

GÜNTER KUNERT

translated by Christopher Middleton

O for our offspring, the computers,
O their impotent compassion for us:
with perforated tongues they talk
logically and without purpose, for logic and purpose,
directed at fathers, is only extravagance:
unrationed irrationalism
of static cubes quick as electrons,
from top to toe nothing but brain
which thinks and thinks
and thinks:
O for our attendants, the oxyginks,
and alas
and woe to the lymphatic ghosts,
incapable of true logic, of pure purpose:
O for our childish progenitors: O O O O
O O O O O O O O O
O O O O O O O O
O O O O O O

CURRICULUM VITAE

ONDRA LYSOHORSKY
translated by David Gill

CURRICULUM VITAE

I am as young as the first human being.
I am as old as the cosmos.
My body contains matter from every galaxy.
When the first man began to sing
—was it from joy or fear?—
I was present there listening.
All living and all dying is a variation of the very beginning.
Unity embraces all diversity.
And the great entirety is as mystifying as every detail.
I cannot err or go astray
for my brothers and sisters are man and beast,
tree and mountain, cloud and river,
the ocean and all the stars.
Through the microscope, through the telescope I see the same.
The galaxies in turn are the cells of the cosmos.
The tiniest and the most powerful are but relativity factors.
Seen from the Omnipotent's point of view
—perhaps it is God's—
the cosmos is like a small gray cloud of dust.
To be human is to see everything in terms of humanity
and, in the knowledge of all things, to act as a human.

HOTEL FOR SLEEPWALKERS

CHRISTOPH MECKEL
translated by Christopher Middleton

Enter from everywhere, in sleep,
my house is an everdark shelter
for will-o'-the-wisperers, for mummies,
winter animals, and for the sleepless peddlers
who sell fatigue from their cornucopias
on the shimmering boulevard of moonlight hotels.

In the convoy of sleep, with freighters and waggons,
you wander along the windless elevated,
out of the light into the dark, the interstitial
tunnels of twilight never delay you long.

You finally knock on my door and beg
with dream-choked voice, with sick wings,
and tattered shoes, to be wakened
from your global voyage through the desolate
night of nightmares.

LAUGARVATN AUTUMN AND OTHER POEMS

HELGA M. NOVAK

translated by A. Leslie Willson

Laugarvatn autumn

softened up by rain and precipitated
the stone on the heart so heavy
that it goes deeper and deeper

besides I had even drawn off wine
the pie in the oven is for you
don't be bashful dig in

when you are full follow the gray geese
that now turn noisily toward the south
and don't fall in the ditch on the way

silken thread

into the sea they speed the harpoon on its rope
he blows bubbles as the sound scrapes him
whishing they split the water with a streak
his neighbor rears up and opens wide his jaws
if his kind cleared the plains
as totally as they do the sea
they would change his name
they haul in the silken thread

bottom

the cast-in anchor has tangled itself in algae
not holding at all fast in the middle of the water
it is pulled by the current toward the outpouring river
when he takes up the anchor feeling for the chain
his arm down over the bows color of ink
his face cut off at the throat looks at him
the focused pupils penetrate the window
bottom   a flying fish moves away under the surface

geysers

man-tall steam columns on the fields
watery mists trickle and fly away
steps beyond a lifeless meadow
sulphur-green with dampened powder
funnel-mouth smoking subdued
at your feet a heaven ultramarine
colorless blades bundled in sand
glassy grass at the rim of the geysers

lost

choked is the outcry of ravens the mink
which lost its way surrenders to white grouse
the stony waste which tosses the foundling
on its belly till the storm has passed
he sees nothing but wings of wind black
curtains before the light sweeps near and
lures him to silvery carpets he has gone to sleep

centrifuge

with back protected at your feet the vortex
pressed against the wall aghast and moved
unable to hold anything fast held fast
another shore unattainable
pressed against the wall uneasy lingering
before your eyes with a fanfare he promises ease
through the vortex no escape

unmasked

when he took off the mask he stopped up the mouth and eyes
and gathered berries in the papier-mâché shell
o don't throw up your hands in dismay
when the sweetness rises in his face

when he removed his disguise he shut the door
he hung the things in front of the window and around the light
o don't throw up your hands in dismay
when he begins to dance after the ball

there must have been a party

shards are lying on the path shattered bottle necks
on the rowan trees the Chinese lanterns swing
the rain is washing off the outdoor stage
tympani grow silent cans are blowing away
there must have been a party to judge by the trash
the flowers of paper are wilted and limp
from the route of the caravan no reflector looks back

stale tea

look at the brown pot with its dregs
the spout is all stopped up and smelly
why didn't he drink the tea
when it was still hot

look at the crust of mold like white satin
that is floating in the pot and gleaming
why didn't he drink the tea
but hurried away instead

look at the teaball sheathed inside with dampness
the leaves swollen have lost their fragrance
what called him away
why is he gone

listen to the crunching underfoot
spilled out tea on the floor
did the news come at five
did he tremble

WERE WE NOT WHAT WE ARE . . .
(for Erich Maria Remarque)

FRITZ VON OPEL
translated by A. Leslie Willson

Were we not what we are
How could we endure
The burden of thought?

Were we not what we are
Where would we derive then
The power of desperation
To confess to our own selves
And to absolve from blame
The eternal stream
Which bears us hence
Into uncertainty.

Were we not what we are
We would not circle restlessly
About our own flame
Like planets
Seeking security of a sun.

O Friend!
We held our lives in a poised hand
But did we not follow—
In our glossy and glistening youth—
The false flag of motley hopes
Still unaware and misled
By the rustling of its silken cloth?
Were we not—
thirsty for approval—
misused as beams for crumbling buildings?
Did we not kiss
In pinkish-red storms of desire
The yawning body of many a honey-aromatic blossom
Always whipped by the wish

To repress ourselves?
Were we not—
Always entangled in battles—
Always in flight from ourselves?

We are punished
By too many tracks.
We are damned
Behind the curtain of beaming life
To see the darkness:
Do we not hear—
Even in greening forests—
The dry rattling of autumn?
Are we not drifting in a perilous dream
On a fragile ship off a rocky coast?
Do we not try—in vain, in vain!—
To cast anchor at too great a depth?

O Friend! Comrade in forlornness!
Let us never forget:
Our escutcheon is defiance
And our pride
Forged us a shield of composure.
Let us therefore—
Broken on the wheel of realization—
Dying but unconquered
Sing as always
Defiant and proud
Even though
With expiring voice.

TWO POEMS

ARNO REINFRANK
translated by Guy Stern

POET OF FACTS

Don't scholars eye me as though I were
an interloper from a different planet?
They think the world in which each day
they move so far removed from worlds
in which the poets move. For it is held
that poets populate a most peculiar zoo,
with Rilke sitting at the ticket booth,
with Goethe, Schiller, Heine in enclosures
for elephants; and Ringelnatz performs gymnastics
in monkey-style upon the climbing poles.
Inside the jungle house, where yawns are seldom stifled,
Nobel Prize winners chatter.
Too tired now by far to visit other species;
a trip, then, to the restaurant
to have a beer. The Sunday tour of
scientists through the poet's garden
has quickly ended. Until they stub
their toes on me, and stop,
and are amazed: Really, there is someone
who aims his lyrics at the vast unknown!
In such approximation do I see the world
in which they daily move, to that
within which facts unfold a lyric all their own.

SEVEN STARS

July is sewing to the velvet cloth of heaven,
with which at night it warmly covers half the globe,
seven golden buttons: they glisten
as on the blazer of a pop-song star,
who—between melody and crazy screeching—
gyrates his hips and shoulders in the spotlight
and all but dislocates them for those whistled cheers.

Therefore to speak here of those seven stars
is like a whisper exercise against a roar of breakers
of fashion's flood. Yet nothing else but poetry
can point man's glances into that direction,
from which comes naught but weather, and which none but birds, smoke,
  paper kites
once touched and the short trajectory of a thrown rock—
Lilienthal's flying machine is not old yet!

And so these seven stars, lustrously engraven
upon the chart of heaven of a cloudless night
shall be discussed here. Septemtriones,
so the Romans named this constellation,
which German calls "Great Bear,"
also "Big Wagon," and which beam more avidly
than fourteen just-constructed radio satellites.

For these—small pellets in their orbits round the earth—
which we have flung up there with rockets,
so that news may bounce off them to all the continents,
a feat my words don't mean to deprecate,
these would by no means circle as was planned,
had not the plan, which placed the stars above them.
been first disclosed to us in poetry.

Before technicians in space laboratories got instructions
to develop means for drifting into space,
for which man, since Tycho Brahe, charted courses,
it was observation, looking, amazement, and admiration
of the firmament, to which belong the seven,

for which poets coined names, pungent and sensuous:
"Haunches of the Steer" in Egypt, for example.

The picture of the "Wagon" whose tongue points northward
was familiar there, where wagons first rolled forth:
in Babylon. The Malaysians
viewed the same celestial diagram as a "Laden Boat,"
and researching further, you will find revealed
the features of a visionary mode of thought,
which affixed to heaven what it found on earth.

In China, where the farmers after threshing
would twirl their grain with shovels, square, of wood,
so that the wind would free the rice of chaff,
they thought the tongue to be the handle
of precisely such a shovel, and they named
the seven stars accordingly. The Portuguese
compared them to a ship, unfurling sail.

The culture of the Celts which persevered longer
and purer in Ireland than elsewhere gave these stars
the name of "Plowshare." In the tundras of Siberia
the hunters were quite certain of their being "Seven Wolves."
Hence references to an experience everywhere and always
related to the essence of man's life:
his deed to conquer hunger through his labor.

Small wonder that I feel enraptured
with all this poetry of stars, quite unlike
the humbug of the horoscope. Anticipated
in it are all the abstract signs and symbols
with which, though they may seem bereft of sentient life,
the scientists today feed their computers.
To them, the cosmologists, I gladly dedicate this poem thence,

that they never will lack in sentience!

THE TREE THAT LEARNED TO TALK AND OTHER POEMS

CHRISTA REINIG

translated by *Julia Penn*

THE TREE THAT LEARNED TO TALK

It wasn't aware,
that it was a tree.
They sawed it in two.
The bulldozer could turn.

Out of its stumps it thrusts leaf after leaf,
stuttering,
it gives answers to questions.

SURVIVAL

Around his mouth the ice
didn't thaw anymore.
For which night I do light a candle
red like the snow.

ROME

I breakfasted and left
and was among many maybe one,
who would survive,
but I hardly thought that far ahead.

I held tight to the thought
that I was already dead, and thus:
ungundownable.
What was laid out, couldn't talk back.

The clock stood still.
I counted on my fingers:
first him, then him, then her, then me
and ate lunch.

That noon Rome quaked,
a *dolce* under glass.
It was the cool of the evening
before I grasped my own left wrist.

BUSKINS

RUDOLF HELMUT RESCHKE

translated by J. Jafkom Blamskag

buskins
buskins
the tragic
mien and sound

imparted
to the soles
through the
stage so wide

astraddle
are both
legs upon
the ground

which is naught
but semblance
like the
sounding stride

in the to
and fro
appearance
on the ramp

when veils
billow and
the fold
is whirled

and
settles
in the beam of
the glaring lamp

and
goes over
into a
double world

WORDS NOT EXTINGUISHED

JÜRGEN THEOBALDY
translated by A. Leslie Willson

There are only words
for things, said Rolf Dieter Brinkmann
in the Rhine Hotel room (another
thing), like describing this
evening (it was
his last), this moment, how
else to describe it but
with words for things, this wallpaper pattern,
the floor, the color of the bed-
spread (where he was sitting
and had been writing
in his notebook), look, remember
what you have seen, today
on the way through London, the ducks
in the puddle on the construction site,
in the middle of the city (where did they come from?),
the construction worker with bare chest, the
young women (secretaries,
stenographers, salesgirls), who
were coming out of offices
to take the subway, where to? and what
will they do now? (The fat
black birds in Kensington Park
mornings) and memories
of 1968 that he talked about,
the rock concerts, the book package
with "Fuck You," here
have a drink,
the bottle of beer (it was
his last), not even
half empty, how will I get that down
in a poem, just
with "patch-words" (the words, older

than machines, how will I describe
the work of machines? everything metaphorical?),
perhaps "formula speech," huh?
And what remains, the moods,
the "vibrations," as you say (they
aren't in the words, they're
in the poem), and what he
left behind,
after the car struck him,
the lights, city lights, extinguished forever
for him, in the evening toward ten
on Bayswater Street, 23 April 1975,
what he
left behind were
this arsenal of words, word-fields,
rubble piles of words, blown up
stocks of weapons, desires, word-nightmares
directed against the daily nightmare,
"word idylls" that he
skinned, without fun, without consideration, what he
left behind was
this "most filthy image" of horror that he
"didn't ask for."

WHO CAN SAY MORE?
on the Death of Rolf Dieter Brinkmann
on 23 April 1975—written 26 April 1975

FRED VIEBAHN
translated by A. Leslie Willson

Fragments of memory not an obituary
a poem without mourning full of mourning
my stone draws wreathless circles
oblique
before the prow of a coming shipwreck
—Who can say more?

1

This morning it said in the newspaper
he had been dead for three days
victim of London traffic
run over by a car
—Who can say more?

2

In '68 I
reviewed his first novel
308 pages
"in any case
too much fuel burned up
without getting into gear"
I wrote back then
—Who can say more?

3

We did not
meet often
and even then
fleetingly

naw he said once he was
not mad
at me
only the Reich-Ranickis
did he want to eliminate
with a machine gun
—Who can say more?

4

Brigitte knew him well
from college days
together they developed
at her birthday party
ten years ago
or thereabouts
a Peepee-Philosophy
—Who can say more?

5

Aliana memorialized him
(that was back in '70)
in her novel about the characters
in Cologne
which he haunted
cryptically
through the broken-down scene
the book was long ago remaindered
—Who can say more?

6

Bill and Elizabeth two
German students from Austin
told me early this April
about their experiences
with him
they

had a hard time with him
at the University of Texas
—Who can say more?

7

Today three weeks later
I read
about his death and again
his novel
maybe back then I wasn't fair
the disengaged gears of '68
wrench me chokingly uphill
—Who can say more?

8

I read and read
308 pages
I read him
and finally
on the peak of the next-to-last sentence
I collapse breathlessly:
"Oh 1979,
everything is better.
You could
die on the spot.
Right on!"
Was his life resistance?
—Who can say more?

9

None can say more:
There are no days of yore.

ATTEMPT TO UNDERSTAND A FEELING

MARTIN WALSER
translated by A. Leslie Willson

1

Who will explain to me my homesickness for America?
What must make up the tone that reaches from here to Texas and lasts as long as the lovely sky there?
What am I to do with the splendid oaks, the cedars, countless, that have begun to take root again in my mind?
How can I handle the immortal phrases from the supermarket, which still are imbued with the Southern tinge of the lips from which they came?
Why does the gas station remain with me as though it were done by Michelangelo?

2

Have I been deceived by the dignity that crime assumes when it is committed by the Big Families?
Did I not have a fraternal feeling for Nixon and Agnew, who did what the Rockefellers did, but at home and too late?
Didn't I feel repulsed at the tone of the magazines in regard to the royal House of Kennedy?
Didn't I witness John Ford's color chauvinism in that Italian who earned as much as one must earn to feel like an Irishman when he sees a Mexican?
Didn't I find out that the middle-class children at recess want to have nothing to do with the Black schoolbus riders whose fare is paid for Democracy?

3

Was it the unrelenting heat?
Was it the roads that always reached to the horizon?
Was it the yellow butterflies that occupied the country path on Sunday in Vermont?
Was it the brass band from Boerne that played in San Antonio on the

Spanish-shaded river like on the postcard from 1910?
Was it Mr. Snake, who lives in the sand behind the mountains and cleaned
my air filter for a dollar?

4

Didn't the renowned New York paper make me shudder by its slanted in-
difference?
Didn't the ritual of right-of-way in our fine neighborhood demonstrate a
patience that is exquisite?
Didn't the Mexican who built my apartment pay for my rent being so low?
Didn't the New York taxi driver demonstrate all the traits of an animal of
prey, and under what condition does that come about?
Doesn't New York disavow what America says?

5

Was it the orange from the Valley in Texas, the pancake house on the
interstate, or the ocean-liner whistle of the locomotives?
Was it the girl on TV, who let slogans from Franklin Savings & Loan melt
totally on her lips?
Was it green Tennessee or cottontop Texas?
Was it the perpetual sky, the consistent friendliness of the people, or the
Pentecostal roar of the passing truck?
Was it the humming bridge in Memphis, the concrete scarf that Houston
wears, or the gentleman-size palace that Jefferson put together on a moun-
tain in Virginia?

6

Maybe I am susceptible to beautiful weather.
Maybe I came upon your Democracy, Walt Whitman, in bars, lecture halls,
department stores, and on beaches.
Maybe it was the venerable Pontiac Catalina convertible that rocked the
five of us through the land.
Maybe I happened onto the sunniest of the many folds of the garment of
the Statue of Liberty.
Maybe it's most of all the effect of the distance from here.

7

America is, I believe, where nobody is quite sure of himself.
Europe is, I believe, where Adenauer, de Gaulle, and Beckett are quite certain of themselves.
Doesn't ceremonious self-assuredness tinge everything here?
Isn't everything here crippled by the narcissistic idyll in which an impression is sanctified and one gets old and rich but talks incessantly about dying?
Think: You could become an American. Europe is, I believe, a vainglorious funeral culture.
Could my homesickness for America be a homesickness for the future?

8

I recognize little in movies about America.
And the America that Kissinger stands for is the Soviet Union, for which Gromyko stands, for which Molotov stands, for which Dulles stands, stood, has stood.
The report that reports that Ex-CIA Chief Helms is being charged with perjury reports the true America.
Representatives have nothing more to do with the represented. Nothing is less typical for a country than its representatives. Even America lives under the cloud cover, produced daily by the communications industry and by the entertainment industry in the interest of the representatives who— incommunicative—lord it over the media-smog.
All of America is the periphery for a center that is not a capital city with imperialistic stucco, victory column, parade grounds, Immortality Boulevard. The center for which America is the periphery is the idea that will also overcome capitalism: Democracy.

9

As though for always bend after bend of the Mississippi glistens up under the airplane wing.
As though for always my frail colleague sits in Austin before the massive Sophie edition of Goethe.
As though for always the football superstars thrust their great strength on the ball disappeared at the bottom of the pile.
As though for always nine students sit around on the grass and sing the

song of the Pawn Shop Corner in Pittsburgh, Pennsylvania, the song of
cotton in Arkansas, the song of the Bitter Lemon Tree, the song of the
House in New Orleans that is called "The Rising Sun." Then Tom says:
If I flunk out, I'm going to work in the steel mills like last year.
As though for always in the city panorama stand the laden telephone poles
that look temporary: America, as though for always temporary.

10

So I admit: I can't reconcile this capitalistic America about which the
globe rumbles and the concrete America that I experienced.
I was in the big small towns on Sundays and weekdays, always in the
middle class, nowhere did I meet the plastic people that the intellectual has
to come across in America.
America made the gods of this century, the most ridiculous gods that were
ever made, Chaplin, Monroe, Sinatra . . . the most human-like gods that
were ever made, yes, mankind finally wants to worship itself, a theology
like a razor blade, made sharpest in America because America is made of
people who left from someplace in order not to have to worship gods and
now get along with gods that are small but numerous and shabby.
I am captivated by America's hells that need less theology to operate than
any other hells in the world: so they seem more easily done away with.
Since history, ever since it began, is the most hurried thing that ever pa-
raded across the earth—so much more hurried e.g. than simple Nature—,
and since history wants what is attainable, were that to be to mark time—
were it insanity and were that to be to poison dialectics, you would forgo
the experiment of America, where socialism infers its redemption from the
evidence of convicted SOUL; in the end we are one landscape, and oxygen
and Democracy are more respected ideas there.

11

I'd like to be on the Rio Grande, mix Apache echoes with those of
Ausschwitz,
I'd like to be in Tennessee, which chases the sun with so many hills, and
nobody is named Hohenzollern,
I'd like to be in Virginia, the land of leaves, to forget,
I'd like to be in Texas and learn how to brag,
I'd like to be far away.

FLIGHT 690 PAA

GABRIELE WOHMANN
translated by Allen H. Chappel

As an air passenger I appear blasé
In no case like a tourist.
I wait bored to death in the
Row of seats Gate B 41
Ha, that's an everyday affair for me, a colorless everyday affair!
My luggage seems to consist
Of almost nothing but newspapers.
I dispatch everything
Like a pro, with forced forbearance.
The jovial couple next to me
Was already in Bali at least once
Flew over whoknowswhich
Great oceans and continents.
I stand out, preoccupied
I get in line to board last.
It annoys me really, it belittles my position
That I find this old lady my co-passenger
She visits my neighbor sometimes for tea.
Oh you beginners
You have to use this opportunity right away
To order cold drinks, you Berlin enthusiasts
You conference hounds and wives enraptured by the front-line city
Who finally get out for once, too.
The women are already whispering one to another
Making plans: the Kurfürstendamm, the jewelers
But also the Kreuzberg and all these Turks
In Berlin one is really always lucky
With the weather, they cross their fingers for each other:
Too bad if the sun doesn't shine.
As a seasoned air passenger having decided
For the lesser of two evils, i.e., against taking the train,
The greater offense to a person
Whose time is money, I sit of course
Not at a window, from my aisle seat I ignore now

This everlasting half-crazy
And terribly reckless thing:
We have left the ground!
Suddenly I know
That no one in this motley group
Of somewhat helplessly exuberant people
Is as excited as I, pro at excitement that I am.
Thus, in such a way that I scarcely catch myself doing it,
I sneak a look out past the newspaper
Into the clouds, at the wings
I bring into focus my starry-eyed feelings
For the sky and for the pilot
(I leave out the co-pilot) I disdain in advance
My intellectually stimulating colleagues and the entire
Intellectually stimulating conference, Berlin included
I'll never ever really be able to stand Berlin
With a happy feeling of revenge
I imagine now already
The lift-off from the runway, day after tomorrow in Tegel.
The old lady who sometimes visits my neighbor for tea
Has actually ordered something after all: juice
The married couple celebrates the flight with champagne
Well, we did make it up into the air.
Even I ought not find that so natural!
The heavenly abodes, first thing I read instead of the newspaper
GOETHE NARRATES HIS LIFE and between the lines
Of Heaven and earth keep my eye peeled for you, dear departed souls
And it turns my stomach
To project my thoughts out beyond our low short-run altitude
To the loftier heights of the scientific cosmos
That I now abhor.
Here suddenly, although I don't quite like my juxtaposition
With those whom chance has destined to be my fellow-sufferers
It would suit me to die in the long-overdue crash
Of this ordinary Boeing 707, oh, no!
What makes my heart stop beating, how childish
Now with this unannounced change
In the roar of the motor, why does the pilot not
Express his regret, speak no parting words
Why doesn't he pull himself together, it must be after all
As important to him as to us

To manage a landing!
With a feigned yawn
I search for the face of a stewardess:
As long as these lady executioners still smile
We can't be in such a bad way.
But everything has gone along completely normally again
The crew is encountering bad weather over the Wartburg
Today for the third time already. And I, rather hardened
Pestered by the passport examiners
Remember at the last moment to return a kind of
Obligatory smile to the stewardess
And arrive once more
Once again among intellectually stimulating colleagues
Slowly and with endless zeal they discuss the project about the TWENTIES
And I stand out, yes, angry and happy
To be away from culture, in the hands of technology
Of Flight 690, I romanticize the runway
Someone intelligent slowly says something intelligent
But the pilot actually got something moving, a plane
Indeed he was able to get it off the ground!

MY LANGUAGE AND I

ILSE AICHINGER
translated by Richard Mills

MY LANGUAGE IS ONE WHO IS PRONE TO FOREIGN WORDS. I PICK THEM OUT, I gather them from afar. But she is a small language. She doesn't go far. Round and around, round and about me, round and around and so on. We make headway in spite of ourselves. To hell with us, I tell her sometimes. She turns, she doesn't answer, she tolerates us. Sometimes customs agents appear. Your papers? We go through, they let us go through. My language said nothing, but I made up for that, I nodded zealously, I did them that favor. Someone, and something around one, above suspicion. But what was it? A spiral spring. No, steam. There is something around everyone, don't you know that? The poor boys, I really do feel sorry for them. Yes, really. Now you're talking nonsense. Why do you feel sorry for them? What do you feel sorry about? Young and that's all, why should anyone feel sorry about that? They outgrow it, that is inevitable. Grown strong and becoming impressively large. While we are stuck in the mud, wearing ourselves out, wearing ourselves out more and more and meanwhile pretending that we enjoy it. And meanwhile losing our enjoyment. Honestly. Who is it who says that? I do. Don't make me laugh. That always reminds me of the man who said I when he wanted into the house too late. I'm outside, I, I. It reminds me of him, what kind of job did he have anyhow. Janitor, I think, yes, janitor. Are you hungry? I sure am. But I have a way of always forgetting that I'm hungry. First once, then twice, then a third time. But then I have a feast, you can be sure of that. Nothing is left out then, everything is on the table then, everything spread out before me. It tumbles about then, all around me, I've got it then. Sleepy? Then go to sleep, go on. I'll watch for you.

I sit there with my language then, just three meters apart from the ones who talk that way. But we have made it, we have gone through, we can sit down when we are out of breath. Enough solitary places, a cloth down on it, the sun is shining everywhere. My language and I, we don't talk to each other, we have nothing to talk about. What I need to know I know. She prefers cold meals to hot ones, not even the coffee should be hot. That keeps you busy. There's enough to get done, covering, slicing, measuring the cold, letting things cool off. While she stares at the sea. My language has it easy, staring while I do everything. I don't hurry like I did at first, I calmly smooth the cloth out, I calmly weight it down with rocks when it gets windy, but it's true: I work and she stares. She doesn't even express any desires. That wouldn't be the least that could be demanded of her, but it would still be something. A good turn, a favor, some encouragement for me. But that is of no interest to her, none whatsoever. That much I've already figured out. She only stares or listens to the surf, my language. We are always near the sea, I make sure of that. I, not she. I'd like to know what she would do if once I went inland, simply made a turn like other people, searched between the hollows for a stone table for us, pine boards. How she would react; would she come along? The coastal wind is bad for my ears, that I know. Sometimes I start singing or clattering about with the silverware, it subsides. Although only a little silverware is needed for our meals, I take all of it out, plates and glasses too. I take a knife and carefully let it fall onto a plate, always from the same distance. The past five weeks it has been quieter. Recently I once tried letting the knife fall onto the plate from a little higher. It struck loudly—I heard it distinctly—but the plate shattered. My language remained calm, her gaze fixed on the sea—and as I believe—always on the same spot. To me she seems to be the opposite of those pictures whose eyes follow you wherever you go. Her eyes follow no one. Sea monsters and trawlers would be lost equally on her, and none come anyway. I then lay out our cold meal, pour the cold coffee, but all in vain. I have carefully set the cloth, often even putting a beach flower in the middle, or next to her silverware. She doesn't turn around. I take her silverware and put it down before her, between her and the sea spray. My joy is gone, the hearing test has made me dispirited, the sea annoys me. My language used to have a lilac shawl, but it is gone. I fear that we are ruining our health here. If my language loses her voice, she will have one more reason not to talk with me. While I, whispering and coughing, continue to overwhelm her with questions and offers. And the lilac shawl looked good on her, it covered her too-long neck and gave both gentleness and decisiveness to her unobtrusive appearance. All that is past. She won't even turn her collar up. As she is now, she sometimes reminds me of a fully grown swan, a swan whose colors are so dull as though all of its growth were yet to come. She'd better not get any ideas. From a distance I hear the voices of the customs agents. They talk on and on—at least the one keeps on talking. It wasn't my idea to sit so close to the customs shed, but my language was not to be forced any farther. The fourth country is behind us, I screamed in her ear, that one over there is the fifth one already. She followed me unwillingly, and no farther than here. We could just as well be customs agents. Only one of them keeps on talking, about eating and about youth, the other one is sleeping. Or, like now, staring over here through the window panes. Earlier he was sleeping while I was searching for our papers. Since she lost her shawl I no longer trust my language with them, they stay with me.

The men over there are bored. Or they are suspicious about us. They are suspicious about my language, not about me. I am normal, I eat and drink, and from that distance it doesn't look like a hearing test when I let the knife fall onto the plate, it looks like clumsiness, and that is what it's supposed to look like. But if we stay here much longer, it won't look like clumsiness any longer, but will seem intentional instead. If my language would speak to me, I wouldn't need this kind of hearing test, but she does little to help keep us above suspicion. Me, at least, she should be more concerned about me, should have been long ago. I suspect that she is concerned only about herself. Or nothing about herself concerns her. Or both, that's it. She hasn't touched what I put before her, she lets the sea spray salt it. To each his own. I maintain that. And I can maintain others as my own too. I can become a cook for the customs agents, a supplier for the customs agents, or even a customs agent. Those two over there won't ignore what I set before them. We will talk about customs, about taxable items, silver and lead and other such things. About card games, I know card games too. And about my language, who, I suspect, won't be moving from here anymore. About her salty meal, her gray gaze. I will do what I can for her. Only conversation will help her, discussions about her, observations that repeat themselves. In time no one will want anything more from her. And I will do my part towards that. Here and there I will insert a sentence that keeps her above suspicion.

WANNSEE

GUIDO BACHMANN
translated by André Lefevere

HEINRICH VON KLEIST, WHO LIVED IN POOR CIRCUMSTANCES SINCE THE start of his affair, at first secret, then commonly known, with Henriette Vogel, wife of Receptor-General Friedrich Vogel because the *Berliner Abendblätter*, the newspaper he published, had gone bankrupt on account of a considerable loss of subscribers, arrived on a cold and foggy afternoon at the end of November in the year 1811, in a coach from Berlin, in the neighborhood of Potsdam, where he had the coach pull up at the innkeeper Stimming's, and, as he alighted, helped Henriette who, taking his hand, looked about her uncertainly. To the innkeeper who stood under the lintel, breathing heavily, so that gray steam emerged from his parted lips, Kleist said he wanted, until further notice, to take lodgings there, two rooms on the top floor of the house. "Hey," called the inkeeper to Riebisch, the day laborer who was loading manure, and again: "Hey, Riebisch, light a fire and take the gentlefolk's luggage upstairs." Kleist whispered something into the ear of his heavily muffled companion and left the hired coachman, who was handing pieces of luggage to Riebisch, where he stood. He stepped into the public room, supporting the woman, and, after he had filled a pipe with tobacco and puffed it alight, ordered coffee to be brought, into which he poured rum. The guest's hand, the innkeeper noticed, watching the pair with suspicion, trembled when Kleist smoothed his black hair which, jagged on his wide forehead, fell down to his eyebrows and curled on his neck.

Kleist got up hurriedly, his coffee hardly drunk, and left the public room with Henriette. Upstairs, where Riebisch had in the meantime lit the stove, Kleist closed the door, opened a bag, and took from the same a large pistol with the butt about one and a quarter feet long and with the inscription Lazarius Comminazzo displayed along the barrel, weighed the weapon in his hand, leveled it, and aimed at Henriette in such a way that she, shrinking back, held up her hands and stammered: "My Heinrich, my mellifluous one, my bed of hyacinths, my Aeolian harp, my sinner, my desire, my sweet care, my forest, my sword, my right hand, my tear, my ladder to heaven, my tender page, my crystal, my reward, my Werther, my frankincense and myrrh, my crown of thorns, my poor, sick Heinrich, my tender, white lamb, my gate of heaven" and suchlike until she, with spittle in the corners of her mouth and her artfully piled-up hair falling on both sides on her, now bared, white shoulders, disheveled, rushed towards him who took aim, whose clear blue eyes were filled with tears, and knelt before him. Kleist clenched his teeth together so hard that the pipe's stem broke in two. He threw pistol and pipe away and pressed Henriette's head against his body. "My dear child," he soothed her, "we must go into the public room, we must be merry, we shouldn't let people notice anything, now, in the middle of this triumphal chant that my soul intones in this moment of death—don't let them notice anything! The whole of my exultant concern can only be to find the abyss, deep enough, to plunge into with you. A whirlpool, a whirlpool of bliss never experienced has taken hold of me, and I prefer a grave with you to the beds of all the empresses in the world."

"Good," she said, "good," stood up, "good, my Heinrich, my Pan flute, good." While Henriette got herself ready, Kleist sorted papers, picked up the pistol, took another, hid them both in the next room and finally, in the company of Madame Vogel, walked down to the public room where the innkeeper poured them coffee for the second time.

They went for a walk, a good hour. When they had agreed on where they wanted to die together, they went back to the inn. There the coachman was still waiting. Kleist paid him. Amazed at the large sum that was handed to him, the coachman curled his lips. He got on the box, and the horse pulled violently, as if it had taken fright. The wheels creaked. Still grinning, wrapped in his black cloak, the coachman turned around and showed his long, yellow teeth.

Kleist, going in, demanded supper. He ordered three flagons of wine, dispelled the innkeeper's misgivings by making outrageous fun, and followed Henriette into the room, where he did not touch the food that was brought in later.

Henriette wept. Kleist wanted to embrace her and console her. He started towards her and under his ample soft-leather boot crushed, halfway, the pipe he had thrown down early in the afternoon. He cried out: "My favorite pipe, damn it!"

"Oh," replied Henriette, "now it doesn't matter any more." Kleist bent over and touched the broken pipe. He acknowledged that it indeed didn't matter any more now, left the pipe where it lay, and felt, when he straightened up and looked at Henriette, revulsion toward her. His eyes clouded over. Henriette, who noticed, asked if he had changed his mind. "Me?" he stared at her and stamped his foot, "me? Me change my mind?"

"You promised! Promised! Remember? Back then. We were playing Beethoven."

"No, we were singing."

"All right. We were singing," she screamed, "we were singing, all right! And what did you say? What? What did you say? That it was so beautiful you could shoot yourself, so beautiful you could shoot yourself. You granted my request, you promised, you did promise, me, me! I am the first to ask you. All the others didn't want to, I am the only one, I want to, I want to, and now do you want to—do you want to?" Kleist, arms dangling from his shoulders, murmured: "I am a man of my word." Henriette ran towards him. But Kleist pushed her away. She stumbled backwards and bumped into the table on which, next to the evening meal, pen and ink lay. She whispered, excited: "Who else did you promise? Who? Who? Who? In Thun already? Young men, I bet? All the young men you went to swim with, naked? You wanted to die with all of them, didn't you? Didn't you? And with Marie, too, even though supposedly you left her for me? Didn't you? But I, I am sick, it is serious, sick, sick, cancer is eating me up, Heinrich, you, I, you know, you, I, you know, I am rotting, my good Kleist, my Sir Heinrich, you scoundrel! Oh," she wept suddenly, "it was so beautiful, the way we imagined it, so," she stopped and searched for a word, "so noble," emphatically: "so noble!"

Kleist did not reply, walked up and down, hammered his fist against his forehead and, after a while, ordered the houseman, who had been summoned, to be so kind as to bring four candles that would burn all night long. He was cold, Kleist said, he was cold, even though there was a fire in the stove, he was cold.

Henriette, who had been sitting motionless and upright on her chair for hours, jumped up when Kleist cried out unexpectedly: "Come, little bird, come, sit down, my bird-catcher, I want to dictate a note to you! Because there are a few things I want to add to the letter you wrote yesterday to your dear husband and receptor-general of the Kurmärkische Landfeuer-sozietät. Be so kind as to write: 'Now, my good, my excellent Vogel, the last request I have to beg of you. —Do not separate Kleist from me in death, and please make the necessary arrangements for a suitable, proper burial for him, for the repayment of which measures have already been taken on his part.' Have you got that? Are you satisfied now? Bon. Let's drink some coffee then."

"Now? At this hour?" objected Henriette. "Oui, Madame, at this hour!" roared Kleist and saw to it that the maid, a Mamselle Feilenhauer, brought coffee, albeit a little sleepily, upon which Henriette, alone, for Kleist was in the next room, said it was her wish that coffee should be brought between three and four in the morning.

The four candles lit up the room. The fire was burning in the stove. Kleist was walking up and down again. His big shadow on the wall was restless.

Henriette started, because Kleist suddenly bent over and, from the brown-lacquered little chest she assumed was empty, took papers that he pressed, trembling, against his chest. "What?" she asked, "what? you—you didn't burn everything at my house?" Her big eyes under the strong brows went glassy with fear. Kleist, his mouth gaping, silent, shook his head. Henriette stretched out her hand and rose slowly. "In Paris, seven years ago, my *Guiskard*, I—I destroyed it, a pox, I destroyed it, tear it to shreds, burn it, I couldn't, I can't, I gnashed my teeth, a terrible renunciation, and Pfuel, I loved him, Brockes too, Brockes too, with him in Würzburg, I—I—no, no, I won't say it, Brockes and Pfuel and others, many others, they were all young, and now, I can't, I can't get away from it, it's ridiculous, I'm thirty-four, it's ridiculous, again and again," he stammered unconnected sentences as he stood in front of his big shadow, until Henriette said slowly: "Heinrich, I shudder to look upon thee," which made Kleist wince, as if he had been hit by a fist. "Ha!" he snorted. "Ha, he has it good. I wanted to steal his laurels, years ago, that man in Weimar, who is now destroying the radiance he brought forth in his youth. But I can't. I have it in my hands, here. I can't, I can't. Here in my hands the proof of my inability! I have been writing on it for years, my loathsome novel; everything is in it, I wake up in it, I grin at myself in it, I grow bigger than myself in it, a ghost, my ghost, it shakes me, seizes, suffocates my cursed self, here, here, here! But I'll tear it to shreds, I am tearing it up, to shreds," which he did, starting to tear the sheets apart like a madman, in such a way that his fingers were bloodied by the sharp edges of the paper, and: "Tear up, tear up and tear to shreds, destroy, this life, these confessions, these experiences in the dark, shining with blood and pain, these missed opportunities, tear it all up, to shreds, crush it, this paper life, this youth, yes, Winter, be gone, old man, kind and wise, who smooths emotions to ice, hahahaha! Spring? Nothing melts, no, nothing, neither rivers nor—no, nothing, I disavow them. My seven plays—tear them up, all of them, no, not *Penthesilea*, she did it right, I know, she said: 'So! So! So! So! And again. —All is well now.' What? What? Still on your feet? Why don't you fall down? Why are you standing there alive? Why are you staring at me? I'm not a man, am I, I'm just a hypochondriac, right? The kind of man who asks everybody to die with him. But I can't do it alone. I mustn't die alone. Not alone! Don't stand there and stare! Mad—oh—you disgust me! Why didn't I die together with Pfuel? Frenzy, frenzy, how often have I imagined dying, death a thousand times, and death again and again, and now, when I know, for certain, I'll do it, yes, I'll do it, I am a man of my word, you goddamn whore, I'll shoot you down, I'll do it, I'll rot together with you, my nails dug into you, rot into the putrefaction of your uterine cancer, that terrible rotting together, without God, without Kant, without Brockes, without Pfuel, without the ragamuffin in Prague, no prison, no syphilis, just this putrefaction, this rotting in the common grave, this horrible coitus without end with a—horrible! with a wife in death, hahahaha! Not to find a sure way to happiness and to enjoy it undisturbed, even among the greatest hardships of life.

"No way, no way out! But a long, crooked, wrong way, Frankfurt, Potsdam, the campaign on the Rhine, Würzburg, Dresden, Göttingen, Mainz, Strasbourg, Paris, Bern, Thun, Leipzig, Berlin, Chalons-sur-Marne, Aspern, Prague—towns, towns, corpses, soldiers, prisons, illness, and these breakdowns time and again—always the last time, and always back to the beginning, always start over again, scream Never Again, final, inescapable, irrevocable. My life on paper, the most terrible corpse. Torn up, torn to shreds! Burn the shreds! Burn it all! All, all! Burn the paper futility." And he gathered the papers together and crumpled them and opened the stove and watched the paper wrinkle, rear up, spew flames, shrivel, be blown upward like ash, charred black, crackling.

He broke down and embraced Henriette's legs. "All burnt," he sobbed, "it's all burnt. My life burnt, my life's novel burnt, my hope burnt, my reputation burnt, my virility burnt, burnt out—clouds, a gloomy spectacle. Hermes, my Psychopompos, has left me. Gray wall, torn apart. Oh how it did hurt, the beauty of the good I only dreamed, and it transfixed me, an arrow, its tip soaked in a numbing poison. But my wishes grew dark in the shadow of my desire. The stinking sweat of my vice. Ah, of the black gush."

Henriette, tired, slowly opened her dress, took it off, stood, white, before Kleist who, on his knees, whimpering, shrank back and kept repeating: "No no no no no," stood thus before Kleist, her hair a dark flame, stood, bent over with shame, stood in tears and waited. But Kleist, with his broken pipe in his hand, closed his eyes, whispered: "Not yet, not yet, I can't," fled into the adjoining room and locked the door. Weeping silently, Henriette knocked. She implored: "Heinrich, my hope and my expectation, my renascence, my soul is yours!"

She lay before the door a long time, and her hand grew hot. When she heard Kleist vomiting, she stood up. The stove had gone out. Only two candles were still burning. Shivering with cold Henriette ordered coffee. Mamselle Feilenhauer brought it and gave Henriette a helping hand in lacing herself up.

When Kleist suddenly knocked violently on the door, she called: "Bon-

jour, mon enfant, un moment,, s'il te plaît, mon cher ami!" Mamselle Feilenhauer curtsied and went away.

Kleist, walking in, went without looking at Henriette to the table, where,
standing, he wrote without interruption a letter with the following content
to his stepsister Ulrike: I cannot die without reconciling myself, joyful and
content as I am, with the whole world and therefore also, above all others,
with you, my dearest Ulrike. Let me take back the harsh expression contained in the letter to the Kleists, let me take it back; indeed, you have
done, I won't say all a sister could, but all a human being could, to save
me: The truth is that there was no help for me on earth. And now goodbye;
may heaven grant you a death but half the equal of mine in joy and inex-
pressible serenity. That is the most glorious and heartfelt wish I can muster for you.

> Stimming's near Potsdam
> dated—the morning of my death

> > > > Your Heinrich

Henriette looked over his shoulder and said harshly: "Your serenity
doesn't seem all that serene to me." Without answering, Kleist strewed sand
over the paper, blew on it, folded the letter, made the documents that were
to be dispatched ready for the messenger, and drank the coffee that had
grown cold. The maid came at nine to look after their clothes.

In the public room, where Kleist and Henriette pretended to be cheerful,
as they had agreed they would, and called each other "My dear child," the
innkeeper Stimming asked about noon what his guests would like to dine
on at night. Kleist replied: "We are expecting two strangers tonight, they
must eat very well." "Oh no," said Henriette, "I thought we'd let that be,
they can content themselves with an omelette, just as we did." "Well," said
Kleist, "in that case we shall eat all the better tomorrow at noon"; and
Henriette turned pale; and both repeated: "This evening two guests are
coming." Kleist, who knew that husband Vogel would come accompanied
by Councilor of War Peguilhen, jokingly handed the innkeeper the letters,
with the order that a messenger should take them to Berlin at once.

Kleist and Henriette went into the garden and played about, in fact Kleist,
in high spirits, even jumped and hopped over the ninepin alley, shouting:
"They're falling, all nine of them!" and told Henriette to do the same,
which she declined. They flirted in the kitchen instead and ordered coffee.
Kleist walked away hurriedly, ran into his room, and got down on his
knees. He looked for the broken pipe but couldn't find it any more. He
got the two pistols, loaded them carefully, put them in a basket that he
covered with a white cloth, and went back into the kitchen, where he wanted eight pennies worth of rum. He took out the bill, which he had asked

for, paid, and gotten back with a receipt that morning, looked at it pensively, and put it away again. Suddenly he proposed that a table and two chairs be taken to the lake, because he intended to have coffee there. Frau Stimming protested that it was too much trouble. But Kleist insisted. Frau Stimming finally gave in and said she would clean the rooms in the meantime. Kleist, startled, objected and said that everything had better remain as it was.

After the pair had whiled away the time, asking occasionally if the messenger would be in Berlin by now, they went, hand in hand, across the Wilhelm Bridge to the Chaussee where they met Riebisch, the day laborer, who was pushing a cart of manure that blocked the way. Kleist said harshly: "Get that cart out of the road so the lady may pass," and so Riebisch did, for which he was given a penny. He looked after them as they hurried away. His wife came to meet him and said: "Riebisch, such madness, just imagine those two people want to drink coffee up there—in the middle of winter!" Riebisch muttered that she got paid for it, so she could take the coffee all right, and he wheeled the cart off. The innkeeper later ordered him to carry a table and two chairs up to the hill by the Wannsee. The day laborer obeyed, dragged table and chairs, and found the pair by the hill. Kleist poured rum into the coffee and said to Riebisch: "Grandpa, tell our host to fill this flagon half full of rum again and have it sent out here to me!" Henriette interjected: "Dear child, do you really want to drink more rum today, you have had enough rum already." Kleist thought for a moment and then said dryly: "Well, dear child, if you don't want to, I don't either. Just never mind, Grandpa, and don't bring anything out here."

Henriette gave the old Riebisch woman, who had brought the coffee, some milk to drink and, squealing with laughter, said when the old woman got some on her: "Look at what a milk moustache you have made for yourself!"

Kleist, confused, asked for someone to bring him a pencil, grabbed Henriette by the hand, and hissed: "Don't you want to be merry? Be merrier, damn it!" And Henriette gave a shrill laugh, and both, jumping, romping, scampering, ran wildly down the hill to the Wannsee and played tag. The old people gazed after the young couple, amused, and went back to the inn. When the old Riebisch woman brought the pencil, Kleist and Henriette came skipping towards her. Kleist offered the day laborer's wife a cup, in which there lay a few gold coins, and said in a friendly voice, while his face twitched: "Little Mother, here is the cup, take it with you, rinse it out, and bring it back." The old woman left.

Kleist opened the little basket and took from the same a large pistol, with the butt about one and a quarter feet long and with the inscription Lazarius

Comminazzo displayed along the barrel, weighed the weapon in his hand, leveled it, and aimed at Henriette in such a way that she, shrinking back, held up her hands and stammered: "My Heinrich, my joy in sorrow, my—"

"Enough," interrupted Kleist, "enough! I am a man of my word." He fired, and Henriette, struck in the left breast, sank into the ditch and died. Kleist grabbed her shoulders and leaned the corpse against the wall of the ditch. Then he folded his victim's hands. "Now, now! I'll manage, now I can, now," took the second weapon, gasped, gripped the hard barrel, pushed the muzzle between his lips, gasped, gasped, "Now," and felt the hot pressure, saw fire, his mother, a hairpin, Robert Guiskard and still heard the shot and saw himself go down in the bright red explosion.

After a short while the Riebisch woman came back with the empty, clean cup. She found both corpses lying in a ditch by the Wannsee. Foot to foot, their faces opposite each other, the upper parts of their bodies inclined and leaning against the wall of the ditch, the lifeless pair sat opposite each other and stared at one another.

The Riebisch woman screamed, dropped the cup, ran into the inn, and was still trembling when the husband Vogel and his companion arrived. Vogel acted inconsolable, took some snuff, and went to bed at eleven. The next day he accepted a lock of his wife's hair and traveled back to Berlin.

But at noon the other gentleman, who had also left with Vogel, came back, had a deep hole dug at the place of the crime, and said two coffins would be brought from Berlin.

In the meantime Dr. Sternemann, the Teltow County coroner, cut open Kleist's corpse, forced his mouth open with great difficulty, sawed the head open, from the brain took the piece of lead that weighed one-quarter of an ounce, ascertained, while rummaging about in the corpse, that Kleist had died of asphyxiation by gunpowder, discovered a lot of thickened, black bile, and recorded that Kleist had been a *Sanguino cholericus in summo gradu* by temperament and that he had often suffered attacks of hypochondria, which allowed the rightful conclusion that *de nati* Kleist had been of a sickly mental disposition.

He did not take part when the corpses were buried in two coffins in the deep hole that night at ten. But after all participants were gone, there came, from the direction of the Wannsee, out of the thick fog, a figure wrapped in a black, hooded cloak. It was the coachman who had brought from Berlin both Kleist and Henriette and today, as well, two coffins. He bent down and stabbed his finger, grinning, into the night-cold earth.

He got on the box, and the horse pulled violently, as if it had taken fright. The wheels creaked. Still grinning, wrapped in his black cloak, the coachman turned around and showed his long, yellow teeth.

END OF THE LINE

JUREK BECKER
translated by Brian L. Harris

MAN, YESTERDAY I REALLY LIKED HER. I WISH I UNDERSTOOD MYSELF. ALL of this agonizing, and I still can't make sense of it. Not that I would have suddenly lost interest in her, that's out of the question; but something is basically different. And it can't possibly be because she came over to my place last night, even though we have known each other only a couple of days. That's what I wanted, more than anything else. At first she did put on a little show of modesty.

The blue lamp is still on, and here it is, the middle of the day. Fine, so they all put on airs, nothing more needs to be said about that. But she went about it in a very unusual way. I don't even know if you could really call her behavior an act. She merely had to overcome some doubts, which she did, without a big fuss.

I won't make a long story of it, but it is true that I had convinced myself that this time was going to be something special. Maybe it is something unique; but even if it is, I'll still need a good long while to figure it out. I had told myself a thousand times that it wouldn't happen again, that sooner or later you have to grow up and settle down a little, and such things people always say. And so, as best I could, I indulged in what I call waiting it out. It's better you don't ask me what exactly I was waiting for, I could only come up with hazy notions. But something had to happen, this extraordinary event just had to take place, I mean, a girl showing up who was so much different from all the others. How, nobody knows, just different. She was bound to be as good-looking as my brother's wife, and she'd have to be as understanding as my mother has been on five or six occasions, and her way of handling people could be compared to Doris Day's, right now I've forgotten the title of the movie. And that would be it, the end of the line, so I thought.

And now, here I am, seeing myself almost like a sailboat that has got a good wind at the start, but hits a lull half-way out, and is just drifting around. Nobody can expect me to fool myself, make myself believe that I've ended up exactly where I always wanted to be. I'd give anything, if right now everything about her would be as it was last night, when I was looking at her like a half-starved puppy might look at a juicy, unreachable steak. On purpose I dispensed with the whole circus that I've always put on for similar occasions, since I was telling myself: This won't be one of those. There wasn't supposed to be a hint of routine.

Those select record albums that had never failed before were left right in the cabinet. We just listened to whatever was on the radio. As soon as we stepped into my room, I switched on the ceiling light, not even glancing at the floor lamp with the blue shade, which a few weeks ago would have struck me as sheer stupidity. We sat politely at the table, she in the arm-chair, I on the sofa, and we talked for a while about the lousy play we'd just seen. Her views were very intelligent, but of course I was already aware of that, she was a bright young woman. After an hour or so I discovered in the cupboard half a bottle of wine, left over from my last birthday. We finished it, but I can swear there was no ulterior motive. The longer I looked at her, the better I liked her. I would've bet my life it was going to be that way for-ever.

It did occur to me how crude and blunt I'd always been whenever some-one else was sitting at the table. But those were such different situations. From the start everything was somehow transparent, the other girl always knew why she'd come along, and I knew that she knew. It was a game played with all our cards on the table. Yet in the theater last night I didn't even dare to hold her hand.

An uncle on my mother's side had told me once that true love makes you shy, and applied to both of us that seemed to be positive proof I was nearing the end of the line in a hurry. I was so inhibited I was getting afraid of stand-ing there like some idiot in her eyes. I didn't want to do anything wrong, for God's sake. I kept on thinking that I didn't want to do anything wrong. It went so far that finally I didn't know what was happening. I couldn't even come up with the next word or gesture, the right ones. Then suddenly I felt certain it'd probably be better if it didn't happen right then. Why, I don't know even, but now I tell myself that I considered it utterly impossible that it *could* happen today. And so in these straits I just took as undeniable wisdom the saying, something to the effect that all good things take a long, long time.

She asked if anything was bothering me, and if so, I really ought to tell her. I seemed so preoccupied, so entirely different than usual, she said. Obviously I couldn't tell her what was going on inside my poor head, but I couldn't just sit silently forever, so I told her I liked her very much. She was glad about that. Now, she didn't say, "Oh, I'm so glad," or anything of the kind, and her whole face didn't brighten up. She just looked at me with those eyes, one of which is just a little lighter than the other, until I knew she was glad. At that point most of the others would have said, "Oh, you're just saying that." Or they would have asked, "Is that really true?" She said nothing at all; actually she's a very quiet girl.

As soon as we had sipped the last of our wine, she got up from her chair, went over to the floor lamp with the blue shade, switched it on, turned off the ceiling light, and sat down on the sofa next to me. My heart nearly stopped. At that instant I realized that all of my deliberations about putting things off until later, just now, about good things taking a lot of time—I knew right then all of that was screwed-up nonsense. Here she was, acting much like Esmeralda had acted from time immemorial in my dreams, like that other girl whom I've known for an eternity, but who had just acquired through her a real name and a face. It is simply incredible what a difference it makes whether you switch on the blue lamp yourself, or someone else does.

When I put my hand on her shoulder, it trembled. My hand, I mean. Someone was reading the evening news on the radio. I've never heard anything that that could have left me more indifferent. I even forgot to kiss her, I was so idiotically content. And you can believe it or not, I'd give anything if it were possible to preserve such a moment. Of course, I realize that you can't spend your entire life sitting in blue light on a sofa, gazing at one another, that's quite out of the question. But I don't mean that either. I mean, if somehow you could save this feeling, this indefinable peace of mind.

When I awoke next to her this morning, it took me a while to get my bearings. Her head was resting on my arm, and my arm had gone to sleep, that's probably what woke me. I pulled my arm carefully away, without waking her, and got up to get a drink of water, my tongue always feels like leather in the morning. It was still very early, and I lay down again and tried to go back to sleep. But it was no use. The floor lamp was still on, as I discovered quite by accident, for the room was as bright as day. In our excitement last night we had forgotten to lower the venetian blind.

I've had plenty of time to look at her closely. Her mouth was slightly open, even though she was breathing through her nose. Now, don't think that I would have suddenly started finding some fault with her, there wasn't any bump on her nose that I might have overlooked earlier. No rash or pimples on her skin, it was as smooth and clear as milk or new snow. If anything, she was almost more beautiful than yesterday. One of her hands was resting on top of the covers, palm up, fingers slightly curled. It looked like a hand that was about to catch some small object. She was sleeping so soundly and peacefully that anyone could be envious. I thought of how beautiful it was with her yesterday, in the blue light, and for a few seconds I thought I would have to wake her. I even had my hand on her arm, but I drew it back and fell asleep again.

GOING BEGGING

HANS BENDER
translated by Jeanne R. Willson

TELL A STORY? ALWAYS ASKING. MAYBE FROM MY CHILDHOOD, THAT IN-exhaustible supply.

Alvina, Amelia, Alphonse were the names of the neighbor children.

Who in the world gave them those fine names that all begin with A?

Their mother went to the cigar factory, mornings at seven until afternoons at five. When it struck twelve, she hurried home to cook a quick midday meal.

Their father was out of work, as many fathers were in those days.

Alvina liked to comb my hair a lot.

I sat on a chair in our yard. She had put a pocket mirror in my hand so I could see how she combed it.

"Your hair is so blond, so fine," she said. "And mine is black as pitch."

"Black hair is prettier," I said.

"But not for girls."

Alvina was skinny, really too tall for her age.

Amelia was still little. She had two blonde pigtails, with the ends fastened together on Sundays by pink ribbons.

Alphonse had short, reddish brown hair that curled around the crown. In March he was already going barefoot.

Lots of days Alvina, Amelia, and Alphonse disappeared.

I played with other children.

"Don't you know, they go begging," said the children.

In Malsch and Malschenberg, in Rettigheim and Östringen, in Rotenberg and Rauenberg they went from door to door; and because they aroused sympathy, people gave them things.

It was certainly an adventure—to go begging.

"When are you going again?" I asked Alphonse.

"In the fall, after the potato crop is in," he said, "when the farmers are all at home."

In the fall after the potato crop was in Alvina said, "Tomorrow we're going to Rotenberg."

Rotenberg was really a town, but it wasn't any different from the other villages. On the contrary. There were no cigar factories, only hired hands and farmers who kept horses and cows.

"The town of Rotenberg," said the sixth grade teacher, "has 365 inhabitants. You can easily remember that. If each day one inhabitant were to die in Rotenberg, the city would be empty on December thirty-first."

"But new children are always coming into the world!" I objected.

"Take me with you!" I said to Alvina, Amelia, and Alphonse.

They were surprised, but they didn't say no.

"Good, that's fine with me," said Alvina.

There were two routes to Rotenberg: the highway along the creek and a lane along the railroad and the hill—a lane through the fields.

We went on the lane through the fields next to the wheel tracks or on the grass between them.

Halfway there Alvina said, "You're dressed much too fancy. You'll have to disguise yourself."

I looked down at myself abashed.

"Put on Alphonse's jacket, only inside out," she commanded. "And Alphonse'll put on your sweater."

The jacket was too big for me. My hands disappeared in the sleeves, and it smelled of kitchen odors.

We could see the first house in Rotenberg already, the mill that belonged to Herr Kefer.

"Just like always, first to the mill," said Alvina. "We always get the most there."

"Not to the mill!" I begged.

I had already been to the mill three or four times. Frau Kefer, the miller's wife, was usually sick, and then she ordered meat and sausage on the telephone, and my father took me with him in the car and said to Frau Kefer: "My youngest son."

"Why not to the mill?" asked Alvina.

"Just not to the mill first," I begged.

Alvina gave in, and we went on into the village, and at the first house we went slowly up the steps with me behind Alvina, Amelia, Alphonse; and the door stood open.

When a woman's voice called from the end of the hall, "What do you want?" Alvina recited with a whimpering voice, as if she had learned it by heart: "We are poor, we are hungry, our father is out of work."

"Come on in," called the farmer's wife.

We had to wait awhile inside the door until the farmer's wife fetched apples from the storeroom. She put one in each of our hands.

Alphonse had a knapsack on his back which got filled up at the next houses—with apples, with pears, with bread and potatoes.

Another farmer's wife, who was really old, even gave us a chocolate bar, and a shopkeeper's wife let us sit at the kitchen table, and she put a pot on the stove.

"I still have soup left over from dinner, chicken soup with rice."

When the store bell rang because a customer had come in, the shopkeeper's wife left us alone while we emptied our bowls. Why, the shopkeeper's wife finally even gave us money; to each of us a ten pfennig piece.

"Thank you, may God reward you," we said.

A farmer, who was unloading beets in the yard, ran us off. "Clear out," he yelled. "If you don't get lost in a hurry, I'll sic the dogs on you."

Little Amelia cried. But the knapsack was full, the old bag, too, that Alvina lugged along.

It was already getting dark as we came to the end of the street, and it was getting colder because the sun had gone down.

"Now on to the Kefers," said Alvina.

We saw Herr Kefer and his boys working in the mill. Bright lights burned in there, and the walls and the sacks were dusty with flour.

There was a stairway up to the house which Frau Kefer's maid had to scrub every day with soapy water.

To the right of the door was a brass knob. When you pulled it, a loud bell rang in the entrance hall.

Frau Kefer opened the door. She had a white cloth tied around her forehead because she had a headache.

She smiled and said we should step in. She invited us into the kitchen for a cup of hot milk and a piece of raspberry cake. For each of us she filled a cup up with milk, and the pieces of cake were each on a plate with a fork next to it.

"You may eat with your fingers if you like," she said and smiled again so friendly.

I reached for the piece of cake with my hand too.

Then she looked at me—much too long.

I held the cup in front of my face.

"Don't I know you?" she asked.

"Me?"

"You surely belong to . . ." she said, and she mentioned the name of my father. "Didn't you bring me meat and sausage?"

"No," I said softly.

"I still think—you are the youngest son."

She still smiled as if she most certainly recognized me, but she said in a no less friendly way, "So, and now empty your cups and go home. It's late enough."

"Thank you, may God reward you," we recited.

Silently we went back along the lane through the fields. It was almost dark, and from the creek came the smell of fog.

"She did recognize you," said Alvina. "And she'll tell your father on you."

"Who cares! He'll just make fun of me," I said.

Alvina wanted to walk on the tracks.

"Can you all dance on the tracks too?" she asked. "In the dark?"

"And what if the six o'clock train comes?" asked Amelia.

"This crybaby; she's always afraid," said Alvina.

"They'll throw hot coals out of the engine, and the Laplander will jump down from the footboard and beat on us."

The Laplander was the conductor of whom all the children were afraid. He had a funny face with slanted eyes and bushy eyebrows. When he punched the tickets, he asked in a strict voice: "Are you six yet?"

Halfway home we sat down to rest in the grass next to the train track. Alvina took a pack of cigarettes and some matches out of her pocket.

"Where did you get the cigarettes?" I asked.

"I snitched these from the shopkeeper's wife," she said and started to blow smoke through her nose.

"You want a smoke?" she asked.

I puffed twice and handed the cigarette on to Alphonse.

Amelia was allowed to eat an apple.

It was nice to sit in the grass and smoke.

"Won't they bawl you out when you get home so late, Hans?" Alvina asked.

"No, I can come home when I want to."

Just then the locomotive whistled before it came to the bridge, and it came up close behind us with its headlights, right and left, like red eyes in a black face.

The train passed close to us. We saw the engineer in front of the fire-box door and the people in the compartments.

There on the footboard stood the Laplander with the carbide lamp glaring in front of him. He lifted his right hand and threatened us, but the train was going so fast that he couldn't jump off.

"Laplander, Laplander," Alvina called after him.

And when the train was even farther away, Alphonse, Amelia and I shouted: "Laplander, Laplander!" as loud as we could.

Laughing we tumbled into the grass and rolled all over each other.

That's how happy we were.

IS IT A COMEDY? IS IT A TRAGEDY?

THOMAS BERNHARD
translated by A. Leslie Willson

AFTER NOT HAVING VISITED THE THEATER FOR WEEKS, YESTERDAY I
planned to go to the theater, but two hours before the start of the performance, during my scientific labor and so in my study—I'm not entirely sure,
whether in the foreground or the background of medical matters that I must
finally conclude, less for the sake of my parents than for my overexerted
head—I wondered whether I should not after all refrain from the theater
visit.

I haven't been to the theater for eight or ten weeks, I told myself, and I
know why I haven't gone to the theater. I despise the theater. I hate the actors. Theater is just a perfidious impertinence, an impertinent perfidy. And
I should suddenly go to the theater again? To a play? What is that?

You know that the theater is an obscenity, I told myself, and you will
write the study about the theater that you have in mind, a study of the theater
that will be a slap in the face of theater once and for all. What the theater *is*,
what the actors *are*, the authors of the pieces, the directors, etc. . . .

More and more I was dominated by the theater, less and less by pathology,
frustrated in my attempt to ignore the theater, to assault pathology. Frustrated! Frustrated!

I got dressed and went out onto the street.

The theater is only a half-hour walk for me. In that half-hour it became
clear to me that I *cannot* go to the theater, that a visit to the theater, to a
theatrical performance is forbidden me once and for all.

When you have written your study of the theater, I thought, then it will be
time, then you will again be permitted to go to the theater, so that you can see
that your treatise is *correct*!

It just bothered me that things ever got to the point where I bought myself a theater ticket—I *bought* the theater ticket, I didn't receive it as a *gift*
—and that I tortured myself for two days in the belief that I would go to
the theater, watch a theater performance, the actors, and behind all those
actors smell a wretched, stinking director (Herr T.H.!), etc. . . . but above
all, that I had *changed clothes* for the theater. You *changed* for the theater,
I thought.

The theater study, one day the theater study! A person can describe well
what he hates, I thought. In five, possibly in seven sections with the title

Theater—Theater? my study will be finished in a short time. (When it is finished, you will burn it because it doesn't make sense to publish it, you will read it through and burn it. Publication is ridiculous! *Unavailing purpose!*) First section, THE ACTORS, second section, THE ACTORS IN THE ACTORS, third section, THE ACTORS IN THE ACTORS OF THE ACTORS, etc. . . . fourth section, STAGE EXCESSES, etc. . . . last section: SO, WHAT IS THEATER?

With these thoughts I arrived at the Volksgarten.

I sat down on a bench next to the Meierei, although sitting down on a Volksgarten bench at this season of the year can be *fatal,* and I watched with an effort, with pleasure, with enormous concentration *who and how* one goes into the theater.

I am satisfied *not* going in.

But, I think, you should go in, and in consideration of your poverty, sell your ticket, *go on,* I tell myself, and while I am thinking that, I take the greatest pleasure in mangling my theater ticket between the thumb and forefinger of my right hand, mangling the theater.

First, I tell myself, there are more and more people going into the theater, then fewer and fewer. Finally no one will go into the theater anymore.

The performance has begun, I think, and I get up and walk a short way in the direction of midtown. I'm cold. I haven't eaten anything and, it occurs to me, I haven't spoken to a single soul for more than a week, when suddenly I am spoken to: A man has spoken to me. I hear a man asking me what time it is, and I hear myself exclaim "Eight o'clock." "It is eight o'clock," I say. "The play has begun."

Now I turn around and see the man.

The man is tall and thin.

Besides this man, no one is in the Volksgarten, I think.

Immediately, I think that I have nothing to lose.

But saying the sentence: *"I have nothing to lose!"* and saying it *out loud,* seems senseless to me, and I do not say the sentence, although I have the greatest desire to say the sentence.

He has lost his watch, the man says.

"Since I lost my watch, I am forced to talk to people from time to time." He laughed.

"If I had not lost my watch, I wouldn't have spoken to you," he said, "spoken to *anybody.*"

Most interesting to him, said the man, was the observation that, how—after I had told him that it was eight o'clock—he now knew that it *is* eight o'clock and that today for eleven hours without interruption—"without an interruption," he said—he had walked in one thought, "not back and forth," he said, but "always straight ahead, and as I now see," he said, "in a circle. Crazy, isn't it?"

I saw that the man had on women's slippers, and the man saw that I had seen that he had on women's slippers.

"Yes," he said, "now you may get ideas."

"I," I said quickly, to divert myself and the man from his women's slippers, "I planned to visit the theater, but right in front of the theater, I turned heel and didn't go in the theater."

"I have been in this theater very often," said the man—he had introduced himself, but I had immediately forgotten his name, I don't remember names —"someday for the last time like every man some day goes to the theater for the last time, don't laugh," said the man. "There's a last time for everything, don't laugh."

"Oh," he said, "what's playing today? No-no," he said quickly, "don't tell me what's playing. . ."

He went into the Volksgarten every day, said the man, "Since the start of the season I have gone into the Volksgarten about this time, so that here, from this corner, from the Meierei wall, you know, I can watch the theatergoers. Remarkable people," he said.

"Of course, one ought to know what's playing today," he said, "but don't *you* tell me what's playing today. For me it is extremely interesting *not* to know for once what's playing. Is it a comedy? Is it a tragedy?" he asked and said at once, "No-no, don't say *what it is*. Don't say it."

The man is fifty, or he is fifty-five, I think.

He made the suggestion that we walk in the direction of the Parliament.

"Let's walk up to the Parliament," he said, "and back again. It is remarkably quiet when the performance has begun. I *love* this theater. . ."

He walked very fast, and it was almost unendurable to me to watch him. The thought that the man had on women's slippers caused me to be ill.

"I walk the same number of steps here every day," he said, "that is, in these shoes I walk from the Meierei to the Parliament, to the Volksgarten fence, exactly three hundred and twenty-eight steps. In the *buckled* shoes I walk three hundred and ten. And to the Swiss Wing—he meant the Swiss Wing of the Palace—I walk exactly four hundred and fourteen steps with *these* shoes, three hundred and twenty-nine with the *buckled* shoes! Women's shoes, you might think, and it may be repulsive to you, I know," said the man.

"But I walk on the street only in darkness. The fact that every evening at this time, always a half-hour before the start of the performance, I walk into the Volksgarten is based, as you can imagine, on something shocking. That something now lies twenty-two years in the past. And it's very closely connected with women's slippers. An incident," he says, "an incident. It's the same feeling as back then: The curtain's just gone up in the theater, the actors begin to act, out here the lack of people. . . Let's walk," says the man, after we're back at the Meierei, "to the Swiss Wing now."

A madman? I thought, as we walked to the Swiss Wing, next to one another. The man said: "The world is totally, thoroughly legal, as you perhaps don't know. The world is just one monstrous system of laws. The world is a penitentiary!"

He said: "It's been exactly forty-eight days since I last met a human being here in the Volksgarten at this hour. And I asked *that* man, too, what time it was. And that man, too, told me that it was eight o'clock. Remarkably, I always ask what time it is at eight o'clock. That man, too, walked with me up to the front of the Parliament and up to the front of the Swiss Wing. By the way," said the man, "and this is the truth, I didn't lose my watch. I never lose my watch. Here, see, is my watch," and he held his wrist in front of my face so that I could see his watch.

"A trick!" he said, "but to continue: The man whom I met forty-eight days ago was a man your age. Like you, taciturn, like you, at first *un*decided, then resolved to walk with me. A natural sciences student," said the man. "And I told *him*, too, that something shocking, an incident, that lay long in the past, was the reason that I stop by here in the Volksgarten every evening. In women's slippers. Identical reaction," said the man, and:

"By the way, I never have seen a policeman. For several days the police have avoided the Volksgarten and are concentrating on the Stadtpark, and I know why. . ."

"Now it really would be interesting," he said, "to know whether, in the very instant that we are approaching the Swiss Wing, in the theater a comedy or a tragedy is being played . . . This is the first time that I don't know what's playing. But *you* mustn't tell me. . . No, don't say it! It wouldn't be hard," he said, "while I'm studying *you*, concentrating totally on *you*, occupying myself exclusively with *you*, to figure out whether at this moment in the theater a comedy or a tragedy is playing. Yes," he said, "gradually my study of your person would explain everything that's happening in the theater and everything that's happening outside the theater, everything in the world, that after all is connected to you completely at any time. Ultimately, someday, the moment could really appear when, through my most intensive study of you, I'd know everything about you. . ."

When we had arrived in front of the wall of the Swiss Wing, he said: "Here, on this spot, the young man whom I met forty-eight days ago took his leave of me. You want to know *by what means*? Watch out! Oh!" he said, "*you're* not taking your leave then? You're *not* saying goodnight?

Yes," he said, "then let's walk from the Swiss Wing back to where we came from. Where did we come from anyway? Oh yes, from the Meierei. The remarkable thing about people is that they constantly confuse themselves with other people. So," he said, "you wanted to go to today's performance. Although, as you say, you hate the theater. *Hate* the theater? I *love* it. . ."

Now I realized that the man also had a ladies' hat on his head. I had not noticed that the whole time.

The coat, too, that he had on was a ladies' coat, a ladies' winter coat.

He actually has nothing but women's clothing on, I thought.

"In the summer," he said, "I don't go to the Volksgarten. No theater is playing then either. But always, when the theater is playing, I go to the Volksgarten, because when the theater is playing, nobody but me goes into the Volksgarten anymore because the Volksgarten is much too cold then. Singly young men come into the Volksgarten and, as you know, I address them immediately and invite them to walk along, up in front of the Parliament, up in front of the Swiss Wing . . . and always back from the Swiss Wing and from the Meierei. . . . But up to now, and this just occurs to me, not a soul," he said, "has walked *twice* with me up to the front of the Parliament and *twice* to the Swiss Wing and so back to the Meierei *four times*. We've now walked *twice* to the Parliament and *twice* to the Swiss Wing and back again," he said, "that's enough. If you like," he said, "accompany me a piece toward home. Not a single soul has ever accompanied me from here a piece toward home."

He lived in the Twentieth District.

He was *housed* in the apartment of his parents, who six weeks ago had died ("Suicide, young man, suicide!").

"We have to cross the Danube Canal," he said. I was interested in the man, and I had the urge to accompany him as long as possible.

"At the Danube Canal you must go back," he said. "You may not accompany me farther than to the Danube Canal. Until we have arrived at the Danube Canal, don't ask *why*!"

Behind the Rossau Barracks, a hundred meters from the bridge that leads over into the Twentieth District, the man stopped and looking down into the canal water said suddenly, "Here, on this spot."

He turned around to me and repeated: "On this spot."

And he said: "I pushed her in quick as a flash. The clothes I have on are *her* clothes."

Then he gave me a sign that meant: *Be gone!*

He wanted to be alone.

"Go!" he commanded.

I didn't leave at once.

I let him have his say. "Twenty-two years and eight months ago," he said.

"And if you think it's pleasant in prison, you're wrong! The whole world is one single system of laws. The whole world is a penitentiary. And this evening, I tell you, in that theater over there, whether you believe it or not, a comedy is playing. *Really* a comedy."

REPORT FROM AN ISLAND

HILDE DOMIN
translated by John K. Menzies

I LIVED ON AN ISLAND. IT WAS COMPLETELY DIFFERENT FROM THE ISLANDS
that you know. Every afternoon at exactly five o'clock the parrots flew over
the house, a green cloud. Like doves, except green. They didn't circle, they
flew past, and they talked together very loudly, in their own language. We
can't learn their language, you know that. But they can learn ours.

I came to the island quite suddenly. A small airplane landed on the water,
off the island. On the sea, that is, which is very blue there, naturally. I was
sitting in the airplane. The door was opened. In front of the door was a
wooden gangway: Two boards and a railing, like when you get into a row-
boat. In front of the boards was the earth of the island. Behind me the airplane took off. I had no choice. No one can stay on the gangway. So I came
onto the island. For many years no airplane came to pick me up. And so I
lived on there. I had it more comfortable than Robinson Crusoe, people were
already living there. I'll tell you about them in a minute.

The best part was that the sky was always blue. Except at night, naturally.
But even at night it was very, very bright. That was because the stars and the
moon were larger. The moon lay down on its back as if it were lying in a
cradle. Quite differently than here. When it was full, you could read by its
light, and it cast small shadows from the trees, more distinct than we have on
a gray day.

Because it was always blue and also very hot, the houses only had window
frames, but no panes. Yes, indeed. Why should the houses have had windows,
if it was always blue and hot? Whenever it rained you only had to close the
shutters. Then it became dark as night in whatever room they were closed. It
only rains for a little while there, and right away it is blue again.

When it rains there, the people take off their shoes. The poor people, of
course. But that is quite a few. For they have only one pair of shoes, and they
care for them more than for feet. In many parts of the world the poor people
take their shoes off, so they won't get wet when it rains.

The people who live there have brown feet. Like café au lait or chocolate.
Many have black ones too. And all in all they are dark-skinned people.
You'd think that would be a big difference. I know better. For once I was in

a hospital, a leg lay in a box there, it had been cut off. "Amputated," doctors say. It was a black leg, almost as black as coal. There it lay in the box, and I couldn't look away, although I didn't want to look at it. At the place where it had been cut off, you saw the inside of the leg. The black skin was no thicker than an apple peel. Underneath it the leg was red. Just like all legs are red inside, including yours. You'll see that if you ever fall down.

As I went home and came up to the banana palms with their thick leaves, and the bananas looked very green and uninteresting, much more uninteresting than apples, a little cat came towards me. It was very pretty and very striped. It had only one ear. I had never seen a one-eared cat. I could tell you a lot about the cat, for we became friends, the one-eared cat and I. But there's no time for that today. I only want to add that it was a tomcat and not a pussycat. You can see right off what is a tomcat; tomcats have much thicker heads.

All that I've told you is true. You can ask anyone.

—Is it true that tomcats have thicker heads than pussycats?

—Is it true that skin is thinner than an apple peel, and that people are the same underneath?

—Is it true that poor people are more concerned about their shoes than their feet?

—Does the moon lie on its back in the tropical sky, and can you read there at night?

—Can the parrots learn our language, but we can't learn theirs?

Anybody who knows anything knows all that. But in regard to the one-eared tomcat you must come to me, for only a few people have ever encountered a one-eared cat in their life, although there is an island on which cats have no tails. No cat has a tail there. And again that's something you can ask anyone about. And it's also a completely different island, much closer to us.

THE ENGAGEMENT

GISELA ELSNER
translated by Minetta Altgelt Goyne

THE CHILDREN DIDN'T FEEL LIKE KISSING ONE ANOTHER, IN ANY CASE NOT yet. That it was she, Ellikins (also called Elli and, only in rare instances when she went to extremes, called Elizabeth), who had lured Bobbikins into violating the rules of the game this way, showed in the facial expression with which she (completely inadequate to her starring role and just short of her majority and far from as slender as would have suited her years) pretended to be the naughty little girl that she stubbornly wanted to be and to remain forever in an almost anti-natural way.

We feel so silly, she said.

Although the circle of guests at the table was to be dispersed so that the first part of the celebration (which, as so often happened at the Leiselheimers, had become just a bit too formal) could make way for the second part with music and dancing, Mr. Leiselheimer (while his wife cast a warning glance at her daughter) asked the photographer to wait a bit before he had the waiter who had been hired for the engagement dinner refill the couple's glasses.

Children, children, I wish I had such worries, he said a bit too cheerfully, because he sensed that the conversation had lost momentum and, thanks to Ellikins' having declined to exchange the engagement kiss, was threatening to stop entirely; and then, not without discomfort, he kissed the hand of Ellikins' future mother-in-law, because he had the strong suspicion(not, indeed, founded on so much as a wrinkle in her face) that Mrs. Wiegenstein (whose figure was almost exciting from a distance whenever and wherever he saw her approaching, and who against his better judgment was able momentarily to arouse in him a purely sexual interest) was older than his wife or the graying Mrs. Ockelmann across from him, who was considered well-preserved.

What, pray tell, are worries? asked Bobbikins (also called Bobbi, Bob, and, only in rare instances when he went to extremes, called Robert), to whom coyness was more becoming by far than to his fiancée; and, as Ellikins (from jealousy, apparently) thrust herself in front of him (now let's kiss, she shouted, and the photographer raised his camera), he made the entire party laugh, even both sets of parents, for whom the joy of their children's having found one another was by no means without consequence.

Children, children, what a kiss, called Mr. Leiselheimer no less than anyone else turning his eyes toward Ellikins, who, because of the continuing applause, leaned back her head as if from an uncontrollable fit of passion, threw her fair-skinned bare arms around Bobbikins, and shut her eyes (which had turned out to be a little too close together) so that her eyelids (painted with a subtle pale-blue crescent that matched her pale-blue ankle-length dress and even her pale-blue engagement ring and the gems in the chain around her neck) were completely visible.

What Ellikins was wearing at her engagement party matched in a way that revealed taste, indeed even lengthy fashion consultation.

Only one thing matched neither the original dress, which had cost a small fortune, nor the antique engagement ring, nor the necklace, which had been made especially by a foreign jeweler just in order to go with the ring: namely, Ellikins, whose congenital coarseness never could be entirely concealed despite all attempts at refinement.

Only when she didn't feel well did Ellikins seem almost pretty or at least cute; mostly, as on this evening (after hours of attention by the hairdresser and the cosmetician who had cleverly made her up for the engagement party so that her face looked not narrow but decidedly less wide and flat than usual, an effect which the skin, increasingly red as a result of the alcohol and the excitement, had long since destroyed) she looked, to put it gently, quite healthy, especially at the moment in which her hair fell back from her prominent right ear (which she had inherited from Leiselheimer) as she turned from the guests toward the photographer during this long kiss, which, had it not been a bit exaggerated, might have indicated a degree of being-in-love that bordered on enslavement.

But no matter how carried away she pretended to be, Ellikins by no means ignored the crowd. She loosened her hand from around Bobbikins' neck and, with her subtly tinted ash-blond hair that curled away from the face, covered the ugly, dark-red ear.

Oh, to be able to fall in love, said Mrs. Wiegenstein, smiling in Leiselheimer's direction without straining her face.

What's to prevent it, asked Leiselheimer.

She's suffering from temporary indifference, Mr. Wiegenstein answered in his wife's stead.

Oh, no, my senses are getting dull, my dear, said Mrs. Wiegenstein.

I'm awfully sorry about that, said Mr. Leiselheimer.

I'm incapable of any excitement, said Mrs. Wiegenstein (while Mrs. Leiselheimer left the room and the three-man combo in the den struck up the first notes right afterward) like everyone else turning her eyes toward Bobbikins, who, in order to whisper something to her, laid bare Ellikins' ear (the left one now) without suspecting what he was doing to her by doing this.

You're tickling me, Ellikins shouted so loudly that she drowned out the dance music, which, growing wilder and wilder, proved what privileges Leiselheimer granted to the young, even though at this point they were numerically inferior to the older people.

However, except for Ellikins dancing out of the room with Bobbikins (gorgeous Bobbikins; no matter how much she sometimes envied him and how often she fought regular contests with him for compliments, she couldn't be angry with Bobbikins for long; a bit too lively now, she seemed more poorly coordinated than she actually was despite her ballet lessons), youth was represented only by Bobbikins' older brother Conni, a girl cousin of Ellikins, as well as two of Bobbikins' girl cousins who had felt more than out of place without male dinner partners all through the meal.

Ostensibly because of these two unescorted girl cousins (but mainly so that she, Ellikins, although engaged and thus spoken for, might seem still to be sought after), Ellikins had invited for the second part of the celebration a handful of young gentlemen, the first of whom, known as Ellikins' showpiece, arrived at the moment when, since the two waiters were leaving the house, the only available servant was Mrs. Loos in the kitchen.

Briefly he stood, with a cardboard tube under his arm, in the gigantic entry hall (in the middle of which was a marble stairway which led to the upstairs bedrooms of the villa that looked very modest from the outside in order not to arouse the envy of Mr. Leiselheimer's employees immeasurably) almost vouched (as he stood there bearded and casually dressed, although he felt uneasy between the men in tuxedos) for the openminded sophistication of the Leiselheimers, at whose house one could appear unceremoniously in a turtle neck sweater for the engagement of their only child.

How nice that you've come, called Leiselheimer and (because on the one hand he sensed the other's discomfort and on the other because he himself recently had begun to value the fact that even artists were entertained at his house) greeted his guest with an over-eagerness that the other would not have anticipated in his wildest dreams, let alone would have considered to be due him. Indeed, Mr. Leiselheimer even went so far as to call this guest, who had long been quite unwelcome, the only free man among slaves (among us slaves, he said, plucking and picking at his stiff shirtfront) before he turned him over to Ellikins, who grabbed the cardboard tube from him with a poorly pretended greediness and (while even Leiselheimer himself now found his favorite intolerable) swung this cardboard tube over her head as she dashed to the gift table in the gigantic, just a tiny bit too expensively furnished den, where the three-man combo (a pianist, a bass player, and a clarinettist) obviously was giving its all, just in case somebody sometime might be overcome by the desire to dance.

That's me, shouted Ellikins, unrolling the gift, a watercolor which bore witness to an above-average artistic sensitivity in so far as it did not show

Ellikins as she lived and breathed but as fitted Ellikins' a bit vague and a bit elevated image of herself.

This image, no bigger than a thumb, dancing on a balustrade that formed a dividing line between the pale-blue cloudless sky and the earth, showed Ellikins' elevated but vague image of herself so far away and tiny that, because of the lack of individualizing traits (only the color of the hair shown matched Ellikins' albeit unnatural hair color) one could not say it was like or unlike Ellikins, whether, like Ellikins, one held the watercolor very close to the eyes, or, like Leiselheimer, looked for some distinguishing feature with the help of a reading glass.

What a gift, said Mrs. Wiegenstein, smiling in the artist's direction without straining her face; and then (perhaps in order to hide a little twitching at the corner of her mouth) she helped Ellikins flatten the watercolor on the gift table, as it constantly kept rolling up automatically, while (to the amusement of the whole company, yes, even the four young gentlemen who had just arrived and hadn't had a drop to drink yet) she weighed down the left edge of the picture with a gilt fork and the right with a gilt knife from the gift chest full of equally valuable place settings which had been made for the children, who had no objection to gold and even thought it very pretty and had merely objected to the customary old-fashioned design, being against grandfather's curlicues and grandmother's little roses.

With one exception the other gifts on the gift table also were appropriately restrained, if one ignored the fact that Ellikins' less wealthy relatives and childhood friends had taken the easy way out by sending flowers or telegraphed greetings. For none of the friends, business friends, or acquaintances of the Leiselheimers would willingly have been deprived of contributing his bit to the household of these two so-called children, who, even if their connection seemed at first to be only an instance of good sense, had playfully come to love one another, not overnight, it's true, but little by little, until now they were affectionate toward one another in a way that everyone found charming.

While Ellikins and Bobbikins introduced the young gentlemen to the girl cousins, Leiselheimer stood for a moment longer by the gift table and looked at what had been given to his daughter (to be more exact, to him, the financier Leiselheimer) feeling satisfied, by and large, before he involuntarily found fault with this and that as he had already done in the morning.

It was not, by the way, the flowers and the telegraphed greetings from have-nots that aroused Leiselheimer's objections. On the contrary, Leiselheimer would have been the last to expect anybody to deprive himself of necessities for something useless on his daughter's (that is to say on his) account. What Leiselheimer objected to (more than that: interpreted as downright attempts at extortion) were the disproportionately expensive gifts from some people (nobodies, as Mr. Leiselheimer generally called them) who used the engagement of his daughter in an almost deceptive way to make the financier Leiselheimer feel indebted to them.

Especially he would have liked to return a Venetian glass bowl, the gift of Mr. Miche, his only recently promoted sales manager (with whom neither he nor Ellikins, unless she had lied to him, had cultivated the slightest social contact), to this not especially appealing but comparatively young man (who was rising in his career and could sell him sand by the seashore, as he put it) in order to put him in his place.

But, while, standing there by the gift table smiling somewhat absent-mindedly at the children as they cuddled up all the more affectionately under his gaze, he would have called this Venetian glass bowl the most embarrassing gift, something else (which he, who seldom failed to consider possibilities, would have forestalled had he foreseen it)—namely, six silverplated napkin rings, the gift of Mrs. Loos—occupied him anew, as it did every time he came near the gift table or Mrs. Loos came into view in the den as at this moment, in her home made black silk dress and her little white apron, passing around a tray with champagne glasses, embarrassed and overjoyed without the slightest reason.

For, like it or not, these shabby napkin rings (hard to come by for Mrs. Loos with the hourly wages of a serving woman and practically useless for Ellikins, who at his behest had cleared a place of honor for them where they more than ever had the effect of a bad joke; but it was too late to change that) stood out so among the expensive gifts that had been paid for with casually written checks and moved and shamed the not very delicate sensibilities of Leiselheimer (who had meanwhile given in to the idealists in theory; but, he asked, of what use would it be to humanity if I gave away my business? None, he said) so much that he had forced himself to look away from the napkin rings which caught the eye (and not just his; the reactions ranged from his being moved to Mrs. Wiegenstein's cleverly overplayed curiosity to his friend Ockelmann's being sarcastic) as nothing this inconspicuous had ever done before, as much as he could recall.

Less from calculation than from impulse (he could not, try as he might, separate the two; he found more and more that what he thought he was doing for humanitarian reasons helped him in business too) Leiselheimer was momentarily on the point of acknowledging Mrs. Loos by inviting her (she got the salary of a serving woman but at the same time had the trusted position of a housekeeper) to a glass of champagne.

However, when he saw her approaching with the tray (not just overjoyed for some unaccountable reason, as has been said, but beyond that so embarrassed that, in the effort to be as little noticed as possible, she walked on the front half of her shoe soles) it became clear to him how this well-meant

gesture would confuse the world as it existed in the mind of Mrs. Loos, who
was already serving the same champagne to the musicians as to Ellikins with
mental reservations that could indeed not be proved, but could be sensed.

And so he simply helped himself, nodded to her, a bit annoyed (as he
always was when he, the financier Leiselheimer, who went fishing with
fishermen, who argued with taxi drivers, who let streetcleaners treat him to
beer, failed in overcoming a social barrier for at least a few hours) put aside
the matter for now as, once and for all, he turned his back on the gift table
when he sat down by the older gentlemen in the club chairs during the now
truly earsplitting solo of the clarinettist (who had still not succeeded in yank-
ing the young people out of their lethargy and into the dance) and began to
joke harmlessly with Mrs. Wiegenstein (just like Ockelmann with Mrs.
Leiselheimer and Wiegenstein with Mrs. Ockelmann) because this was
what good taste dictated.

Only they didn't stay alone that way for long. While Mrs. Leiselheimer
and Mrs. Ockelmann (in contrast to Mrs. Wiegenstein, by the way, who accepted compliments in an almost insultingly relaxed way) burst out laughing as if they had been tickled, the children (not knowing what to do about
the young people, at least for the moment) came running up hand-in-hand
to those who, more than they themselves, had helped provide them their
happiness in order to kiss and embrace Mommy and Daddy and Mom and
Dad on the one hand and Mommy and Daddy and Mom and Dad on the
other (Ellikins with a charm that seemed to have been pounded into her;
Bobbikins with a seemingly innate one), both, indeed, to the sorrow of Mrs.
Wiegenstein, who, during the demonstrations of devotion from the children,
held her oversized evening bag before her as if for protection, because her
face (which had cost a small fortune) had, like so many another valuable,
been intended more for looking at than for touching.

Don't you want to dance, Mrs. Leiselheimer asked.

If we have to because of the band, then naturally we'll dance, said Bobbikins.

We feel so silly, Ellikins said.

They play excellently, said Wiegenstein.

Heavenly is how they play, insisted Mrs. Wiegenstein, although she too
did not in the least want to dance. Maybe later, she said (as if incidentally
answering that question of Leiselheimer's, because what she was mainly
concerned with was rooting around in her oversized evening bag), but not
just now.

That nobody wanted to dance was clearly disturbing to Mrs. Leiselheimer,
who, stemming from modest circumstances, always felt great uneasiness
when people did not avail themselves immediately or did not avail themselves at all of something that was available. She, who constantly wanted to

prove what all but she took for granted: that the Leiselheimers could afford heaven-knows-what-all, had to restrain herself from urging her guests to dance too, having already urged them to drink, to switch rooms, to eat, drink, switch rooms, and so forth. Yes, she had to restrain herself from standing up and dancing so that somebody would "make use of the band," as she had been phrasing it in her thoughts for some time while sitting there as if on a bed of coals. For she danced with neither skill nor pleasure.

Even after the practice she had had meanwhile and the arguments she had had year in and year out with Leiselheimer every time she had thrown herself almost pathologically into demonstrating what she considered to be an elegant life style and luxury, Mrs. Leiselheimer showed (albeit not with dexterity and not without lapses but, at any rate, with an advanced degree of skill) how capable she was in what was accepted as an endearing or at least an amusing foible.

Go into the bar for a while, she proposed to the children, urging, even almost begging, despite Leiselheimer's glances.

Maybe later, said Ellikins, just as unyielding as her father.

If we have to, said Bobbikins, then we'll do it, naturally.

Nobody has to do anything here, children, said Leiselheimer, while next to him Mrs. Wiegenstein emptied the contents of her oversized evening bag on the carpet.

Or go into the summer house, his wife requested, her discomfort becoming visible only because the veins on her temples were a bit more prominent than before as well as because of the slightly fixed smile with which she acknowledged Ellikins' headshaking and the torturously affable "maybe- later -but-not-just-now" that followed nearly every entreaty and was adopted from Mrs. Wiegenstein by Ellikins, who, like everyone else, turned to where Mrs. Wiegenstein knelt on the carpet before the heap of cosmetics from the evening bag.

Good Lord, she shouted, I've forgotten my comb.

Are you sure, asked Wiegenstein.

For Heaven's sake, said Bobbikins and brought his hands together in front of his face.

If that's all, shouted Leiselheimer while his wife arose, not only relieved, but yes, ridiculously intent.

Unfortunately, said Wiegenstein, urging her with a gesture to sit down, there is a lot more to it than that.

It brings me luck, said his wife, suddenly so disconsolate that even Leiselheimer, who thought he had long since seen through Mrs. Wiegenstein, would not have been able to say what he thought of that.

The chauffeur will fetch your comb immediately, Wiegenstein silenced her.

Does he know my comb, his wife inquired.

Everybody knows your comb, my child, said Wiegenstein, who was a much better father to the mother of his sons than to his sons in any case, already underway with Leiselheimer, who as host felt likewise duty-bound to pursue this puzzling matter personally.

I only hope she hasn't lost it, said Wiegenstein, who was quite obviously worried.

What's it all about, asked Leiselheimer, if I may ask.

How should I know, said Wiegenstein, for goodness' sake.

A secret, said Leiselheimer.

I only know, said Wiegenstein, that her hair has been combed with it ever since she was a child.

A talisman then, said Leiselheimer.

Possibly, said Wiegenstein, mostly to himself.

At the moment when the gentlemen, surprised by the heaviness of the snowfall, stepped outside, Wiegenstein's chauffeur (although it was the duty of only Leiselheimer's chauffeur to stir the fire in the hearth every quarter hour in case somebody sometime might after all be overcome with a wish to have a short sojourn in the summer house at the other end of the quite extensive estate) also held in his arms an armful of firewood which he laid down close to the lighted silver fir which annually provided a bigger Christmas tree, before he, careless in his excessive zeal, more slid than ran on the sleet under the cover of snow in the direction of the gentlemen, who, because of their dress suits, stopped under the overhang of the roof.

You see, you see, Director, it's a good thing I stayed, he called as soon as he knew what was to be done, with a self-righteous obstinacy that Wiegenstein would not have allowed himself, if it had not been so selfless. Because the chauffeur, having slid immediately in the direction of the snowed-in line of cars, was now stopping again and warning Wiegenstein in a reproachful tone of voice; you'll catch cold, Director, he said, still acting superior by no means for his own good but solely for the good of his employer.

What enviable zeal, said Leiselheimer.

He stays content only as long as one keeps prodding him, said Wiegenstein and stepped into the house, on the one hand a bit repelled although on the other he did know how much such overzealousness was to be valued.

He has so overexerted himself, he added, that he and his wife and child would starve without his bonuses.

What was his latest demand, asked Leiselheimer.

His own new car, said Wiegenstein, and then he joined in Leiselheimer's ringing laughter, even though meanwhile he didn't consider the story funny anymore.

When they came back into the den, Mrs. Wiegenstein was holding shut Bobbikins' mouth (so that he couldn't give away any information about the comb), for from it was issuing for the first time this evening some conversational material that went beyond platitudes and included everyone but Mrs. Leiselheimer, who, with her fixed smile, was clearly pretending to listen; did the chauffeur change the candles in the bar, she asked.

Even Ellikins, however, who, since she had discovered how important the world of emotions was to Mrs. Wiegenstein and she to it (it is true, it was far more to Mrs. Wiegenstein than breadwinning was to others), tried to compete with her future mother-in-law, being so much impressed by this foible that she, despite her almost primitive naturalness, managed to bring forth something like a hysterical giggle.

Will it really bring you bad luck, she asked.

She has proof, said Wiegenstein.

It occurs to me, his wife called, that he won't be able to find the comb.

Where did you hide it, inquired Wiegenstein.

In the left snakeskin boot, said his wife.

My chauffeur will get it for you right away, proposed Leiselheimer.

Does he know it, Wiegenstein asked.

I'll go along, called Bobbikins.

We'll all go along, called Ellikins, apparently without knowing what she was doing to her mother by saying this.

While suddenly, high-spirited because of the upset in the plan of the formal engagement party which had been so strictly followed up to now, the young people left the den as the sounds of several motors starting and then dying again penetrated from outdoors, Mrs. Leiselheimer got up and slowly went out, because she sensed that she wouldn't be able to control herself for more than a few minutes more.

Don't you want to dance with me, she suddenly heard Leiselheimer ask.

Maybe later, she let slip out, but not just now.

After glancing to check through the leaded-glass window in the cloakroom whether the young people had truly driven off in the middle of the party (and some had probably even run away, because the Wiegenstein's villa was at most five minutes' walking distance from the Ockelmanns', since there was only one fashionable area in this town), Mrs. Leiselheimer went resolutely on a kind of patrol of the house, because she thought the correctness of the engagement party she had planned for her daughter was still in question. But no matter how thoroughly she checked details, her instructions seemed to have been carried out perfectly. In the bar, to which the music was carried by loudspeaker (although it penetrated through the door anyway), the candles had been replaced, just like the ice cubes in the buckets; the first crock stood directly under the tap of the barrel in the wine cellar; in the ping-pong basement the celluloid balls lay just as carefully arranged next to the net as the freshly cleaned caftans lay on the divan and the hookahs lay on the camel-leather cushions around the dice cup in Ellikins' Moroccan room, which (no less than the camel-leather cushions, the hookahs, the caftans, the ping-pong table, the crocks with wine on tap, the bar) Ellikins said she had "up to here," making a gesture as if to cut her throat. To be honest, Mommy, Ellikins had admitted to her mother before the engagement party began, I've had the whole engagement "up to here."

Knowing quite well how bitterness spoiled her appearance, Mrs. Leiselheimer avoided glancing into the wall-sized mirror next to the exit as she left the house before she went (through the snow, past the illuminated silver fir and the likewise illuminated swimming pool full of snow) to the summer house, where during parties one occasionally took care of the sudden (yes, even almost spasmodic) needs of some guests with a rather bucolic simplicity.

But the fireplace was just being stirred by the chauffeur, who had already returned because the young people had suddenly decided halfway there to go the rest of the way on foot.

Should he go on stirring, he asked Mrs. Leiselheimer.

Why, of course, she said, more or less incidentally, because she was mainly seeing about the bottles of beer that had been kept cool for hours and the cooker, where for hours the hot sausages had been kept warm.

Did you do that, she asked, pointing to the burst sausages, which had been kept much too hot.

Not I, insisted the chauffeur.

Then it must have been Mrs. Loos, said Mrs. Leiselheimer, and then, despite the warning of her family doctor, she waded back through the snow with the pot of sausgaes, through the cold wetness next to the trail the chauffeur had made running back and forth every quarter hour and on the often enough but less often trod path left by Mrs. Loos; she was exclusively concerned with the question of what would have happened if somebody sometime had been overcome with the desire for hot sausages.

Did you do that, she repeated, so convinced that she would find Mrs. Loos alone in the kitchen that she really gave a start at the sight of Bobbikins' brother Conni, who was squatting on the refrigeraor in a tuxedo, eating chocolate pudding.

We're just discussing art, he said, jumped down from the refrigerator (gallant toward Mrs. Leiselheimer and affable toward Mrs. Loos) and, taking the pot before either woman could prevent it, took a burst sausage and dunked it, as one usually does in mustard, in the chocolate pudding and devoured it without changing his expression.

Have you ever tried that, he asked Mrs. Leiselheimer.

Didn't you say I could depend on you, she asked Mrs. Loos.

How could I have forgotten that, asked Mrs. Loos, herself again; and then, embarrassed as she was by the presence of a Wiegenstein in the kitchen (because Mrs. Loos had so much admired the Wiegensteins ever since, as she put it, she had "known them," that she had expressed the wish to be allowed to clean at their house sometime; I'd simply love to do that, she said afterward repeatedly), she carried the pot with the burst sausages, murmuring, I'll put new ones out right away.

I think she thinks I wanted to make fun of her, said Conni, while he accompanied Mrs. Leiselheimer (who was thinking he had had the same intentions toward her) into the den, where she saw just then Mrs. Ockelmann with Ockelmann and Wiegenstein and her husband suddenly dancing wildly.

Why don't you say we should dance, asked Ockelmann.

All you had to do was say the word, said Leiselheimer breathlessly and stretched out his arms toward his wife.

Please leave me alone, she said and then sat down by Mrs. Wiegenstein.

Just imagine, I really feel like dancing, Mrs. Wiegenstein admitted, and I can't risk a single step.

Without a comb, you mean, inquired Mrs. Leiselheimer.

When every step can be a misstep, said Mrs. Wiegenstein, who actually permitted her fingertips, with which she constantly drummed on the black leather arm of the club chair, a certain freedom of movement. During the again ear-splitting clarinette solo she even refused the champagne being served by Mrs. Loos, who made not only an arc around the dancing group but also bent her entire body away in an arch in her efforts to be as little noticed as possible.

It was probably mostly because of this clarinette solo that even Mrs. Loos didn't hear the children ring the doorbell, that is to say the chimes that more pleasingly served the same purpose at the Leiselheimers. But, though the solo lasted only a few minutes, the children, even Ellikins, felt locked out and, finger on the doorbell, felt so silly that they climbed over the fence and approached the den from the other side to the alarm of the two women who sat very close by the terrace door on which the children pounded with their fists; for, what these children, who could do so many things other people's children couldn't, could do least was wait.

It wasn't in the snakeskin boot at all, said Bobbikins, and (amid the laughter of the young people who, in their high spirits, were grinding the lumps of snow into the carpet with their shoes) handed his mother the comb, an almost toothless little rose-colored baby comb.

It was simply too much, said Ellikins.

The chauffeur is still looking for it, called Bobbikins.

Did you really not tell him, Wiegenstein inquired.

A little searching won't hurt him, Ellikins shouted.

He bet his life, said Bobbikins.

It was simply too much, said Ellikins.

Somebody has to call him, said Wiegenstein, already on the way to the telephone.

Tell him the matter took care of itself, said his wife, who sat there caressing her baby comb.

Don't you want to comb you hair in the bathroom, asked, almost begged Mrs. Leiselheimer, who for a moment envisioned Mrs. Wiegenstein standing before the mirrored walls which made the indisputably imposing room like a salon, tiled as it was with pastel green, leaf green, and bottle green and which had floor and ceiling covered with algae-like and fish-like ornaments.

But she doesn't need the comb, Ellikins shouted with irritation, as if she couldn't muster any understanding for the lack of understanding on her mother's part.

I simply have to have it, said Mrs. Wiegenstein, whose rose-blond coiffure artistically piled on the back of her head needed grooming just as little as did the symmetrical little curls on both sides of her cheekbones, as, smiling without straining her face (which always began to decay a bit about midnight), she put the almost toothless baby comb in her oversized evening bag and then stood up, debilitated, as though the matter of the comb (though she hardly seemed relieved now that she had it) had brought her to the end of her endurance.

Don't, for Heaven's sake, think I'm awful, she said primarily to Mrs. Leiselheimer, but I have to go.

While in the immense entryway (which, like everything at the Leiselheimers', was a bit too expensive) Mrs. Loos (who had to stand on tip-toe because she was shorter, but with self-righteous obstinacy would not let Leiselheimer deprive her of doing this) helped her slip into her coat, Mrs. Leiselheimer, trying to save her face, smiled with a warmth bordering on hate, ready for a moment to wager any amount that all evening she had been made a fool of as never before.

But the next moment this suspicion, hinging on the way she kissed Mrs. Wiegenstein goodbye, seemed to her far-fetched; you just don't know how sweet you are, she said.

Mrs. Wiegenstein kissed all the other ladies after her in exactly the same way she wanted to be kissed: tenderly but quickly. She didn't even leave out Mrs. Loos, who blushed. Mrs. Wiegenstein wasn't the way people said she was, at least not the way those who knew her only by sight or by reputation said she was.

You will come to my house sometime, won't you, she said to Mrs. Loos, in a way that anyone who didn't know anything about Mrs. Loos' wish to be permitted to clean as extra help at the Wiegensteins' would have taken to be a completely normal invitation.

I'd love to do that, said Mrs. Loos.

THE WOMAN BEHIND

WOLFGANG H. FLEISCHER
translated by Astrid Ivask

IT WAS THE SAME DARKNESS THAT THE CREATIVE SPRINGS OF HIS ENDAN-
gered and dangerous mind had always been able to fill with contents—to
which his words would give the shape of truth—yet now he did not dare to
sing; he had to listen to the footsteps of the woman behind him. He fell silent
prey to undulant shapeless shadows and a groundswell of many-voiced noise
which did not fill time and space and was no longer measured by the magic
metrics of his syntax, but by the footsteps of his wife. Probably one before
the other, her feet touched the ground (defined only thereby in the dark)
and he depended on this as the last measures of his ebbing life, through which
he stepped only lightly now.

Her steps sounded steadily in his ear and in an entirely different rhythm
from that of the song from which she had emerged, stepping immediately on
the earth with her respectable legs, growing away from the image in his
heart, toward a person in her own right whom he was not allowed to see any
more: so that she would not once again become eternal in the form of his
words, having stepped outside of space and time, out of reach of his swift
impermanence. She followed him in the dark, behind his back, she trusted in
his oath not to mirror her in his eyes again, doubling her image and bringing
her into the world once more through his glance. And he knew that she, for
the second time replete with a hope that had no relation to him any more,
unfolded an unverifiable life on her death mask.

She followed him out of love: His voice had called her forth from an order
that had prepared her to accept destruction by his sex for the sake of a new
return of the ancient laws. Her eyes held his figure, walking straight ahead
of her, as if certain that she would follow without his glancing backward,
and so bent on his own way that for her, too, there could not be one more
clear and definite: far ahead, toward the light of the world that was waiting
to be entered again and again by all those after them who would have united
the superior qualities of them both—:

thus she drove him forward along a road to which he had to present a face
that did not exist for her—his own, showing wrinkles that had not been there
before her time. He listened for her footsteps and felt a longing for her legs
whose every single tiny hair was strung on his lyre for the song of his life; her
delicate sense of smell determined the scents he gave his daily life, and he

knew all the variations of her lightly trembling nostrils. Now, in the timeless smell of decay of an inexorable nether world, where he had sought her image and found her free of all illusion, which had to be replaced by the past in the enduring darkness of their featureless shared time: a smile, teeth, earlobes, fingernails and birth mark, armpit, naval, ring on her finger and the play of her kneecaps; hair fashion and the colors of her clothes: turquoise, scarlet, indigo, white (he had to ask her!); the darkening of the eyes, when; the yielding of the hand, at; and the short, swift twist of the body in; with; against; without. In the large dark caverns his voice created, his spirit animated, his prosody filled: her—she only had to decide, to accept one of the emerging forms for him.

He did not perceive her footsteps any more and stood stiff in the stillness, struck by the renewed and final decision to silence him. Excited, he was at the mercy of the variety of his own images among which none seized him with physical force, embraced him with smell and sound, consented to a realization. It was quiet, and if by chance his glance should alight on her in the mere shadowy space between dark and dark, he would, finding her, lose her again, bringing her to life, kill her. He called her name: Yet from how many different directions could his voice's echo reach her? What sound would scatter over her face reflections that he could no longer know? Where was she and who was she at any other place, changing under the weight of his voice as under the impact of her silence? But had she ever been able to give him an answer, had she ever been able to step out of the silent immediacy of her love: fervent between her thinking and his, and even now?

—Since he would never be able to find her on her own way, only on his, to which he was indifferent without her, he walked on. Since he could only make her real in the light that was, without her, a torture of the truth, he walked straight ahead towards the distant goal. Since his love could only seek her person, a landscape stretching ahead under the sun, with all its passionate unevenness, its threats and transcending promises, only this one ephemeral and singular person, he did not hesitate.

Again the stranger's enigmatic footsteps followed him through the darkness, linking his future in a trusting and familiar way to a past now drawing near. The steps echoed immediately behind him now, tapping much quicker and lighter than his own, which went quietly and slowly ahead of the skipping that had already become a challenge and a swift readiness. When before him in the incipient twilight he saw the dark shimmer of the waters dividing death and dying, he felt the stranger's hand on his unbending neck; and yet he stopped, touched to the quick and disarmed by this message that concerned his life's happiness. And she attacked, with incontestable hands she sought to overcome his shielding back; with assured matter-of-factness she covered his eyes and face with a scarf and fastened it. Unseeing he faced her and held her entire weight in his arms until it rested securely and he found the place of fulfillment and of Now, the womb: between distress and distress, between himself and the individuated woman. She followed him.

As he approached the darkening river, the ferryman looked attentively into his face; then he scrutinized the stranger behind him, approached her, and spoke in another tongue.

Orpheus had meanwhile stepped into the boat; here he turned, his eyes now free; singing, he left her behind, thus, again dead for him, and crossed the river. He never revealed whom he had seen.

His heart-rending lament for Eurydice is well known; also his terrible end.

MISHAP

KARLHANS FRANK

translated by Paul T. O'Hearn

Slowly, ever-so-tortoise-snail-slowly, an old man padded along the street.
To his right there hurried, hastened, raced passersby. Farther right, the
metropolitan quitting-time traffic boomed, zoomed, roared. It was thirty-two
minutes past five, according to the synchronized clock on the building in
which a jeweler identifies his trade through two display windows, when I
caught sight of the man. To his left there was nothing but wall, housefronts,
interrupted here and there by display windows, by entry ways, which—if
they had steps tacked on in front—forced the old man to make sharp devi-
ations to the right. Gramps required three little steps to traverse one flag-
stone. He appeared to have a game leg. He had no cane with him, wore a
threadbare but tidy bottle-green suit, a white shirt with blue stripes length-
wise, also clean; but he wore no tie. His face was beardless, but the stubble
protruded like feather quills. His shoes had a new look; only a little dust
dimmed their luster. Had he laboriously polished them before he went out
onto the street? Had he just bought them, because the old ones had fallen
from his bare feet?

On the metropolitan street the man aroused no mockery, no goodwill, no
disgust—no notice whatever. I alone looked over at him repeatedly, and for
longer duration. He held his head, with its white hair ruffling on his temples
like down, stretched forward on a relatively long and thin neck. His nose
jutted out, its edge sharp and hard. His posture was no more lax than
could be excused by the age he displayed. "Displayed," because I don't
know his age, know nothing about him—except that ever-so-tortoise-creep-
slowly, tail-tottering, he stiff-leggedly bore his bottle-green suit along the
street, and that he pressed his arms and hands to his sides in a peculiar way.
That was an oddity which—like the unusualness of his eyes, composed as
they were almost entirely of blue pupils, small, filmed over as if by gray veils,
half-covered by lashless lids—became apparent only after repeated observations. His arms lay tightly against his sides, fingers and thumbs pressed against
one another as if in a cramp, thumbs toward the thighs, hands edge-outward,
fingers bent out from the palm at right angles, so that they jutted away from

his trunk at the level of his backside like the tips of a tail—the illness or quirk of a certainly uninteresting Gramps (from the viewpoint of market-economics), of a boring average man—at least, one could assume all that.

At the street crossing Gramps kept waddling along straight ahead, had no wall next to him any longer, no possibility for orientation, drifted off insignificantly to the left, no longer had protection from any side, was bumped into inadvertently several times by people overtaking him, meeting him, but he did reach the edge of the curb. In the traffic signal across the street the light burned behind the red glass.

Gramps waited with the others. The yellow-colored circle shone. Several young adventurers started out. Most of the other people stepped onto the pavement with Gramps, on the green light. The result of the race could have been predicted: The field spurted ahead of Gramps. No one tore him along, no one fired him on. When the bulk had already reached the outpost, the next curb's edge, Gramps was still padding along his way, alone, on the first quarter of the pavement. Late-starters, stragglers passed him by. He was midway on the pavement when the traffic signal changed to Yellow = Caution. Gramps tried to quicken pace, fell into a strange hopping. The drivers lay in wait. Nearest Gramps's right side a powerful Porsche shuddered, blood-red, when the signal indicated that the cars could go, and to Gramps, Stop = Danger. Cars roared off. The Porsche advanced threateningly, honked a hoarse hunting-blast, came on relentlessly, almost had him, and then . . .

. . . quite gently the old man raised his arms, wagged them a bit, rose up, flew, circled the Porsche and didn't twitter, didn't gaggle, but he smiled as he let himself down on the traffic signal.

You should have seen the stricken face of the Porsche driver.

COMMENTS ON A CITYSCAPE
AND OTHER SHORT PROSE

WALTER HELMUT FRITZ

translated by Charles Merrill

COMMENTS ON A CITYSCAPE

Well, then, there is the city, murky with zeal, noisy as ever, earth. People longing for improvement, craving to fill out their lives at last, wanting something to come into sight, these limitations to be lifted, this rigidity to give way. They speak with one another in order to maintain equilibrium; otherwise, the intelligibility of what occurs and surrounds them would become even more questionable. Many things project lines, extensions beyond the area in which they happen to be. Are visible, become invisible for a time, reappear. Are familiar with expedients, prepare for a new goal, take hold of a new distance, traverse as yet uncharted stretches. The present: The days hesitate to turn into history. Have not yet turned aside, do not agree with what was.

PRECARIOUS BALANCE

What we see, after years, is a language which we learn more laboriously. There are some few accidents which may now be reaped. Not attaining the goal, not fooling yourself, getting to know the anatomy of disappointment— all a concealed vice, someone says. The first losses, unnoticed for a while. Forgetting unreconciled with memory. Without ceremony, thoughts enter the body, which casts a slighter shadow.

DARK BOAT RIDE

Where is the deepest darkness? There, where we are underway—drifting between vortexes—talking when something startles us, talking so as to dream up something? How can you live on ground from which you are perpetually moving away? Are we ourselves darkness? Is time that of which we consist? What we have thought peers at us. Now and then you can hear light scream.

BORDERLINE

Where someone leaves his inventory behind, deviates from the path he might never find again, thinks he's approaching an exit, sees himself driven into a corner again, knows less and less what he sees, thinks he understands the absolute necessity of figuring out the world, perceives that precision permits above all the recognition of the monstrous.

MARIONETTES IN THE STORM

In the windless calm. They admonish us to keep on inventing transience, to understand words as truth or as lies. There they are; they hold up for a moment or pass on by, with no wish to try something, no wish to get involved in anything, no wish to sleep.

THE STEP

One step—that's many steps. An answer, an action, a life: why do they multiply? One step. How to go on? Same old question. Before his window a city, behind that the river. He's in a room rented for a few days. Later— quite unlike himself—he goes walking a good ways out, and a bit farther. A chill day, which drives him back. Another part is long since somewhere else.

THE MAN OF CONFUSION

He pursued a goal and forgot it, while he sought. He was on the way and can't tell whether he's come back. But he got to know a few of the outlines, which things project from themselves. He grasped that what has been found returns speedily to obscurity. All the while there were countless complements to all that was transpiring. What he could no longer shake loose was the question, to what extent is a thing true?

DESTRUCTION AND HOPE

Take this away, add that on. Simultaneously take away and add on. Right there much begins anew. Are destruction and hope stipulations for each other? Do they rival each other? This exertion in both directions. Halfway, all the way, the way. The ghostly way to the foundation of the future. For a long time perhaps no waystations, just way, on which it is possible to be removed from oneself, to see outlines and cross-sections unified. Touch tentatively. Remove this, add this, add tentatively.

NO THREAD

It was difficult to remember yourself. Events succeeded one another, but formed no sequence. At the end there was no surprise. Still there was no reason for relief. Eventually you kept wandering into the vicinity of conditions you didn't understand because you'd observed them too long; and you saw how things got lost, moment by moment, incalculable quantities. Much was no longer comprehensible in terms of the original postulates. Cause and effect—a remote contrivance. People still thought of what had earlier been thought of, but it was no longer the same; it was something which wasn't, and which nonetheless pulled the rug out from under you.

TOO SOON

We understood that too soon, inexplicitly. Thus the difficulty of recognizing it. This business of walking around, for instance—or lying down, and becoming immersed, and getting up, this doing and desisting. Too soon understood. This wall, this speaking, whispering, shouting in front of a wall . . . But how to get from one day to the next; not even that is really clear now.

THE LAST SNOW

It lets the things become once more invisible, pardons them, transports them into the distance which they love; composes another land out there. The new snow doesn't show up this time. Soon you'll run more suddenly into what happens. But still silence. For because of the snow much can no longer be made reversible. For example, we will remain prisoners of vastness!

AS I WENT FORTH

The more you held onto the nearest things, the farther out you got, the more distinctly you saw that something was on its way into visibility . . . or dissolution. A good thing that the sentences abjured more and more. They still accepted that which abruptly struck out in unexpected directions. Detached from everything: How else could you be in a position to see anything? Occasionally something threw the facts into sudden confusion. Then they seemed at last to stabilize at moments; they retreated and approached simultaneously.

VEILED FORM

Who is more ahead—we, or our words? Why are we unlike one another so often? Isn't it possible that emptiness props us up? Can you have a hope without also desiring its fulfillment? When you've gone on ahead, isn't clarity there again where you used to be? How long does the mask look for its face? What kind of trick is this thing death? How will we die—each of us first?

MEDIATION

A body: a person, but also that which first he finds outside of himself; something which sees and can be seen; which makes itself known to its shadow; which has a history pointing to something else; which keeps alive by fearing that it is inadequate to the task at hand; which finds words to be possibilities daily growing stronger; which knows that comprehension is inextricably entwined with what is done the wrong way.

SCALES OF TWILIGHT

Plots. Pantomimes. Asides. It turns out that we get unacquainted with ourselves, that contradictions concern us more than many other things, that we learn how much the simplicity of results comes to mean to us, discern movement's origin in resistance, grasp the pointlessness of invention not accompanied by discovery. Twilight already? To begin, to cease, to find no end. To be chained, hoping for a way out still.

TRIP

On this trip out of one area into a new one, which only sporadically approximates existence, we see things because we imagine them. They greet thoughts and protect them. We speak of them so as to have a supply of silence. They teach us what approximate values are, simultaneities, counterforces which oppose petrification.

SEAWEED CALLIGRAPHY

On the limestone along the coast. Imprinted millennia ago. Interrupted there, where the rock was not sufficiently yielding. Or interrupted by deposits, by fossil remains, mussels, snails, coral. Come to rest. But still stirred in the reflection produced by shallow waves lapping across. Script not to be obliterated—and yet so, as if one were reading it elsewhere.

ANTITHESES

Found, lost again. All the better, so much the worse. Are we estranged from each other? In any case, no more oratory is needed. No more mountains of words. Nor the final word. Not now. That could come some time as if through an oversight.

SHOALS IN THE CHANNEL

They rarely can be identified. No familiarity is of avail in the attempt, nor any preparations made. If you fail to avoid them often enough, then much becomes no longer imaginable, many words become incomprehensible. Whirlpools—there, there too. Somebody says, there's this death, and the next, and the last. But he says it as if he'd already forgotten it.

METAMORPHOSING

There you have something in your hand; suddenly it's there, you discover it to be a bit of defunct life, are amazed that you have it in your hand once more: Who could have foreseen that? You hear it approach again, it's no dream, it comes with cities, streets, faces, questions—it comes again, point by point: Maybe there's even something there that wasn't at all before. Now and then it really looks that way. That's unexpected enough, how is it conceivable? But as usual, you clutch at it, you hold it in your hand, there it is . . . why, of course!

LANDSCAPE FOR LOVERS

—No, nothing is at an end.— You'll hear that. —That's really no reason to lose courage.— You'll hear it on this street; the construction site is there, the laundry, the café with tables and chairs, inert, gaily-colored bugs. A postman passes by, a girl stops and then turns about. Clothes are there, voices, hands, brilliance leafing through the city: dainties for the sweet tooth of our dreams.

MASKS IN THE TWILIGHT

In them, too, emptiness gets to know itself, at once gets to know itself through what is there. Becomes its own translation, aftereffect. Does it age? Is it like anything? Twilight, the extension of late afternoon—very short-lived. This done wrong, that too. No point in hiding befuddlement.

VISIT TO AN EXHIBITION

MARTIN GREGOR-DELLIN

translated by Brian L. Harris

HE ENTERED THE EXHIBITION WITHOUT HAVING BOUGHT A CATALOG AND SO did not know who had made the dog or the tiger, or whether it was a dog or a tiger at all or something else. The dog or the tiger or whatever it was, perhaps a wolf or a wolfhound, stood, sat, crouched in the hall one entered first, looking inward, if it did look, from the door into the center of the exhibition room, ready to spring. It was, as the man who entered the exhibition discerned immediately, not an especially good exhibition, and only the dog, or the jackal, which was cast in metal and which at first he had not made out, because only in the middle of the hall was he obliged to turn around, only the dog began to interest him. For a short while, after he had discovered nothing worth seeing on the walls but only pieces reminiscent of an exhibition of thirty or forty years ago, he turned and stood opposite the dog (let's leave it at that), the dog, which sat erect with great shoulders of splintered metal and looked at him with hollow eyes. But he could not make up his mind to go back on the animal's account and buy the catalog. He sought to soothe his vexation by telling himself the dog would gain nothing, if it were connected with anyone's name, for there would always remain the uncertainty of what kind of animal it was supposed to be, which he so simply called a dog, only because everything spoke in favor of this assumption.

To end his uncertainty and since he had to pass by the dog again when he left the exhibition, he entered the second, adjoining hall; but there a group of foreigners were conversing loudly about the pictures on the walls, on which predominantly planes and dots in the divided planes were to be seen, except for two winter landscapes. And since he could not bear it whenever one launched too loudly into words about divided planes and dots—the same with winter landscapes, when it was not even a question of landscapes, whatever that might mean, and whatever significance a cow had which gave no milk: obviously, not a cow—anyway, because he could not bear it, he stepped into an adjacent passage which led along from the first room to the steps at the rear of the building.

Here he stopped before constructions, compositions which disintegrated into the fantastic and were a little better painted than all the others, went on stooped-over and with sidelong glances—and heard suddenly steps behind him, or something like steps. He stopped again before an oil painting, moved a little to the side and stepped somewhat closer, was about to continue his tour and go on, when again he heard steps, noises, footsteps, a sliding, and now he was certain that except for himself no one and nothing was in the gallery, for he had made certain with a quick glance over his shoulder that no one and nothing was following, no shadow, no form. Then he perceived it more distinctly: There were sharp noises, as from hobnail boots or spiked shoes, but in quick succession, as though someone were jumping light-footed with metallic hooves across an iron grate—if that was possible, if such a thing existed, but these noises on the stone tiles of the art museum did seem so unusual to him. He glanced cautiously along the walls, back where the glass panels of the display cases in the corners of the gallery would have reflected any shadow, any form. Yet there was nothing. He went a few steps, passed by some pictures, and the metallic footsteps were behind him. When he moved, there was movement on the floor behind him, too. It could be only on the floor, otherwise he would plainly have felt on his back if the air in the empty hall behind him had parted—nothing, only feet on the stone, and now, too, he heard that there had to be at least four feet, for two legs would not run so fast, unless they belonged to a child, and it would not tread so heavily. He reached the stairs.

To get out of the way he simply omitted the room to the left, perhaps also because it had no staircase, and climbed quickly up the steps. Above he stopped before screen-printed surfaces, figured out inversions and reflections, movements of the horizontal against the vertical, longed for wind that would move the pictures, or that something would move in the pictures, even as sentences themselves move, phrases move within a sentence, or anything at all is moved in that way. He saw things moved, since he heard movement, and he kept hearing it. And now he saw in a cubistic picture planes elongating, slanting lines, he saw lines of streets, lines of houses. He could well imagine that something fit in there, let us say a dog, and certainly then that was the reason why suddenly he saw on the picture in the gallery a dog that moved into the picture, moved off along the lines of houses; it moved farther and farther away, became smaller and smaller and turned almost into a point, a point in the surface, amidst walls, rows, and lines which now, however, stood still; no longer was anything moving in front of him, rather he heard something rolling by behind him, directly behind his legs, almost felt the current of air, or would have said, I feel a draft, if anybody had asked him.

Those were confused results of an exhibition, had he reflected on them carefully. He was imagining things, for he saw nothing. There was no dog in the picture, nothing moved in the pictures, something was moving on him, a jostling and jerking on his suit, he was noticing changes, there was a jostling and jerking, his suit didn't feel comfortable, what was happening to his suit, to his arm, the sleeve of the suit, something was missing, his right arm was missing. There was nothing in the sleeve, it hung slack, it had lost the arm. He turned on the spot, he ignored the pictures in the gallery, he ran away from them to find his arm again or to complain to the management, no, not to complain, what about? Merely to report that he had lost his arm, perhaps it would be returned to the checkroom, then he could pick it up with his umbrella and take it along when he left the exhibition. With this thought he rushed to the stairs, but halfway down, right where they made a turn, a pair of legs approached him—not his, clearly, not his at all, he was running on his, downstairs, but now no longer with the same assurance. What was going by him were a woman's legs, he could tell a lot from that. So back upstairs, what was he to do down there where legs went astray complete with stockings, preferably on up a level to the third floor, to the graphic arts section. As he reached the familiar room, heads rolled toward him, heads like spheres, neckless—that won't do, most extraordinary, what is all this, dismantled visitors, bellies in the halls, hands with catalogs, senselessly opened, for who was reading them, no one was reading them if heads were rolling through the graphic arts.

The noises had diminished; better said, he heard the sounds only half as loud, everything was softer, or was he hearing with just half an ear? And since everyone possesses two ears, it has to be: with one ear. Exactly, for now he had also lost his right ear, a fact he did not establish immediately, since he no longer had his right arm either, but he could grab at the right ear with his left hand, or for the place where the ear had been; he had nothing at all in his left hand, no catalog, fortunately.

The pictures now lost all attraction for him, although up here everything was getting better, more serious, more startling, as he recognized with one eye—the other simply had gone away, for who knows what reason—in any event he could still see, though only without perspective, and so now he had to hold fast to the railing with his left hand in order to descend, which he did now decide to do, without missing the steps, in going down or jumping down, hopping, however you want or don't, he however did not want to, had not wanted to, but had to now, had to want to, jumped, hopped on the left leg, for where the right one was, who could say, he no longer possessed it, at most it possessed itself, was possessed, perhaps was wandering in the exhibition, my God, he hoped he had put on clean socks, he hoped it (singular) was wearing a clean sock, he hoped it was fit to be seen by itself, alone; regardless, he had to worry about himself, what was left of him, and see how to get on downstairs the fastest way. It was impossible without crutches, he could not simply cross the room, it was too large for that, the stone tiles were too slippery and, also, with only one arm he lacked jumping power, there was nothing left for him to do but lie down—lying down was easy with only one arm and one leg—start himself off and roll and rotate away and hope that nothing got in his path. He heard then how he made noises, how his left arm slapped in turning, he saw with half an eye, or with one, how the room revolved around him: ceiling, distant, the walls, closer, the floor, close, and again the ceiling, crosswise, he rolled diagonally and he saw the pictures move, caught up in rotating motion, now finally they were in motion, now finally vertical lines were running into the horizontal, the visit to the exhibition had been worthwhile.

He rolled toward the door, but there, right before the exit, something intervened. The rotating was over, he lay still, for the dog, the tiger, or whatever it was, perhaps a wolf, or a wolfhound, which crouched there, sat erect with great shoulders of splintered metal, stood suddenly over him and looked at him with hollow eyes. What actually had happened to him, and why had it happened to him? An unexpected event, all right, what did he have to complain about, everything was all right, no one would talk about it, one way or another he would leave the exhibition, look for his arm, his eye, and his ear, as soon as he had his leg back, go home and lead a middle-class existence, as if nothing had happened, not betray himself, forget, behave calmly and live on, towards his natural end.

*UBU*VILLE—THE CITY OF THE GRAND EGG

HERBERT HECKMANN

translated by Thomas I. Bacon

MY HOMETOWN IS *Ubu*VILLE. IT IS LOCATED IN A NAMELESS COUNTRY, BE-
cause our government still can't decide upon a name. They do not like to
commit themselves when confronted with so many alternatives. Our neighbors think we are backward; perhaps, if I may say so, because we deplore
the wearing of clothes. Even tourists must comply at the border with our
regulation on nudity. The Great UBU, whose works we study most carefully
and exactly in order to enrich our lives, states at one point, "He who clothes
himself has something to conceal."

In our country we drill for oil, but with little success. However, we do
have peanuts here, and graves from the Stone Age. UBUville is a rapidly
growing town of 50,000 inhabitants, most of whom live in egg-shaped houses.
From a distance the town looks like the egg depot of a gigantic bird. The
Great UBU considers the egg archetypical of life itself. In our language it is
called "uch." "Uch" is also the word for thought or idea, when you pronounce it somewhat more gutturally.

The seat of the government, which we call the Council of the Great Egg,
is in UBUville. Every year the Great Egg is elected, generally a small child
just learning to talk and think, and an old man who also can barely think and
talk. These two then brood over the future of our country. The Little Egg
is the parliament, which determines whether or not the decisions of the Big
Egg are to be taken seriously. On the other hand, everyone is free to do as
he pleases. Every year on the fourth of April we celebrate our one and only
state holiday with a huge egg dance.

The Great UBU, whose monument, by the way, can be seen in UBUville—
a ten-foot-high egg with human features radiating deep understanding—
shapes our lives with his teachings. His first axiom is, "Truth through Error;
Error through Truth." Once a week everyone must laugh at himself; the rest
of the time one may laugh at others. There is, in fact, a lot of laughing here,
an observation I made only after visiting other lands. Our language requires
the use of muscles with which one laughs much more than those for frowning,
so that the mastery of it is well-nigh impossible for persons of a melancholy
disposition.

Our main dish is the soft-boiled egg. We have approximately seven hundred egg recipes, from the raw state to its highest refinement through fire.

The presence of egg-laying hens in our society is thus quite comprehensible. Sometimes, though, it gets to the point where we can't hear ourselves think for all the cackling. The Great UBU is probably exaggerating when he boldly states that cackling is a kind of hymn to life. On this one point, at least, I disagree with him,

In contrast to our neighbors, we have a three-day week—relaxation comes right after exertion. The Great UBU says, "Work should be recuperation from recuperation—and recuperation, recuperation from work." Moreover, he who wishes to display affection and love in any manner may stop working. Such intermissions are even encouraged.

I place these indiscriminate comments at the beginning of my travelogue so as to render my mode of behavior in Germany more comprehensible. I am especially indebted to Herbert Heckmann, who was quite helpful with the review of my notes. Of course, I must admit—and I do not wish to wear my heart upon my sleeve, as the Germans say—that he helped a great deal with the editing, because the Germans prefer only the essentials. We, on the other hand, love details. As the Great UBU says, "Truth is the juiciest part of the whole thing." (By the way, I intend to use the language which is customary in Germany, the one which the great DUDEN requires of his subjects.)

March 14

About ten o'clock our time the boss called me in and disclosed that I was to fly to Germany on business, in order to ascertain whether there was any interest there in our oil. I was alarmed, for I had only a very vague conception of Germany, The Great UBU had been through Germany once and had shouted from the Rhine, "Oh, you Germans, you are always looking through binoculars, so that everything becomes extraordinarily large." On another occasion, he deplored their obsession for titles. Even he himself felt compelled to make his appearance with a title. He called himself "Omahu-UBU," which means, roughly, "Joyful Event UBU."

March 15

Great difficulties mastering the German language. For one thing, because the German teacher whom I requested fainted at the border, when she learned about our custom of living without clothing. Only after unnerving arts of persuasion did she agree "to decode the secret of the German language," as she described it.

"If I were naked," she screamed hysterically, "you'd just start getting ideas."

"If it suits you," I replied soothingly, "I'd just like to learn German."

On another occasion it turned out that Fräulein Grabert had very little command of our language. There is a big difference between UBURU, as our language is called, and German. We have almost no abstractions whatsoever, and our vocabulary for sense perceptions is at least three times larger than the equivalent in German, Three years ago an Englishman attempted to compile a grammar of UBURU. Our students of UBUology still consider it a masterpiece of involuntary humor. When the Englishman found out about it, he departed this life, Our language is not spoken, but sung, in which respect Fräulein Grabert wasn't altogether talented. The nakedness also confused her. She was ashamed of inadmissable thoughts. Finally, I could say some polite phrases, after a fashion, count to one hundred, ask the time of day, comment on the weather, and sing "Am Brunnen vor dem Tore."

But these were not the only preparations I was to undertake: I also had to adjust to the awkward business of wearing clothes. I wired my measurements to a tailor in London and, draped with fine woollens, for the first time in my life I felt ashamed as I strolled back and forth in my room. I couldn't imagine how I was to distinguish one clothed person from another. Suddenly, I was one among many.

September 25

Departed UBUville for Cairo by plane. My friends brought me a case of eggs. They were afraid I might starve in Germany. They also mistrusted German hens. I felt quite silly, standing there in my suit, and began to perspire. From a bird's-eye-view, my homeland really looks very ordinary.

During the flight I attempted to read several German newspapers that I had brought along in order to facilitate the transition to a new language. As the Great UBU is my witness! I understood not one single word.

Boarded a German plane in Cairo. The stewardesses fed me all the way to Frankfurt. They had the curious notion that one can overcome fear by consuming incredible quantities of food. My stomach was upset several times. I also got to rehearse my first courtesies and learned how to listen intently without understanding a word. One particular stewardess caught my eye, and I casually attempted to communicate this attraction to her. Somehow I must have used a wrong word, for she turned red even to the roots of her hair and replied, "I am on duty." The word "duty" seems to bestow strength, when one says it.

It was raining in Frankfurt. The clouds over Germany are somewhat grayer than at home. Herr Ocker, whom I had informed of my arrival, ran toward me with an umbrella, said he was Herr Ocker, and shook my hand vigorously. Fräulein Grabert hadn't told me about this duel one must endure in Germany upon meeting a person. When at last Herr Ocker lay flat on the ground, several men in elegant suits grabbed me by the arms and demanded my passport. Herr Ocker soon calmed down, beat the dust from his coat— and would have offered me his hand a second time, had he not noticed my horror. My case of eggs elicited great mistrust at customs.

"What's in the crate?" they asked me.

"Eggs," I replied, in conformity with the truth.

"Anyone can say that," said a customs official who, in addition to his elegant suit, was wearing a hat-like headgear on which he placed his hand at particular intervals. Why, I do not know. He took an egg, cracked it on the side of the crate, and behold—it was an egg.

"You could have told me that in the first place," he growled and permitted me to pass. I was in Germany and I took a deep breath. It smelled like damp clothing. The people were in a hurry and they seemed to be very proud of the little suitcases they were carrying around with them. They behaved as though they had nothing to do with one another.

Herr Ocker carried the egg crate along behind me. I had put him into a good humor with the golden egg, which we present to persons whose merit we anticipate, I was driven in a taxi to the hotel in which a room with a private bath and a view of a construction site had been reserved for me. Herr Ocker said goodbye at some distance and suggested that I rest up a bit from the trip. He would pick me up the next morning in time for a conference, he said, and made a bow this time, which I attempted to imitate as best I could. In this country courtesy consists of conveying for a moment the impression that one is meeting his fellow man on the same level.

Mostly out of curiosity I pressed a button on the wall and a man dressed in white appeared, He reminded me of a dove.

"I'm hungry," I said, in order to say something to which I could in turn

respond, and pointed to the case of eggs. "Would you kindly cook some eggs
for me?"

"Sir," he replied, smiling discreetly, "that will not be necessary. We have
plenty of eggs."

"Well, then, may I offer them to you as a gift? They're eggs from my
country." He hesitated, said something I did not understand, lifted the crate
to his shoulder, and departed.

I just had time to undress, when he reappeared with a tray upon which
there stood the three egg cups.

"Excuse me," he stammered, upon seeing me naked. He stared where I
wasn't, namely at the ceiling, and tripped over a chair. The eggs rolled across
the rug and disappeared under the bed.

"I'll take care of it," he stuttered. To come right to the point (Herbert
Hackmann thought this incident unimportant): He brought me three new
eggs which, as I was eating them, brought forth a feeling of nostalgia.

"No one egg is like any other," said the Great UBU.

September 26

Slept quite restlessly. Depressed. The sound of running water next door.
Gargling. Then, in the restaurant, kidney-shaped ornaments and pictures
of amoeba. People reading newspapers with disinterested expressions, Shuf-
fling of papers and yawning. Well-groomed heads. Self-assured obesity.
Weary faces, surly hands that beheaded the eggs with a tableknife. Women
in dresses that sit up straight. Their lips color the cup's rim with lipstick.
Some stare crossly at their husbands, who appear to have enjoyed a good
night's sleep. The waiters dance in ill-humor. The look of importance that is
not destroyed even by a smile is remarkable. When someone laughs, then
and only then, because he can think of nothing better. They laugh during the
pauses. I forgot to eat my egg for watching, I should have forgotten it altogether. It tasted like an exhausted rooster.

Read in the Great UBU. Underlined the sentence, "When confronting the
question as to whether the hen or the egg came first, the rooster crowed."
Precisely. (Here Herbert Heckmann deleted something. I mention it only
because it annoys me.) Herr Ocker arrived at ten o'clock on the dot and
paid me his compliments. I asked him, "Did you sleep well?"

"Right now I'm a grass-widower," he replied. Suddenly the expression on
his face changed. He cleared his throat, in order to outline in serious terms
our plan for the day. (Clearing the throat has several different meanings in
Germany, at which, unfortunately, I can only guess.)

"How can you be so sure that all of this is going to happen?" I asked, noticing that I had insulted him with the question. Where I come trom, we believe in the self-determination of things. Decisions have to mellow for some time. "One should not meddle clumsily with the future through hasty planning," said the Great UBU.

"One has to proceed systematically," replied Herr Ocker, almost defensively, as he straightened his tie. "Otherwise, how would we ever get anything done?"

"You mean there is a plan for everything?" I insisted.

"In all modesty, I assure you there is," he replied. I didn't know exactly what Herr Ocker was up to, though I suspected that that which he called "plan" was nothing more than the best opportunity to cheat me. I restrained myself completely and quietly studied his broad face, which was confined to practiced gravity. The fleshy parts were flabby and tired, nose sagging, and the mouth sullen from having spoken so many important words. It would take an onion to make Herr Ocker cry. Then he began to explain lots of things to me. He made use of his hand, which had been strengthened by pounding on the table, and glanced occasionally at his watch, as though it were his beloved. I reveled in sweet incomprehension, laughed when it seemed appropriate, and, finally, I said, "We shall see." (That, by the way, is the figure of speech which we often employ in UBURU, especially after we have commented on things we know absolutely nothing about.)

My first conversations with German businessmen during a luncheon in front of toothpicks and flowers. I suffered from the absence of eggs. I spoke memorized sentences about my homeland and for sheer enthusiasm I broke into song, as is customary in my mother tongue,

"How do you like Germany?" inquired a Herr Doktor, a name that one hears frequently in Germany.

"I can't really say much yet," I replied to disappointed faces.

"We're getting ahead of things again. We're meddling again."

"Do you know UBU?" I asked across the table, in search of a topic I knew more about, as I played with the toothpicks.

"UBU! Of course, completely out of date. Now we have the pill."

"I mean another UBU," I replied.

"Of course, how could I forget. You mean UBU, the president of your country."

"We don't have a president."

"Then I was misinformed."

"UBU is our great teacher."

"But not one of these pocket-sized Marxists,"

Herr Doktor always knew just what I didn't want to say, so he could talk about what he knew. He asked me questions that he was only too happy to answer himself. When he took issue with something, it always seemed like sublimated murder.

My head was buzzing, and in desperation I said "Please!" in hopes that they would leave me in peace. I also began to mix up my hosts in their well-pressed suits, and with golden rings on their fingers they looked so similar that I proceeded to address them all as Herr Doktor, which they received with pricked-up ears (a pricked-up ear is our designation for enthusiasm).

After the meal jokes were told, apparently a form of entertainment in which one elicits laughter from the listeners with little stories, by being the first one to laugh. I laughed the way we do back home, with stomach in and head thrown back, but not at the jokes, which I didn't understand. Instead, I laughed at the laughing of the storytellers, which apparently had nothing to do with the humor of the joke. If one of them momentarily left the table, those remaining moved closer together and talked about the absentee, which amused them even more than the jokes. I recalled a comment from the Great UBU: "The value of one's fellow man depends upon how much one can talk about him."

When they all had exhausted themselves, they shook hands and said they had to hurry along. I stayed on with several gentlemen in order to talk business. Herr Ocker sat next to me, fishing papers out of his briefcase, shoving them under my nose, and saying:

"I've already drawn everything up."

The briefcase must be invaluable to Germans. One could almost consider it the national costume. Wherever you see a briefcase, there is also a German who appears to be carrying his life's work around in it. Herr Ocker led the discussion. Every time he spoke of logic, I paid very close attention, for I had discovered that he employed the word "logic" only when he was unable to convince me in any other way.

In the Great UBU it is said that with strangers one should pay attention not so much to what they say as to what they do not say. I remained silent and finally said, "We shall see."

Herr Ocker shut his briefcase disapprovingly.

Evening in the theater. Herr Ocker smelled like peppermint. The women in expensive gowns, the men with sharp creases in their trousers. A piece was performed which, as well as I could judge, attacked German society fiercely but very clumsily. Strangely enough, the critique was enthusiastically received by the audience. Were they blind? Or do they consider the dramatist a paid, and therefore innocuous, fool, about whose criticism one laughs but does not reflect? In this country knowledge of oneself seems to be a social game in which one appears in one's best suit and sucks peppermint.

The actors strained every nerve and screamed as though harpooned. But the best actors were the spectators themselves. They behaved as though they were thoroughly enjoying the critique aimed at them, and hid their eyes behind opera glasses. The applause at the end strained me a great deal. I tried to outdo Herr Ocker, who was working at it like a madman. The whole affair resembled a military maneuver, and I could almost see gunpowder smoke above their flushed reddened heads.

In the lamentations of the Great UBU one finds the thesis: "Woe unto the country that hushes her writers with applause."

As we were leaving, Herr Ocker told me, "Above all, there must be culture. It elevates us to the pinnacles of humanity." (Herbert Heckmann, whom I consulted about the meaning of the statement, unfortunately was not able to interpret it for me.) Though I was very tired, I accompanied Herr Ocker, who wanted to teach me even more about German life, to an after-hours bar.

When does it all cease to be theater and begin to be life? Or at what point does it become theater and cease to be life?

The Great UBU writes: "In the beginning there was sublime boredom; then mankind invented entertainment, and it wasn't long before sublime boredom prevailed once more." Herr Ocker ordered a bottle of champagne, nevertheless. I watched him watch girls, who were watching him. Some other girls were stripping to very loud music on the stage. In this country, for reasons unknown to me, nudity must be something so rare that one needs music with it. Apparently, the play that I saw in the dimly-lighted room was by an inexperienced dramatist, for the scenes recurred too often.

After the third bottle of champagne, Herr Ocker began to talk about his past. At first it was not at all clear to me what had led him to these confessions. "No one who has not been through it knows how it really was. My very existence was at stake."

I clapped my hands with fear. Still not sure what he was leading up to, I thought of a family tragedy and cleared my throat sympathetically. Soon, however, I knew what Herr Ocker meant: Herr Ocker wanted to vindicate himself, but, as is customary with Germans—I permit myself this generalization—they love generalities. Herr Ocker was no longer Herr Ocker, Herr Ocker was a case study. Herr Ocker had been deceived.

"After all, we're only human, and every man must see to it that the homefires keep burning."

Did I really know what Herr Ocker was talking about? I took heart and asked, "About what do I have the honor of hearing you speak?" (I love to formulate questions in German. They are the next best thing to singing.)

"I am speaking of the Hitler era," replied Herr Ocker, ashamed to have been so frank. A dark-haired girl on the stage was doing a handstand. Herr Ocker observed her in a state of melancholy. I remained silent.

I have engaged in similar conversations with other Germans: that is, I have listened to them. Germans live with a past that was really quite different. Cloak-and-dagger stories are among the most beloved children's books. Only on the rarest occasions can you find them living in the present, and then only in the presence of grand stories about their history. But let us return to Herr Ocker. I shall never forget how he paid the check.

"Charge it ," he said proudly. (Charging, as Herbert Heckman explained, is an opportunity to deduct personal entertainment expenses for the benefit of the community.)

September 28

I requested a day off, in order to look around some by myself. I was completely exhausted and suffered from gas pains. German cuisine is torturing me. I regretted having given away the eggs from home. Read in the Great UBU, "A sound stomach makes a strong mind."

At the hotel I rented a bicycle, the chief means of transportation at home, because the noise from automobiles encroaches upon the hens' egg-laying and poisons one's mind. I am revived once I am on a bicycle seat. The upper part of my body stretched over the handlebars, feet pressed against the pedals, with trembling calves I rush over the streets. The wind whistles in my ears and the tires sing.

"Only he who kicks about can liberate himself from diapers," says the Great UBU.

In anticipation of the pedaling, unfortunately I forgot to get dressed and left my room in customary nudity. I walked about fifteen paces, when a woman caught sight of me, screamed, and fainted. For the Great UBU's sake! The hotel was transformed into a mob scene, and the German language into a thunderous rumbling. They threw a raincoat over me and led me away. At headquarters, which in Germany is always nearer than you think, I was required to state my name and, as briefly as possible, explain why I had approached the woman.

" I was going to ride my bicycle," I replied quite truthfully.

"You must be drunk."

"Why no, not at all," I countered emphatically.

"Let's start over from the beginning." The elegantly-dressed policeman rubbed his forehead in hopes that in this manner he could illustrate his approach to the problem. "You approached the lady at 10:11 a.m."

"I had to approach her, because she was standing right in the middle of the hallway I was hurrying down. As I just mentioned, I wanted to go for a ride on the bike."

"In the nude?"

"Where I come from, we detest the wearing of clothes."

"Must be *some* place. May I see your passport?"

I couldn't help laughing, and replied, "Let's see you search the pockets of a naked man."

"Do you realize to whom you are speaking?" he asked abruptly.

"A human being, if I'm not mistaken."

"An officer of the law, to be quite specific. And I will not tolerate your attitude. Now let's start from the beginning."

I hate repetition. So this time I told a different tale, and when I noticed the degree of malicious pleasure with which the policeman was listening to me, I decided to tell yet another version of the event.

"What, then, is the real truth?" he shrieked.

I almost quoted the Great UBU, who said, "Truth is a lie's stroke of luck," but I preferred to remain silent, and watched the second-hand on the wall clock. I had discovered that Germans love to look at clocks and now I hoped that imitation would begin to alter my miserable situation. It didn't help much. Without a passport I was a clean slate, upon which any well-dressed policeman could write whatever he wished. In spite of my heated protest, I was led to a room that had a single window with bars. Not bad, I thought, at least I'll be safe from disagreeable callers. Suddenly the door for which I had received no key was flung open. With a very serious expression on his face Herr Ocker appeared and handed me some clothes, with which I departed from the police, a free man. He was quite upset, and insisted that I extend an apology to the woman. I attended to the matter by bringing the customary golden egg to her room. I stayed so long, that I never did get back to the bicycle ride. (Herbert Heckmann advised me to omit this most comical passage, as such scenes are already all-too-common and graphically portrayed in contemporary literature. So anyone who isn't sufficiently familiar with these things can simply look them up.)

As usual, on this day I saw nothing more of Germany than a hotel room.

This event had stirred up considerable dust. A reporter came up to my room and began to pump me.

"What do you intend to accomplish with your nudity?"

"Immediacy."

"Have you no shame?"

"Sure, but only when I have done something stupid."

"What do you think of Germany?"

"It is a very industrious and serious-minded country."

"Wherein do you see the future of your own country?"

"In bicycling."

The reporter looked at me helplessly and left. I read in the Great UBU.

October 1

Finally on the bicycle. Herr Ocker had definitely advised against it and added that in the first place it was too dangerous; secondly, it did not become a person of status. He wanted to drive me around a bit in the area. But when he saw that I was determined to ride the bike, he wished me well and regretted that he could not kick around with me. When he was a boy, he too had ridden a bicycle and had once pedaled through the countryside.

"We Germans have an intimate relationship with nature," he said sadly. I attempted to envision Herr Ocker as a child of nature, with a dirty nose and red cheeks. Instead I saw only a well-groomed gentleman tugging away at his briefcase. Herr Ocker waved to me, and as I turned the next corner, I knew exactly what he would say about me: "That man is really out of his mind."

Unfortunately, my ride ended very soon, because I had forgotten to acquaint myself with the street signs in Germany, which lead you where you don't want to go.

An impressively-dressed policeman halted me and inquired, "Apparently you can't read."

I contradicted him in all modesty, but it didn't help things. I really should have known that policemen are always right. Paid a fine and, intimidated, I pushed my bicycle back to the hotel.

My attempt to reach the Rhine by train was more successful. Everyone had recommended this trip to me. The Rhine, they said, is the very heart of Germany and is sung about in many a song.

In my compartment there sat a very fat man, who was wearing suspenders in addition to a belt, and he was breathing very heavily while reading a newspaper primarily composed of headlines. When he noted that I too was reading his paper, he grumbled, "This is my newspaper."

"Of course, whatever you say," I replied, and glanced out of the window.

"It's my newspaper and mine alone, and if you want to read one, then you can buy one for yourself. These foreigners are always so nosey." He stared at me hostilely. I didn't know where else I was supposed to look. The newspaper crackled seductively under my nose, and again I began to read the headlines. Enraged, the fat man jumped up, folded the newspaper, and left the compartment, cursing foreigners from whom there was no escape.

"They'll take over the government next. Things were definitely better back then."

This was not the first time I had heard the expression "back then." In German it has a very solemn ring to it.

Mountainous vineyards swept by, small train stations and station signs. I saw many construction sites. The Great UBU phrased it accurately: "Whosoever builds much, leaves many rocks behind." The Germans must abhor vacuums. Any time a speck of nature becomes visible, they quickly cover it up with houses.

Finally on the Rhine. I rode a steamer and watched the dirty water flow by. A teacher was explaining rock formations of the bordering hills to his pupils. I listened with one ear. A young man in a corduroy sport jacket was kneading a girl's hand. The teacher proceeded to history. The young man said, "Am I glad I'm not in school anymore. We had to know the tributaries of the Rhine and the dates of the emperors and kings."

The girl stood on tiptoes.

"But you don't know when I was born."

The teacher was talking about some authors. One little boy asked softly, "Is Loreley spelled with or without an h?"

"With two l's," whispered his neighbor. The young man pretended to throw the girl's purse into the Rhine. The girl was clinging to his arm. In this manner they got closer. The teacher said, "I want a report on our excursion from each of you, but no copying." A woman in a colorful peasant costume was selling souvenirs and peanuts. The castles to the right and left were almost all ruins. They were also to be seen on the postcards he was selling.

I mustered the courage to ask my neighbor, a thin, disgruntled-looking man who was looking on and feeding paper to the fish, "Excuse me, but why don't they restore the demolished castles?"

He stared at me almost enraged.

"I won't take offense at this question, as you are obviously a foreigner.

They are ruins—and ruins are part of the grandiose trappings of the Rhine. They are symbols of the grandeur of the past."

I glanced to the right and the left. There was that troublesome word "symbol" again. The Germans appear to be living on symbols. That's probably why they are so well-nourished. When they eat an apple, they aren't just eating an apple, but also that which the apple signifies.

I went ashore at Rüdesheim. The school class left the ship two-by-two. Since it was raining heavily, I fled to a tavern, where a frolicsome crowd greeted me loudly. I had to sit next to a young man who was so loud that I was able to understand only the echo of his words. They were singing songs —and their songs never seemed to end. They were about love, parting, wine, about youth, and once again about love and Father Rhine and the hazelnut and the Westerwald—and once a song finally ended, they raised their glasses, looked at each other very earnestly, as though they were about to come to blows, drank, raised their glasses again, clicked their tongues, and began a new song.

One-two-three! They sang, squalling with fat cheeks and trembling Adam's apple, and slapped themselves and those next to them on the thigh, laughed, snorted, groaned, and panted. I feared the worst and started to leave.

"Hold on!" screamed one of them. "No party poopers around here."

And once again I was sitting there, drinking to the health of unknown personages while destroying my own. With a wild lunge I jumped up and ran out of the place. I can't say for sure whether the wine drinkers then killed each other off. I never saw them again.

Too tired tonight for the Great UBU.

October 2–5

Spent some time with Herr Ocker, who showed me the sights around Frankfurt. I learned the song, "Ach du lieber Augustin." Herr Ocker was very exuberant and told me all about his first love affair. Whenever he sang, he closed his eyes.

Wearisome attendance at cultural events. Observed Germans listening to music. They love to wag their heads, each a conductor in his own right. Under the influence of culture, great severity steals into their faces and resides there for some time. The Great UBU says, "Culture is the ability of mankind to look down upon itself." The Germans look up to themselves through culture.

Herr Ocker pressed for the signed contract. He was still carrying the briefcase along behind me.

October 6

In Germany there are lots of dogs. Their owners walk them in the mornings and at night. When one steps in dog's dung, they say, it's a sign of good luck. I must be the luckiest person on earth. During my walks through the city I was occasionally approached by women who asked me, "Got some time for me?" I didn't know exactly how to respond. At the next opportunity I asked Herr Ocker, who did know. Now I understand the expression I hear so often, "I don't have time."

First ride on the streetcar. I'm still surprised that I ever got in and out again alive. The Germans always want to be first: in science, on the street, and in the streetcar. They have rather well-developed elbows and knees. The thesis of the Great UBU suits them: "The straightest path goes up the wall."

Spent the evening with Herr Ocker at a lecture by a German professor of philosophy, whose name I have heard time and again. The lecture room was packed. Students were standing in the aisles. The highbrows sat there wearing glasses. Women were putting on rouge. When the professor mounted the podium, a small bird-like man who, it was apparent, thought about life rather than living it, a paralyzing silence descended. A young girl was sharpening her pencil.

Then there resounded a sublime sing-song, which is widespread in Germany in the name of philosophy. I heard the word EXISTENCE and the word ESSENCE and the word VOID whirl about in confusion, as far as German grammar would allow. I heard the word BASIS and everything was underscored by self-conscious coughing and clearing of the throat. There was hissing and rumbling, an aria consisting of dissonant consonants and lengthened vowels. His voice hopped from word to word, slurred in the lows and screeched in the highs, and the audience nodded approving heads. The sing-song became more and more hortatory and, with flapping gestures, the bird-like little man seemed to be taking off from the earth—into a realm in which existence, not life, prevailed, freedom with no one free, love and no lovers, a realm in which concepts alone flew around and were captured by bloodless creatures with butterfly nets. Once the professor had concluded his sing-song, he gave us his profile, whereupon an almost enchanted silence grew loud. I applauded first, in order to get my feet back on the ground.

The Great UBU once noted, "Contemplation is supposed to remain in one's head, not dissipate like bubbles in the sky. Compose thyself, many have been lost before."

Herr Ocker was quite impressed by my applause. "I see," he said, weighing each word, "you have peered into the heart of Germany."

"Yes," I replied calmly, longing for the cheerful clucking of the hens back home, for soft-boiled eggs, and a bicycle.

October 9

Nothing special. Walked aimlessly in the streets. The creases in my suit lost their sharpness. I bought myself a hat, so that I could remove it for pretty ladies. I aroused the mistrust of elegantly-dressed policemen because I was talking to myself in my mother tongue.

Spent the evening at Herr Ocker's home. His wife received me with many apologies. I met their son, who was suffering from being so much like his father. Tense atmosphere. We ate for want of something to talk about. After dinner I drank some liqueur. Herr Ocker casually asked me whether I had decided to sign the trade agreement. I promised to do so the following day. Then Herr Ocker became very relaxed and related part of his life's story.

"You're exaggerating, Carl," his wife cried out.

"It's all a big lie," said the son contemptuously, leaving Herr Ocker all alone with his boasting.

I mentioned the thesis of the Great UBU, "Sometimes it would be better, if the sons would beget the fathers."

"Some father you'd bring forth," gloated Herr Ocker to his son.

As I was taking my leave, I resolved to translate the Great UBU into German but immediately thereafter abandoned the resolution. The Germans would only write thick books about UBU. They can't contain themselves. They are compelled to classify everything. They would make an anthology out of the Great UBU. I shuddered at the thought and didn't sleep at all well.

October 12

A large dinner, after business was concluded. Several speeches were about me and the negotiation that joins two peoples. I received a barometer and a calendar for the next century. For the last time in Germany I mentioned the Great UBU. They laughed when I accidentally sat down between two chairs.

October 14

In the air again. I could hardly wait to get home again. Below me lay Germany.

Most of all I would like to have shed my second skin, which they call clothing. I would like to have sung, but I know how difficult it is to be onself in the temperate zones. They have a law against your every wish.

More later from UBUville.

MOZART'S LETTERS

STEPHAN HERMLIN
translated by Peter Spycher

AFTER THE PRETTIFYING CULT OF MOZART HAD BEEN SUPERSEDED BY THE beginning of a more adequate understanding, after terms like "light-hearted-ness" and "rococo" had been recognized as being inapplicable to his person-ality and thus had gradually been abandoned (cf. the interpretations by some great musicians, among them Bruno Walter), people also began to read his *letters* in a different light. His letters had been read as documentary evidence of his apparently ineradicably childlike nature, his exemplary love and respect for his parents, and a propensity for coarse, occasionally risqué jokes. What a wag Mozart was! Incidentally, the off-color quality of certain letters caused quite some embarrassment to their most conscientious editors. Now and then I indulge in the pleasure of looking up, in my personal copy, the falsifying expurgations which the renowned Albert Leitzmann perpetrated in his edition of Mozart's letters published by the Insel Verlag in 1924. Bash-fulness is a wonderful character trait.

Mozart was a great letter writer; of the eminent composers it was un-doubtedly he who left the largest number of letters behind. They were prompted by the long journeys he undertook as a so-called child prodigy, and subsequently by his attempts to obtain a suitable position, his concert tours, his financial difficulties, his family affairs. At the age of fourteen he writes to his sister from Naples: "I have no news to tell you except that Mr. Gellert [he spells the name as "Gelehrt"—"Learned"], the poet, died in Leipzig and that since his death he has produced no more poems. The opera in Mantua was nice, they performed Demetrio, the prima donna sings well but so softly that if you didn't watch her acting, only singing, you would think she wasn't singing, for, being unable to open her mouth, she sort of whimpers her part; well, we are familiar with that phenomenon. La seconda donna looks like a grenadier and also has a sturdy voice and sings remarkably well considering the fact that this is her debut. Primo ballerino: good. Prima ballerina: good, and they say she ain't no dog, but I haven't seen her at close range." And so on and so forth in the same vein. Childlike nature? Hardly. The steely look cast here at the world, at people and their talents comes from someone who not only has acquainted himself already with many places in Europe and is talked about everywhere, but who is also distinctly aware of his enormous technical skills and must, and indeed does, demand high stan-dards. His consistent contempt for dilettantism is already noticeable; a certain impatience, even cynicism. This look, to be sure, is full of curiosity but could scarcely be called naive: "The dances are miserably pompous. The theater is handsome. The King betrays his crude Neapolitan upbringing, and during an operatic performance he always stands on a stool so that he appears to be a bit taller than the Queen. The Queen is beautiful and courteous; she greeted me most benevolently no less than six times, I'm sure."

His letters are addressed at first predominantly to his sister, then more and more often to his father, a musician at the court of the Prince Elector and Archbishop and author of a famous textbook on violin-playing, who admires but does not understand his son and reacts to his thirst for independence with anger and distrust; these letters demonstrate respect and occasionally a kind of intimate comradeship; Mozart gets his own way but never risks a break between the two of them, instead, he acts as though he satisfied the wishes of his old man. Once again we observe his ability to get along with a world in which he is a total stranger. In addition to these letters there are those addressed to friends such as Abbé Bullinger or Puchberg, finally to Konstanze, also one petition or another submitted to some prince. To be singled out are the famous or perhaps notorious letters to the "Bäsle," his female cousin, in Augsburg, who was close to him for a while (he was twenty-two at the time). All of these letters are written in an unpretentious, very vivacious style; they deal with artistic, aristocratic, and bourgeois aspects of the times, they constitute a body of most interesting historical documents. In a natural way they frequently assume a dramatic form since Mozart was a born dramatist. Picture him being with the Prince Elector in Munich and thereupon reporting to his father: "Count Seeau passed by, greeting me very kindly. At your disposal dearest Mozart! When the Prince Elector was approaching, I said: 'Your Serene Highness, Lord Prince Elector, allow me to throw myself most humbly at your feet to offer you my services.' 'Well, are you completely removed from Salzburg?' 'Completely removed, yes, Your Serene Highness.' 'Why on earth? Did it get too tight for you?' 'Oh no, not at all, Your Serene Highness; I merely requested permission for a journey; you denied my request, therefore I was compelled to take that step, even though I should admit I had been planning for a long time to leave Salzburg. It is no place for me.' 'Yes, quite so. My goodness, a young fellow like you! But your father is still in Salzburg, I take it?' 'Yes, Your Serene Highness, I have been to Italy three times already, I have written three operas, I am a member of the Academy at Bologna, I had to take a test, which I finished within one hour, while many maestri labored and sweated over it for four or five hours.' 'Well, my dear child, there isn't any vacancy here. I am sorry. If only there were a vacancy.' 'I assure Your Serene Highness that I should hope to be able to do credit to Munich.' 'Well, that doesn't do any good. There just isn't a vacancy here.' " In the next letter it says: "He knows nothing about me. He does not know what I can do." This utterance does not simply refer to the Prince Elector. Basically speaking, all of them knew nothing about him, and there was no vacancy for him, neither here nor anywhere else.

Nor in that country that he thought about in despair later on: "If Germany, my beloved fatherland, of which (as you know) I am proud, refuses to accommodate me, then it must, alas, be France or England that will be made richer by yet another gifted German—to the shame of the German nation." We might note, though, that his despair, just like his other emotions, never gets out of bounds. Not in his letters, at any rate. This, by the way, helps to explain why "he," why everybody knew nothing about him. For example, we do not know a single genuine love letter by Mozart, at best some amorous ones, among them of course those addressed to his "Bäsle." What do they look like?

"Ma très chère Nièce! Cousine! Fille! mère, soeur et Epouse! For heaven's sacred sake, to hell with the Croatians, devils, witches, bitches, cursed battalion and no end, blasted elements, air, water, earth, and fire, Europe, asia, affrica, and America, jesuits, Augustinians, Benedictines, Capuchins, minorities, franciscans. Dominicans, Carthusians, and Gentlemen of the Holy Cross, Canonici regulares and irregulares, and sluggards, rogues, scalawags, and the whole pack of capons and pricks, jackasses, dolts, muttonheads, fools, simpletons, oafs! What kind of behavior is this here, 4 musketmen and 3 bandoleer? . . . I hope you, too, on the contrary, as it were, have duly received my letters, to wit, one from Hohenaltheim and 2 from Mannheim; and this one, as it were, is the third from Mannheim but, in all, the fourth, as it were. Now I must close, as it were, for I'm not yet dressed and we're going to have a meal any minute, so that we can shit afterwards, as it were; if you still love me as much as I love you, then we'll never stop loving each other"—at this point he starts parodying absurd opera clichés—, "even though the hard-won victory of doubt had not been planned well and the tyranny of the savage potentates furtively sneaked away, nevertheless, Codrus the wise philosophus often gobbles up snot in lieu of porridge, and the Romans, the pillars of my ass, always are, always have been, and always will remain—free of the caste system." The letter concludes with this sentence: "Je vous baise vos mains, votre visage, vos genoux et votre . . . afin, tout ce que vous me permettés [sic] de baiser." A sentence which not even Leitzmann suppressed, hoping that very few readers would understand it.

There is, to be sure, a different tone in his letters to Konstanze (whom he married in place of an adored sister of hers), a pretty and trivial woman, a kind of Papagena, to whom he was slavishly attached because of a mutual sexual compatibility, also because of jealousy, for although he deceived her fleetingly on occasion, he frequently had to remind her of his honor as her husband since he "permitted her calves to be measured by young people," as it is stated in one of her letters; Konstanze, moderately musical, impulsive, scatterbrained, cheerful, as incapable as he was of managing a household and money, and totally ignorant of the true stature of her mate. Thus he writes to her: "While I was writing the previous page, many a tear dropped on the paper; but now let's be merry! catch! there are surprisingly many kisses whirling about! The devil! I myself can see lots of them. Ha Ha! I just got hold of three of them, they're precious! . . ." This he says at a time when his health is broken, his financial troubles overwhelm him, his final string quartets are in the making, also *Cosí fan tutte*, the most delicate, mysterious of his operas, in which, not surprisingly, many a tear is shed and in which we come across the phrase "But now let's be merry!" And in which four marionettes move with and against one another and the two male lovers put their loved ones to a test on account of a silly wager and a fictive good-bye suddenly turns into the most heart-rending, the most shattering of all farewells in the world's art.

Are the letters to his "Bäsle" really jocular, facetious? Only on the face of it. Their feverish verbal cascades, their bowdlerizations, their obscenities, particularly in the fecal area, throw no more light on the character of their author than do the gallant expressions of tenderness offered to Konstanze. They are an extremely remote, distorted echo of his music, which was his sole authentic language. When we read these letters, we hear an inner echo of a reality which they themselves do not manifest. They somehow remind us of the wretched mechanical cheerfulness of the first and the last movements of many concertos, or the stylized triviality of the late *contre-danses*. They are a stammering dream language from a realm in which the essential, the real thing takes place: music. Significant though the documentary value of these letters is, they do not reveal Mozart's innermost mind. Not because the creator of the most discreet and disciplined music had aimed for this effect; rather, because there was no other language at his disposal.

Long afterwards, people felt sad and angry when they recounted that the thirty-five-year-old Mozart was buried in a mass grave in December of 1791 and that no one had walked behind his coffin. It was not until seventeen years later that Konstanze, who had married the Danish civil servant Nissen, an upright man full of admiration for both Mozart's widow and his music, finally did find the time to visit the cemetery; but by then nobody even knew the spot where Mozart had been buried. Actually, all of those things were perfectly appropriate. He was buried, and thus there had indeed been a vacancy. Yet they still knew nothing about him.

I FIND MY WAY

WOLFGANG HILDESHEIMER
translated by Patricia R. Stanley

ONE EVENING, IT WAS ABOUT A YEAR AGO NOW, MY UNCLE VISITED ME. HE brought two pictures which, as he said, he had acquired at auction at a good price. They were two large, genuine, heavy oils on canvas with a display of thickly applied paint, in bulky, gilded frames. Both represented Alpine landscapes with snow-capped mountains, shelters, and homeward-bound woodcutters. The only noticeable difference was that the light of a setting sun shone in the one landscape while a storm was gathering above the other. At first glance it was clear to me that they must be called "Alpine Glow" and "Before the Storm."

My uncle suggested that I hang the pictures immediately. I could think of no reason not to do this, and I hung them while he watched. "The pictures are called 'Alpine Glow' and 'Before the Storm,'" he commented. "Right," I said. "I was just about to ask you for the titles."

Later I opened a bottle of port wine and we talked. As we were drinking the second glass, Roeder came. Roeder, a friend of mine, is a painter of the modern school, from whom I had acquired a picture several days before. His visit was inopportune, because for some reason I had not yet hung his picture, and now in its place hung the two large landscapes.

"Ah, look here," he said in a tone of skeptical astonishment after he had greeted us both and now moved towards the miserable pictures. " 'Alpine Glow' and 'Before the Storm.' "

"That's what they are called, really," said my uncle in amazement. I explained to Roeder, as I sought to give him a meaningful look, that I had just then received the pictures as a gift from my uncle. Roeder, however, did not seem to want to enter into the spirit of the occasion. He murmured again and again with an absentminded air, "Very pretty, very pretty," and I had the feeling that villainous thoughts were at work behind his absent-mindedness. I found his behavior extremely tactless and was therefore glad when he left soon afterward. At the door he tapped me on the shoulder in a friendly way. This, too, had never been his custom. I became very uncomfortable. My shoulder bothered me for the rest of the evening from this tap.

My uncle, on the other hand, remained until the bottle was empty. When he left, I breathed a sigh of relief: The moment had come to take down the pictures and hang Roeder's abstract. But I felt suddenly dejected and curiously paralyzed. It might have been the effect of the visit or perhaps the wine had tired me. Port makes one sluggish. In any case, climbing the ladder and changing the pictures seemed to me a mighty undertaking. I put it off.

The next morning a large crate was brought to me. I had just fetched my tools in order to undertake the rehanging of the pictures, but now I used them to open the crate. A letter lay at the very top. It was from Roeder and read:

Dear Robert,
With this I am sending you some objects which I assume will suit your fancy.
Cordially yours, Roeder

Suspecting nothing good, I began unpacking. First there was a porcelain vase wrapped in wood shavings; it pictured a gaily feathered crane whose open bill was meant for the insertion of flower stalks. Beside this, between layers of tissue paper, lay a bouquet of artificial roses and a table lamp of cast iron in the shape of a naked woman who bore on her shoulder a light fixture and a shade of green silk covered with frills and pleats.

My mood darkened at the sight of these objects. To be sure, I did not let the shipment lure me into thinking that Roeder seriously believed in my sudden change of taste, but I thought that he had gone too far with his mischievous, consciously childish misunderstanding. Where was I to put the things in my two-room apartment; I did not have a storeroom or a junk room. I was still brooding about the tastelessness of this joke when Sylvia came. Sylvia is impulsive and always inclined to unconditional pursuit of a moment's inspiration. She often goes too far, and she did it now, too. She must have taken in the situation at a glance. But instead of helping me, she acted as if the only difficulty lay in where to place some new acquisitions to best advantage. Without a word she went into action. She took a light bulb from a drawer, screwed it into the lamp, and carried it to my bedroom. With feminine affection she arranged the artificial flowers in the vase, placed it on a bookshelf between the pictures, stood back a few steps, and regarded the effect. Then she sat down beside me and stroked my cheek.

I turned to her in exasperation and said, "Listen, Sylvia, this is all a frightful misunderstanding, nearly even a plot. My uncle gave me those pictures yesterday evening. I should not have hung them, but unfortunately I did. Then Roeder came and saw the pictures. On the strength of that—." Here she interrupted me and said, "Why make excuses? It's a matter of indifference to me how the things came into your possession. Now they belong to you." The significance of these words puzzled me at the moment, but it soon became clearer in the course of events. Sometimes I think she said, "Now they are attached to you." In any case, that must have been the meaning of her words.

When she left, she parted from me as if from a patient whom one dare not rob of belief in recovery. She looked into my eyes as if she wanted to give me courage, stroked my cheek again, turned swiftly, and was gone.

She returned in the afternoon and brought her friend, Renate. Renate went immediately into my bedroom and began hammering. Sylvia, meanwhile, unpacked a number of lace doilies and said she wanted to put them on the arms of my chair; that would surely suit my taste. Moreover, they would also protect the upholstery. I was so irritated I could not say a word. Speechless I watched as she placed the doilies, smoothed them down, and then fastened them with pins. Then she dragged me into the bedroom where Renate had just mounted a huge Black Forest cuckoo clock on the wall.

That was going too far. Furiously I began to tear the thing from the wall, but it was attached with two steel hooks; and when I pulled on it, the cuckoo shot out and shrieked furiously six times in my face. "Oh, it's six already," said Renate. "We must go." As they left, a fact of which I took cognizance in stony silence, Sylvia assured me she would embroider me a few table covers in cross-stitch. Then both of them gave me a quick kiss and ran laughing down the stairs. Their laughter rang in my ears for a long time afterwards. It was as if an adversary in the wings were laughing after the curtain had already fallen.

The cross-stitch coverings came two days later, but there was even more. An architect named Mons, an intimate friend, had come to see me the previous evening. He had, as he said, heard from Roeder of my new acquisitions and had come to see them for himself. I had attempted to explain to him, this time in a nervous excitement to which I gave free rein, that everything was a malicious mistake. But he had only looked at me observantly with the seriousness of a diagnostician, as if he were attempting to discover in my manner further symptoms of a progressive illness. That increased my agitation, and when he pressed my hand in farewell and said, "Good night, old boy," I slammed the door furiously behind him.

And now there came, with a card from him, a huge ivory-colored varnished stand with shelves that projected to several heights and in several directions. I knew immediately that it served as a repository for cactus. The cactus, in various sizes and forms, came the same day, as well as an illustrated volume entitled "The Cactus Grower." With a calmness that surprised me I arranged the cactus on the shelves and placed the notebook on my night table.

This night passed restlessly. The cuckoo woke me several times. Then when I turned on the lamp, I saw the bronze woman; I could endure this sight only with difficulty, and I took "The Cactus Grower" from the night table in order to divert myself. I could not become interested in its contents —not yet—; I put the book aside again and turned off the lamp. I cherished unfriendly thoughts towards my uncle, towards Roeder, Sylvia, and the whole group. With these thoughts I fell asleep until the cuckoo awakened me again.

This same week I caught myself several times in the act of arranging the artificial flowers in the vase or smoothing a lace doily on the chair arm; and when the case with the twisted candlesticks and balance scales came, I unpacked each piece eagerly. I took no cognizance of the sender.

Summer came. Sylvia was traveling and therefore the previously regular shipments of cross-stitch coverlets and sofa pillows had ceased. In their place, however, she sent colorful picture postcards representing diverse destinations. I arranged them in an album.

Renate visited me one evening and brought me a record album. She insisted that I play some records immediately. At first we played a fantasy entitled "From Weber's Magic Forest," then "The Most Beautiful Choruses from Wagner's Operas," and in conclusion the finale of Beethoven's Fifth Symphony. Then she left. When she was gone, I played the ballet music from "Rosamunde" and went to sleep. The cuckoo clock struck twelve. I had begun to orient myself to it.

I attempted to rebel once more; it was the day when Herr von Stamitz, who had meanwhile become engaged to Sylvia, sent me the bookcase of mottled walnut and the fake bookbindings. It is no longer clear to me today why I became senselessly angry on this occasion, because the thing was flawlessly handcrafted. I remember that I ran around in my apartment as if in a cage. I attempted to pull the lace doilies from the chair; I had forgotten that in the meantime I had sewn them down. I wanted to tear the cross-stitch covers to pieces with my teeth, but they were stubborn, made of good sturdy farmer's linen. Sylvia had always despised inferior material. All that broke on this occasion was a costly African sculpture, one of the few mementos of the time before my uncle's visit. I had to laugh at this exemplary casualty, and my anger subsided. Passively I went to work, arranged the book facings in the walnut bookcase and secured then on both sides. At the same time I read the names Gibbons, Macaulay, Mommsen, and Ranke. It was a selection for historians. Moreover, I have always been very interested in history.

This night I dreamed. I was wandering through empty halls in which there was here and there a functional piece of furniture. I sat down on a steel footstool. Immediately it grew an upholstered back and arms, with pillows of velvet and rep. Crystal chandeliers dipped down from the ceiling. Women in flowing gowns, hair rolled into spirals above their ears, trundled heavy goldcut volumes that they opened before me. The pages were pasted with prints and photographs under which were to be read such titles as "Franz Liszt in a circle of friends," or "Evening mood at the Walchensee," or "Hiroshima, mon amour." I woke up as the pendulum clock in the living room struck three and turned on the night table lamp. The bronze figure in its hideous actuality stood before me. I turned off the lamp. The cuckoo cried three—it was obviously slow—I turned on the light again and threw "The Cactus Grower" at the cuckoo; it missed. I attempted to hit it with the deer of Rosenthal porcelain but hit the obscene copperplate engraving, "la surprise," which hung beside the cuckoo clock. Glass splintered and I grew calmer. The crisis was over.

Thus my apartment slowly became overgrown. Fewer and fewer visitors came, because it required an effort to wind in and out among the pieces of furniture in order to find a place to sit; and if one found a place he could no longer sit down, because on the chairs lay framed engravings, dishes of all sorts, and also many a piece worthy of a prize for its realistic excellence.

My uncle visited me once more; but I did not see him, for I lay in bed and he could not find the path to me. I asked him to put the picture he brought, which this time, as he called out to me, was something modern, on one of the teakwood end tables, some of which must still be in the foyer. He called to me that the tables were already covered with all kinds of ceramic pots, things moreover of obviously artistic value. I did not answer and therefore do not know whether my uncle left the picture or took it away again, because I have been lying in bed since then. My uncle was the last visitor.

I do not get up any more, for if I were able to find my way through the bedroom, I would get lost in the living room. I lie and daydream, look at postcards or photo engravings, or play, on the phonograph that stands beside my bed, Schubert's serenade or the "Ave Maria" sung by a Negro singer. She has such a beautiful soothing voice. Also I sometimes read in "The Cactus Grower," from which I have learned, for example, that cactus sometimes blooms. Perhaps one of mine is blooming; but I don't know it, for, as I have said, I no longer visit my living room.

I can sleep again now, since I hit the cuckoo one night with a vase of Swedish glass just as it was about to glide back into the clock. The pendulum clock in the living room stopped a long time ago and I can no longer get to it to wind it up. Besides, I don't want to, because it would be senseless.

THE BLINDFOLD

SIEGFRIED LENZ

translated by E. W. Gundel

THE PROOFREADER INTERRUPTED THE GAME. HE FOLDED HIS CARDS UP, threw them on the window table, and slowly rubbed his eyes, then raised his head and looked through the compartment window into the darkness outside. "That was only Wandsbek," said one of the other two; whereupon the proofreader picked up the cards again, spread them out with his thumb into a fan, and silently led off. After two hands, which he lost, he folded his cards up again, let them fall lightly slapping against the window, and said: "It's not in any book. I've looked it up everywhere."

"It's your lead," said one of the other two, an old man with steel-rimmed glasses.

"It just wasn't to be found," said the proofreader.

"Don't start again," said the man with the steel-rimmed glasses, "I'd just forgotten it."

"Well, are we going to play or aren't we?" said the redheaded man.

They went on playing. They played silently as on every evening that they sat in the last local leaving Hamburg, each absorbed with his weariness and the wish not to be left to his own devices on the trip home. For twenty or even thirty years now they had played cards like this all the way home, not indifferently, but not excitedly either, three men of that patient brotherhood of commuters, who had met one another almost inevitably and who met now time and again in a sort of instinctive agreement, always in the next-to-last compartment, which they entered and likewise left again with only a curt greeting.

They played without a sound, no one seemed to care to waste even a single word about gains or losses, and then it was the proofreader who again interrupted the game. "But I've got to find out," he said, "surely you ought to be able to learn how Tekhila is spelled."

"My deal," said the redhead.

"Why do you have to know that?" said the man with the steel-rimmed glasses.

"There's a lot a person would like to find out," said the proofreader.

"What for?"

"You shouldn't leave everything as it is."

"Cut," said the redhead, and dealt.

"The thing will come out tomorrow," said the proofreader. "Tekhila is mentioned four times in the story and each time it is spelled differently."

"I'm listening," said the redhead.

"Is it a village?" asked the man with the steel-rimmed glasses, and put his cards together.

"Tekhila is the name of a village in a story," said the proofreader.

"Who has more than twenty?" said the redhead.

They looked at their cards, no one could find more than twenty, and it was the redhead's game. The rain sprayed against the compartment window. The train had slowed down now and braked next to an empty, poorly lighted platform; they heard doors slamming shut, and then hasty footsteps on stone tiles. When the train started up again it was the proofreader's turn to deal, and the man with steel-rimmed glasses asked: "Why Tekhila of all things?"

"I don't know," said the proofreader, and he lifted his gray, unshaven face.

"Do you know Tekhila?"

"No."

"Do you have an urge to go there?"

"No."

"What is it then?"

"They are blind," said the proofreader, "in Tekhila everyone is blind: They are born blind and grow up and marry and die blind. It is an old Arabic eye disease."

"Does the story take place in Morocco?" asked the man with the steel-rimmed glasses.

"No," said the proofreader, "I don't know."

He left his cards lying unheeded on the window table and rubbed his eyes, while the others looked over their hands and at the same time folded them up with a gesture of resignation.

"You have the winning hand," said the redhead.

"It's called: 'The Blindfold,' " said the proofreader.

"What?"

"The story, the story there in Tekhila. It is an old leather blindfold which the mayor keeps."

"For whom?" asked the man with the steel-rimmed glasses, and likewise laid his cards on the window table.

"I don't know," said the proofreader, "perhaps for everyone in Tekhila. It is a small village on a plain, not much shade, a river with mud-clouded water goes by there, and the people, the blind inhabitants of Tekhila, work in the fields."

"Does the story begin like that?" asked the man with the steel-rimmed glasses.

"No," said the proofreader, "the story begins differently. It begins in the house of the mayor. The mayor takes a leather blindfold from its hook. It is dark, spotty leather, dusty, and the mayor wipes the blindfold clean on his pants. He polishes it with his finger tips, and then he leaves the house. In front of his house sits a basket weaver at work. The mayor holds the blindfold out to him, lets him touch the cool leather; the basket weaver jumps up alarmed and follows the mayor, they go together across the square and down the parched street to the fields, and everywhere they meet a man, they stop, the mayor mutely holds out the leather blindfold to him, to alarm him."

"And each one follows him," said the redhead.

"Yes, each one who touches the blindfold gives a start and follows the mayor," said the proofreader. "They interrupt their work or their lazing. They don't ask questions. They simply follow him, and even the mayor does not say a single word while he gathers the men of Tekhila or summons them by holding out the blindfold to them, and in the end he has all the men of the village behind him."

"And that's how the story begins?" asked the man with the steel-rimmed glasses.

"Something like that," said the proofreader. "Tomorrow it will be in our paper. Tomorrow you can read about it. Tekhila is mentioned four times, and each time it is spelled differently."

"And the fellow with the blindfold?" asked the redhead.

"Who?"

"The mayor and all those he's got behind him: Where are they headed?"

"To the school," said the proofreader. "It is noon, I think it's noon, and they head silently to the school and surround the building. They take each other's hands and form a ring. They stand there alertly. They test here and there the strength of the ring. Their readiness, their silent agreement, the rapidity with which they surround the school building—all of this seems to indicate that this is not happening for the first time. They stand motionless in the sun, and then the mayor leaves the ring and goes up to the building. He knocks. The blind teacher of Tekhila opens the door and the mayor has him touch the leather blindfold. The teacher asks him to come in. He knows that the building is surrounded. He asks, 'Who?' and the mayor says, 'Your son.' The teacher says, 'You don't even believe that yourselves,' to which the mayor says, 'We have proof.' They talk quietly in the hall, each trying to persuade or outwit the other. The mayor demands to speak with the teacher's son. The teacher keeps on offering assurances for his son."

"What has he gotten into—the son?" said the man with the steel-rimmed glasses.

"You couldn't give me that dump," said the redhead.

"While the two of them are talking," said the proofreader, "the son suddenly appears, no, he is already there, he is standing upstairs and listens to the men, and all at once he says to his father, 'It's true. You don't know it, but it did happen: Since the accident that time when our boat overturned and we drifted against the rocks, since that day I can see!' "

"Is it that way in the story?" asked the man with the steel-rimmed glasses.

"No," said the proofreader, "but something like that, or maybe it is that way. Both men tell the son to come down. He refuses. He remains standing at the top of the stairs, and since he seems to know what awaits him, he says to the mayor: 'Yes, I have been able to see for eight weeks now, just so you know; and for eight weeks I have come to know Tekhila.' He dares them to come up to him. He scornfully invites them to catch him. The teacher talks quietly with the mayor, and then they both go up towards the boy, who flees from them without effort and in his flight makes them an offer."

"What offer?" asked the redhead.

"Tomorrow you can both read about it," said the proofreader. "The boy wants to show them the potentialities of Tekhila, he wants to help them to get even more out of it for themselves. Backing off from them he tells what he has discovered in eight weeks."

"And that doesn't interest them," said the redhead.

"They don't understand him," said the proofreader.

"I can see that," said the redhead, riffling his cards with his thumb.

"In any case they chase the boy upstairs," said the proofreader, "he flees easily ahead of them, and they silently follow him side by side. They chase or crowd him ahead of them. The boy opens the attic window—no, that is unlikely: He opens a window, climbs out, hangs there, his body dangling, and then drops. The fall, the impact is heard by the others. They seem to have waited for it. They tighten their hold on each other's hands. They move closer together. The way they stand there! With alert faces, bent, one foot forward, as though they had to stave off a charge. They stand there like that, while the boy gets up, his ankle in pain. He discovers the ring which surrounds him and the house. He looks along the circle of alert faces, tries to remember: What's his name, who is *he,* where is the weakest point? Then he ducks, runs at them. They hear him coming and automatically strengthen their hold. The boy throws himself against the ring. The ring gives way and catches him and closes around him: He is caught in it like a fish in a net. They hold him fast, take him to the middle, until the mayor comes back."

"With the leather blindfold," said the man with the steel-rimmed glasses.

"With the blindfold," said the proofreader. "But they don't put the blindfold on him yet. They lead or drag him through the village, through Tekhila. They don't hesitate. They know what is going to happen. You get the idea that this has happened before. In any case, they bring him out to the old water pump at the edge of the fields."

"There they deliberate," said the redhead.

"No," said the proofreader, "they don't deliberate. They don't deliberate at all in the story. The mayor calls on just one man. It is a man who has experience in these matters, you know right away. No name is mentioned. This man has a wound-up cord in his pocket. He ties the boy fast to the beam of the pump wheel; then he puts the blindfold on him, and while he is doing that you notice that they have done the same thing with him too, a long time ago."

"Is the boy standing alone at the beam?" asked the man with the steel-rimmed glasses.

"A mule," said the proofreader, "at the other end of the beam a mule is tied. The men of Tekhila wait until everything is done. The mule pulls, the boy goes with it, round and around."

"How long?" asked the redhead, "how long will he wear the blindfold?"

"As long as it is necessary," said the proofreader.

"Maybe they have to do it that way in Tekhila," said the man with the steel-rimmed glasses.

"Yes," said the proofreader, "maybe they do."

"I'll read about it."

"Four times Tekhila is mentioned, and each time it is spelled differently."

"That sounds like that dump."

"Yeah, sounds like it; I've looked everywhere. I couldn't find a thing."

"Not a thing?" asked the man with the steel-rimmed glasses.

"Oh, sure," said the proofreader, "a few names which sound something like Tekhila."

The redhead put the cards away, looked through the compartment window, and took his briefcase from the luggage rack. "I guess it's not worth dealing anymore," he said.

"No," said the proofreader. "It's not worth it."

THE DISCOVERY OF SWITZERLAND

HUGO LOETSCHER
translated by Peter Spycher

WE FOUGHT OUR WAY UP THE RIVER. NEVER BEFORE HAD WE SEEN THIS kind of water, the only kinds we knew till then were fresh or sea water, but what we found here, in such a strange region, was indeed a new variety of water. It smelled rather nauseating and had a brownish color; the current was sluggish, the white crests that formed were not caused by the flow of the river. One morning we discovered fish drifting in the water with their pale bellies turned up.

We asked the prisoner who served as our interpreter what this meant; but he seemed to be puzzled by our question. We offered him a ladle filled with this water; he drank it without any hesitation and then looked up beaming. He said that in all his life—he is still a young man—he had never seen any other kind of water in river beds. We ordered him to drink a second and a third time, but it did him no harm.

Since we failed to get a clear explanation about the nature of the water in this river, we called it the River of the Dead Fish. For the people living along the banks of the river do not seem to agree on a name for it either. Our interpreter mentioned several different names; this was due to the fact that the tribes inhabiting these banks speak patently different languages. They are said to have waged quite brutal wars against each other in earlier times, but presently they are at peace, having grown weary of all those wars. As far as we could judge from our ship, they walked and dressed in much the same manner on both sides of the river. But after all, we did not want to stay on these banks, we wanted to push ahead up the river; for we had heard stories about a secret country, rich in gold, an El Dorado, where immense wealth was supposed to be hoarded. During a stopover on an island that is situated close to the mainland, we had learned that this hoard was guarded by gnomes.

But what impelled us to forge ahead towards the province called Helvetia was not just this treasure guarded by dwarfs, but also the existence of fountains of youth promising eternal life. Their magic charms and formulas are said to be kept strictly secret. Yet we hoped to find ways and means to provide our own great ruler and our people with such blessings, too.

Suddenly, our prisoner called out: "Here we are!" We were surprised because what we saw was, at least for the moment, no different from what we had hitherto observed along these banks. But our interpreter was quite excited; he told us that we had arrived at the meeting point of three countries. To be sure, we had not yet reached the province proper of the gold-guarding gnomes, he averred; but we were at the border of their territory. What we saw in front of us, he said, was the legendary location of the fountains of youth.

We marveled greatly at the sight, fell down on our knees, and gave thanks to our mighty god for this unexpected, but most generously granted, privilege; thereupon we sharpened our swords and readied our bows and arrows.

At first, we thought we had been detected and word had been spread concerning our arrival, because there were smoke signals going up wherever we looked. Soon enough, however, we learned that those smoke signals were not intended to broadcast any messages; this was not possible, for one thing, since they were not replaced by visible fire signals at night.

Rather, people were performing sacrificial rites. All along the river bank, smoke was rising towards the sky. Earlier, we had wondered why people would erect tall buildings without any rows of steps, yet we were told that they construct stairs inside and also that these stairs keep moving of their own accord, which, naturally, caused hearty laughter among us. They also build houses for the smoke, round and slim ones, looking like tubes. This was not a holiday, though, but rather an ordinary workday; these people do not sacrifice human beings, slitting open their chests, as we do, taking out their steaming hearts, and offering them up to Heaven; nor do they sacrifice specially chosen victims who prepare themselves for the deadly rite by singing hymns; they sacrifice indiscriminately; they subject their victims to a lifelong sacrifice by forcing them to work; it is not a large number of people who sacrifice a few, it is a few people who sacrifice a large number of others.

Nonetheless, we remained skeptical. On our way, we had already lost one ship, a loss still weighing heavily on the minds of our crew. The natives have larger and faster craft, but so far our own flat-bottomed ships have proved to be superior. To be sure, we had heard that the tribe of the gold-hoarding gnomes was peaceable; that for a long time they themselves had no longer waged any wars, but had kept a careful eye on wars waged between others, refraining from taking sides, doing business with both participants. On the other hand, we had found out that the able-bodied men annually turn into warriors and play war games that last up to three weeks.

In order to test the willingness of this tribe to keep the peace, Kamilk, the brave son of the Kaziks, swam to the river bank in the dark of the night, where he laid out peace offerings: precious wood, some jewelry, and many perfumed cloths. At sunrise, we took up hidden positions, after having investigated the condition of the river bed and our anchorage. I had ordered our lead ship to move towards the bank up to the range of a bowshot. While waiting for things to happen on this morning, we became aware, for the first time, of the barbarity of the custom of constantly sending smoke up into the air. People impregnate the virginal sky and thus befog the face of our highest god, the sun. At that time, we actually began to suspect that these natives, notwithstanding their peaceful intentions, are brethren of the night.

The one who found the gifts examined them at length, then he ran away, and we waited for him to return along with his chieftain. Yet he turned up with two identically dressed men. They were two policemen, as they soon told us themselves, at least that is what they called themselves, pointing with their fingers at their chests; we were to find out soon enough what that meant.

First, they searched the bank, until they discovered us floating on the river. Then they waved to us and boarded one of their fast boats. It would have been wrong for us to try to escape them; thus we made preparations for a fight and took shelter in our ships, being firmly resolved to sell our lives as dearly as possible. But after they had approached us by way of a loop, one of them made unmistakable peace signals in our direction. We returned the same signals to express our gratitude and let the first of them come aboard. The man wanted to see our papers, but we did not know just what he was looking for. Even when the interpreter explained to us the matter at hand, we did not fully understand what he meant. Soon enough, however, we noticed that he was not satisfied to simply look at us and our ship with his own sound eyes.

All natives carry papers with them, on which the place and date of their birth are entered. This is all the more understandable since their hairdo and attire no longer indicate their different origins. The life of these people starts, not with their emergence from the womb of a woman, but with a bureaucratic entry. We would have loved to know if the same applies to death, too.

The native in uniform scribbled something on a piece of paper and held it out towards us. We thought it was a return gift and broke out into a shout of joy. But our mood became more subdued when we learned that it was a penalty. It was really baffling news to us that we should be penalized for having laid out perfumed cloths, jewelry, and precious wood. But the man informed us that there was a regulation against anchoring ships here and swimming ashore. We laughed at him, and this made him angry. We realized quickly that this was just a stratagem on his part to engage us in an argument. The man denied it; he repeated several times what he had told us and insisted again and again that it was indeed a regulation, which made us curious to find out what this word signified.

He produced these regulations from one of their sacred books, which he was carrying on his person; it contains innumerable regulations arranged according to symbols, which resemble a double gallows and a noose about to be drawn tight.

These regulations may be likened to those slowly working poisons that some of our Indian tribal members extract from lianas, maniocs, and cactuses. Except that the regulations are extracted not from plants but from the juice of brains that have been trained for years. These regulations do have an effect, although afterwards you could not determine exactly how long ago it was that you "swallowed" them. Many of them have such a neutral taste that you do not notice anything special when swallowing them. Thus their effect sets in without a noticeable transition after years have elapsed. The regulations lead to some kind of paralysis, without slackening your zest for work; on the contrary, the result may be an outright obsession for work. The most conspicuous effect is a gradual loss of memory; thus, under their influence, most people forget the dreams of their youth and the things for which they once struggled.

The regulations also cause a certain degree of intoxication. Yet this intoxication is experienced not by those who swallow them but rather by those who enforce them. We could distinctly perceive that the policeman's pupils, while he was reading the regulation to us, were dilated with ecstasy and that the cornea was changed to a lustful red color. Since our peaceful intention had been misunderstood, we had to try to lure the second policeman aboard. He was more than glad to climb on and wanted to know whether we were refugees. When he received no reply from us, he asked us whether we had any money and, if so, how much. We were evasive, telling him we had come from the region of the sunset. Then he inquired whether we were looking for work; again we decided not to respond, since we did not want to let on that we were searching for the gold of the gnomes and the fountains of youth. Thereupon, he wanted to shackle us, but we forestalled his move. I felt compelled to give him a sound thrashing. While we were beating him, he asked us whether we were policemen, too.

In the process of searching them, we came across the most heretical objects we had ever seen. Each wore on his arm, attached by a thin band to his wrist, a round object, fashioned after the solar disc, with a myriad of circularly arranged ciphers that had been carefully engraved and painted. They were so-called watches, which indicate the hours even during the sun-less time that belongs exclusively to the moon and its slow waxing and waning. We smashed their idols and forced them to kneel down to beg our god's pardon. For the disc is the unique attribute of the sun god, and any profanation must be punished with the utmost harshness. The fact that these objects and fetishes tell them the time even at night proves once again with whom these sons of darkness are in league.

When the two prisoners saw their smashed idols, they wailed more loudly than they had while being thrashed, and their wailing and moaning went on and on. They said that anyone who had been deprived of such a thing was threatened by misfortune because everything depended on the right time. Yet they were unable to answer our question as to how they knew when someone died at the right time. They have divided time into an infinite number of units in order to store as many things as possible in it, as though it were a huge warehouse; they do this without fearing for a moment that some day time might burst. At any rate, we were surprised to note that they were engaged in crude commerce with time, one of the most sacred gods.

While searching the two of them, we found maps in which all streets and the most important buildings are recorded. We thought this would help us find entry into those houses that enclose the fountain of youth. Nevertheless, one has to bear in mind that the place was too large to be explored in one day even by the hardiest walker. We discovered that there were no fountains of youth in the strict sense of the word. To our surprise, the natives turned out to be rock and soil eaters, although they first pulverize the soil and rocks and then use this powder to bake tiny breadlike pieces in the shape of globules and little tablets in all sorts of colors. In order to cover up their often repulsive taste, they very often sweeten them with a sugary coating.

New for us was that you do not have to push your way into the place where these globules and little tablets are devised, cooked, and concocted, but that they are sold everywhere in the streets by members of a guild called pharmacists or the like and also by members of related occupations such as barbers and sellers of detergents. The guild of the pharmacists does not enjoy a particularly high reputation because of its greed; the pettiness of their character is said to originate in their use of finely calibrated scales; nonetheless, in many respects they have become models for their fellow natives.

Thus all we would have to do was to go out into the streets to acquire these globules and little tablets of eternal youth. We thought this was marvelous. But we were informed that you have to pay for them. We asked the two prisoners why a miraculous mystery such as that of life eternal

was not meted out to all and sundry. Our question made them laugh so
hard that afterwards we had to tighten their shackles. They said you had
to pay for everything and those without money had no share in this miraculous mystery.

I am telling this, implausible though it may sound, to offer a complete
report on everything we experienced, even if it should benefit nobody, except in terms of learning the truth.

Our search of the prisoners also yielded something they designate as
money; again it was some sort of paper. One habit of the natives is never
to go anywhere without such papers because they bestow power and status
on them; they also provide them with as much safety as would weapons,
but they are not as heavy as those forged or carved things and above all
they are invisible, which makes their bearers look harmless. But suddenly
they pull out these papers, and woe to the other fellow! What is dangerous
is that these weapons work secretly; we have observed countless cases of
individuals wasting away as a result of invisible wounds inflicted upon
them by these papers.

We ourselves lost one of our best people because of this money and the
consequences it triggered. We detailed him to acquire globules and little
tablets with the pieces of paper we had taken from our prisoners. While we
were debating whether or not our man could walk along the street unrec-
ognized in view of his alien appearance, we received the reassuring answer
that our tribal friend would attract scarcely anybody's attention since the
people here were dressed in such motley fashions. You can imagine, therefore, how worried we became when he failed to return. We sent out a
search party, numbering as many people as a little boat may hold. They
found him just at the moment he was being carried off. At first they
thought he had been slain by an armed person, but the information we received was far more frightful. Immediately after acquiring those globules
and little tablets, he had eaten many of them and had at once dropped
dead. Our men were unsuccessful in their attempt to recover his body by
force; thus we had to abandon this warrior, who had gloriously distinguished himself in his life both at the helm and with his weapon, to an in-
glorious death.

I do not have to use many words to say that we were most profoundly
surprised and dismayed upon learning that the first effect of such a fountain of youth was death. Certainly, dealing with the fountain of youth
seems to be a dangerous enterprise, but now we were all the more tempted
to pursue this secret further, and we threatened our prisoners with death if
they gave us any misleading information. We played the Yaki flute and the
Queche drum for them, but they are not accustomed to dancing when taken
prisoner.

An older helmsman declared himself available for the next foray; he had volunteered for it because he was of an already respectable age but no longer capable of enjoying the pleasures of life, let alone of asserting his virility. This man, however, had to state under oath that he himself would not eat anything he acquired. He brought back not only globules and little tablets but also countless receptacles of the most different sizes and shapes, all of them fitted with a lid one turns rather than lifts to remove, as the prisoners showed us. To our general amusement and cheered on by our youngest companions, our helmsman immediately began to rub his body with ointments. But since he underwent no change, we went off to get a night's rest, while the old helmsman rubbed his entire body with ointments and particularly a certain spot all night long, so much so that on the following morning he was totally exhausted; despite all his efforts, not one of the wrinkles we had jointly counted the evening before was gone.

At any rate, we had decided to take along as many little tablets, globules, little jars, etc., as possible. But because the problem of how to use them seems to us to be rather complicated, we captured a pharmacist wearing the white coat typical of his profession. He said he would tell us the secret of entering one of the buildings where all those fountain of youth things were manufactured, and he also suggested that we capture a so-called chemist to take his place. But we did not let him go free, we kept him because we planned to present him to our great ruler. Incidentally, I had to protect him, for when it became known that he was one of those privy to the secret, our crew immediately wanted to auction him off among themselves.

Now the temptations mushroomed everywhere. Being so remote from our homeland, under such an alien sky, and exposed to more than the inclemency of the weather, I was compelled to resort to disciplinary measures when one of our youngest crew members busied himself with the packaged articles. However, I was at liberty to exercise leniency since he used the globules he had stolen not for himself but to fashion a necklace for his young wife back home. It is necessary to recall that our expedition had witnessed several full moons and I had to see to it that our men's pent-up sexual drive did not become a liability.

Undoubtedly, the matter of the fountain of youth and of the nutrition that keeps death at bay gives rise to rather weighty reflections, on which I will try to report as succinctly as possible.

The people here believe in a life after death. Nevertheless, they are exceedingly avaricious or at least extremely cautious. They do not give their dead anything for their journey, no arms, no food, only a shirt, not even any footwear. As for married couples, they stretch their parsimony remarkably far: A wife takes from her dead husband and a man from his dead wife the golden band which they have worn ever since their wedding. Admittedly, they make up for many such things by laying or planting flowers on their graves, but those flowers are really more enjoyable to the bereaved than useful to the dead. You can draw the obvious inference that it would be a waste of time to loot their graves.

But it is something of a surprise indeed that the people spend so much effort on preserving their lives while at the same time they believe in a blissful life after death. Their supreme god, too, has a tear in his eye, but this had nothing to do with the irrigation of deserts as it does in our homeland. It does remain a puzzle, though, that they try to postpone the very death that would finally bring them the happy life. But fear of happiness seems to be a widespread phenomenon among these natives.

In the course of our expeditions we had come into our first direct contact with the natives. What was bound to strike us first was their stature; we had anticipated meeting with dwarfs, but most of these people were of normal or even superior height; therefore we had to assume that only the guardians of the white and the yellow metal were gnomes. Yet at first we noticed something altogether different. We observed two separate types of human beings: those who carried on their noses thin frames to which two pieces of glass were fastened. We thought they were insignia of a certain caste; but we quickly found out that they were actually crutches that were placed on the nasal bone and artfully hitched to the ears so that you can bend down without dropping them. People carry these supports on account of their poor eyesight. Their vision has deteriorated generally, though, and so has their hearing, which latter deterioration has doubtlessly been caused by the horrible noise in the streets; since these people no longer wage any wars, they do not emit cries of war, but deafening cries of peace. They have long since lost their hunting instinct and do not even miss it.

It is not very easy to perceive social differences with one's naked eyes. But you can identify the members of the servant class quite well by their use of a foreign language. Ordinarily, they live in houses specially reserved for them, houses often built of wood rather than stone; and they are crowded together; as they are not allowed to have their families with them, they secretly smuggle their children into their rooms, and only at night and only for a few minutes do they take them outdoors. And if these members of the servant class do mingle with the natives—there is no law against it—the stares and the general behavior of the natives constantly remind them of their origin.

These servants are also recognizable by the fact that they are noisier and merrier than the natives. But there are some among them who have managed to move up a few steps on the social ladder; in that case they behave less noisily and merrily than they had before. What is interesting is that these servants are not captured in military campaigns but come here of their own accord or, more precisely, are driven by need. When you consider to what kinds of masters they prefer to subject themselves, you can imagine how appalling the misery must be in their home countries, where the sky is far less gloomy than in these parts.

At first, we were convinced that the natives we approached were telling us lies. For virtually all of them claimed that they personally had never seen a single one of the dwarfs guarding the gold, and that the dwarfs were not really dwarfs at all; the rumor that they were was perhaps fed by the fact that they act as if they were smaller than they are in reality.

But what seemed to us to be even more implausible was that the people we approached had never seen the hoard of gold either with their naked or their bespectacled eyes. We then asked them if the gold was not shown and exhibited, say, once a year on the occasion of a big festival; but they said no, and we had to take note that all are convinced that this gold does exist, even though none of them has seen it.

Furthermore, they claimed that this gold was hoarded in the form of bullion, since this method of storage was better than others. When we asked why they did not fashion goblets, vessels, bowls, or rings, clasps, and necklaces out of this gold because only thus could it display its beauty, we became quickly aware that possession as such is more important to them than beautiful things you make out of it.

When we asked them if they would not even wish to have a look at this gold, their eyes lit up and they nodded. When we asked them why they did not enter these sanctuaries where the gold was hoarded, by force if necessary, they were frightened and placed their index fingers in a vertical position on their lips, which, in their sign language, means: silence. As we pressed on with our questions, they implored us with their looks to be quiet and to desist from any further probing. We could not help noting that these natives are afraid not only of happiness but that they fear nothing more than questions, particularly those asked by strangers like us.

In all likelihood, it is anything but easy to penetrate to this gold. You can easily go into these temples, there is an uninterrupted coming and going there; even though the visitors act busy, they cannot conceal a certain feeling of reverence upon entering these halls. The halls themselves are already under guard, but this is nothing compared to the protective measures which have been taken by the dwarfs to prevent anybody from coming near their gold. These gnomes appear to have secret powers; for example, they possess cloaks of invisibility by means of which they spirit whole fortunes away; no matter how impossible it seems to locate these fortunes, at the proper moment they turn up again. And then the gnomes bring the dead paper back to life and potency, so that it multiplies, by the work of other people, for them; but the gnomes set up some kind of screen between themselves and these people, so that they do not have to watch the toiling and suffering the work entails.

Such powerful and skillful gnomes naturally guard the gold with consummate cunning. They store it in deep cellars to which access is gained through an endless series of extremely heavy doors that can be opened only with well-nigh nonduplicable keys. This is just one of the traps on the way to the gold and into the heart of El Dorado. Thus, mechanical birds have been mounted everywhere, which immediately begin to sing and to utter shrill cries if anybody goes near them, regardless of the nature of his intention. For this gold, as we know, is guarded not only against foreigners but also against natives.

Insuperable obstacles obstructed our way to this gold. Not that our men would have let themselves be intimidated. But the enterprise as such seemed to me to be awfully foolhardy. And not only because the continuation of our journey would have become more and more burdensome; we had found out ourselves that there are artificially created rapids upstream; at those points we would once again have had to drag our ship across a stretch of land at night. This enterprise seemed to me foolhardy because we were just a small, though brave, band which could achieve nothing against the mighty gnomes, at least not single-handedly.

Thus, my judgment was that we should take our time and ally ourselves with those who hitherto had not seen this gold either; they constituted a large crowd and were those you met in the streets everywhere, men and women, youths and old people. It was relatively easier to approach them, although they are none too accessible either. But first of all you have to free them from their fear of the gnomes and show them that these dwarfs are not stronger than they are, that their superior strength is based exclusively on the gold guarded by them. And it should be easy to break this power. There was only one means by which to get at this gold: an alliance with the people.

That was the task we decided to carry out, we who had sailed eastward, and I believe we have a right to be very optimistic; for I am ready to attest that in the last analysis these natives are beings of sound reason. I pledge myself to this with all my manhood and with all my fearlessness.

BLEKPOINT

MAX MAETZ
translated by Michael P. Elzay

fer a long time didn know either what that wuz sposed to be a blekboint but now its clear its on the road on the roads on the autobahn an all over the place a black dot like its called in austria where therer more accidents than elsewhere an so the yanks say the word comes from american they call the spot blekboint comes from black an blue and the like where more accidents happen than elswhere an in austria theres a guy who marks all these places onna map all the accidents an creates an overview.

ya kin see clear over blekboints an ya kin go on a meadow next to the auto-bahn with possibly a chapel or bench in fronta it an ya sit down an light a hand-rolled an ya wait with patience an it duznt take long if its the right blekboint an theres a crash that kin happen anytime if yer sittin at the right place its like usin a dowsin rod but on the previously mentioned maps ya kin pick one with ten twenty fifty an more fatal accidents a year those are the best an it gits to be a sundayspecial like it used to be in the mountins

so later theyll make group fieldtrips to the fabulous view spots an to the most famous blekboints hikin with knapsacks and red hats an the teachers are gonna stan an say see children thats the famous blekboint number 17 warmly recommended by the cops of the area even with an inn theres a conterversy ragin however whether 18 or 17 is better but now lets pitch our tents and open our sanwitches here an wait an if were lucky therell be lotsa material fer tomorrows essay

one a our cornfields borders on the autobahn witha corner an theres one a the best most famous blekboints cause the autobahn comes down here from the blekboint i mean from mönchsberg in sorta deadly though gentle descent connected witha gentle curve an the drivers from salzkammergut that wanna go to vienna fast cause its really nicer there than in the stone an waterpuddle world theyre awways inna special hurry cause vienna is vienna an only in vienna is there a royal ridin academy an beamin streets with stores an happy

the farmer like i mentioned hired a few wetbacks fer the worst work with the beets an hind the taterdigger cause ya needs one on the tractor an another

or sevral crawlin behind in the dirt on their knees in rain er heat pickin up
the tubers an one or more gotta load the sugarbeets onto the wagon an ones
gotta be on the machine that cuts an shucks corn fills the sacks im sure about
that but since we now gotta duzzen wetbacks fer our acres once in awhile
with a cigrett we kin

drive to the blekpoint see whats new the air is mild an the air is fulla sulphur
fulla stink comin from the steelworks an whatever else ya kin say or write
bout the air even the farmer ruins the invironment with the stink a his real
homegrown tobacca but generly those a us on the land don make as much
to do bout the air air is air an nature is nature and that duzn change even if
ya comes an wants some moonshine er bacon er screw up yer eyes lookin
bout the farm an breathe in deeply an say how nice aint nature great

but i like to sit at our blekboint cause here theres awways something going
on fer exampel heres three cars comin side by side down the mountin an one
duzn make it starts skiddin an drifts rolls slides thunders on its roof wheels
up toward the center strip toward the oppisit lane on which to his good luck
but to our bad luck there just happins to be no traffic an the farmer with the
pipe in his mouth next to me nods his head sevral times an the car comes to
a stop across the way an the whole autobahn is sown with flowered garments.

yeah exactly the kine my mother left me fell outta the car outta the suitcases
of the travelin representative an salesman of fancy unnergarments the way
he crawls outta the car nothin happened to him an not much to the car cept
fer gettin bald no more paint on the roof and the shock he lost an ear but
he laughs it hurts he cudda afterall lost his heart or an eye or the steerin post
cudda rammed like ya often read through his lung and thats not outta cardboard and awreddy the cars are stackin up on both sides an the cops

they all thinks it was a panty raid its so colorful little shirts panties bras
belts whatnots in all colors stockins girdles slips an what all that stuff is
called that the women wrap around their bodies jumpers an socks an nighties
an scarfs as if it wuz spring in beautiful contrast to the autumn landscape an
the accident squadcars are awreddy soundin their sirens an awreddy ever-
bodys there an lookin an are secretly pleased that finally somethings happinin
agin in our

yeah now we kin help the roads closed off were collectin an the farmer with
his pipe in his yap sez nothin only shakes his head an duzn unnerstan why
the drivers are in such a hurry in both directions only in one that he could

unnerstan but in both thats too much fer em an he sticks his face in one a
them things outta light brown or pink rasberry an thinks cause i know him
that ole stinker bout my mother an someones bandagin that guys ear an the
firetruck comes too an stans the car back on its feet an theyre all honkin

meanswhile the wrecker pulls the car up and puts it on the shoulder of the
oppisit lane and now the AAA comes bringin the auto repair club with the
st bernard insignia with em an the driver the monteur the mechanic sez
professionally he sure was lucky the car although dented is driveable the
spilt battry has gotta be immediately refilled at the next workshop an hes
gotta get the engin washed or the acid will eat itup like acid does battrys
gotta be checked could be damaged inside just like witha human things kin
be destroyed internally

but outside of that its a miracle that its all workin an hes checkin the turn
signals left an right all the brake lights high beam left high beam right parkin
light left parkin light right gears ok starter ok inside light ok an now even
the repair club guy is comin an a hearse that somebody called a little hasty
an the auto repair club guy gives a new battry to the guy who had the accident very cheap cause hes a member a this association an the policeman
has done enuf measurin an knows the width of the road an all the distances
here an everbody wants to in five minutes

yep in five minutes at the latest the twelve-mile-long line a cars is wantin to
be in salzburg fulla impatience everthins ok first aid bandaged em up hes
gotta white turban thats holdin his torn ear in place sos the wind dont blow
it off an its all measured an noted down an closed off an now it all opens up
an the advice-givin is over an everthin costs money an a hunnert bills change
owners an theys all writin down the number of the wrecked car gainst which
this or that driver has a claim fer all that happens now an

he duzn look too happy the undies is packed up collected stowed away roads
clear all start drivin off the wrecker the firetruck the line an finally awso our
sad guy who had the accident an were sittin at our blekboint an smokin an
are actually quite content there hes drivin off steps on the gas drives slowly
an carefully an drives in the direction of salzburg where he came from but
before we kin look after em hes back in his elemint an races back like he
came racin an flat out up the hill the way he came down before sos that its
smokin

the farmer shakes his an i shakes me head an were thinkin the farmer duz
it by pointin with his pipe that mebbe it duzznt matter where yer racin to just
sos yer racin surely thats the way it is an i wipe my nose an accidently i
pocketed one those things a web a panties an the farmers lookin at me sorta
sad like an hes thinkin the old scoundrel hes thinkin bout my mother an

were lookin in the direction of salzburg an that guys drivin back like i sez an
the only difference is that now hes gotta white turban on his head an a
hunnert bills in his diffrint pockets

cause so much time has passed awmost two hours the farmers pointin with
his pipe to go back to work and we still got all kindsa things to do an dont
matter how satisfied ya are farmin drives ya on its really nice havin sech a
reliable blekboint on which ya only gotta sit an awreddy all kindsa cars er
flyin through the air so clime up farmer les drive an in the theaiter in linz
ya wont see sech an exact direction an sech a straight-out life like stagin but
nevertheless we gotta go back to work sos we clime in an i slam the gear

theres another crash awreddy an we look back from the tractor thats drivin
away cause farmins no happy profession where ya while away time by lookin
rather anyway therere two that slammed into each other like two goats a
buttin an the air is fulla thunder all the way to ems an one cars burnin an
that musta caused at least two deaths with broken skulls an awreddy theres
a fender flyin by us an buryin itself into the earth like a bomb tin in the otherwise healthy air an screams glass black smoke an sure nuf agin another
accidents happened while were drivin back

yep an we gotta go to work thats the way it is ya caint just have fun an the
farmer pokes my shoulder an there it goes again the autos stack up the
screamin the wreckers the sirens but we stick to our guns the wetbacks re
waitin wanna be supervised the sugarbeets re waitin the sugar factorys waitin
susies waitin an ya shuddnt shamelessly take advantage of sech a reliable
blekboint right away two performinces in one day thats too much but on
sunday i sez lets have a farm picnic here with the wetbacks an the girls from
holawibuly

in a rundown neighborhood

FRIEDERIKE MAYRÖCKER

translated by Michael P. Elzay

A STORM OF IMAGES, HE SAID, LIKE A WIND, HE SAID, THEY COME.

and it's all so limited by time, he said, and i would have thought, he said, one day i could have won him to our side, he said.

back then, he said, when we all drove together to the fish restaurant and i helped her out, she had answered while she placed her right foot down and immediately thereafter her left and at the same time ducked her head so she wouldn't bump it, had answered, why not, why not, who knows, maybe one of these days you can win him for your people, he said, but then it became clear that the time was all too limited, he said.

coming from a rough world, he said, from a rough world, returning from a rough world into a smooth world, he said, it's all limited.

her letter, he said, was written in an old fashioned way, adorned with flourishes but the tone was sincere and the space between the lines like the breath of a person much moved and then, he said, we drove to new orleans, he said, all of us together, he said, and i believe he loved the old city where once the french ruled and later in a rundown neighborhood, he said, the jazz negroes.

i look forward very much to your being here, he said, it will be spring.

i have a rose, he said, on my windowsill, i have a rose today.

i also do not have much more time, he said.

on my windowsill i have a rose today, he said, picked for me by my wife this morning, he said, roses bloom here like that even in december, he said. i hope, he said, you will be able to meet your translator, he said, a young banker.

i know exactly, he said, what he will then say, he said, don't draw those damn symbols all over, he will say, reality is really damned attractive, he will say, reality, he said.

as we were leaving the hotel in cologne, he said, there stood beuys, somewhat elevated, in the gateway, he said, with outspread arms, thin whitish eagle-nosed face, surrounded by young people, spoke, was asked, answered, and the rain poured, and because of the strong gusty wind some had lowered their umbrellas, he said, because of the wind.

and as beuys moved his arms up and down, he said, i thought all he lacks
is a monk's cowl, he said, in a rundown neighborhood, he said.

it really rained, he said, and she called us at night though she lived directly
below us, and could just as easily have come up those few steps to knock at
our door, and when she suddenly called us up, he said, we shouldn't make
such a racket, he said, because they couldn't go to sleep downstairs, he said,
we have to put up with that, he said, and it is also only this short moment,
he said, snuffing out, he said, or maybe to be snuffed out, he said, this diony-
sian stupor, he said, this dirty mutation, he said, that awaits us all.

when the green sides of the leaves, he said, are interspersed with white
dots, spots, and stripes, he said, it will be a beautiful season, and i am very
happy about your being here, it will be spring, a beautiful season.

the alpine republic, he said, where once the french ruled and later, in a
rundown neighborhood, the jazz negroes.

that with just half a gesture, he said, in order to evoke calmness in the
other guy, he said, the freezing over of friendly waters, he said, on the telephone, he said, she had told me that she was as fond of me as before, but that
she does not believe she could stand my presence at this time, let a couple
of weeks pass, we might let weeks pass, he said, we have to resign ourselves,
he said, to this and that, so that it will all be limited, he said.

the effort, he said, that we spend to maintain our existence, he said, how
in vain, he said, she wore a pink bathing cap, he said, stood in the annex of
a shoe accessory store and asked to go along.

yes, he said, better to receive injustice than to do it, and in the end one is
marked by what one has done, he said, human vipers, wolf people, he said,
sirenes.

she wore a pink bathing cap, he said, a misunderstanding on his part, he
said, that's the way it's got to be.

and basically, he said, one could divide people into two groups, into
groups of those who are important and those who aren't important, he said,
and beuys stood again with raised arms while it stormed, and prophesied
something, it poured and blew through the gateway and the people had
lowered their umbrellas because of the storm, despite the rain, he said.

out of the hand of a pastry baker, he said, who actually drives a caterpillar
tractor, he said, the tin shears, he said, places, he said, the placelessness, he
said, and still always better, he said, to receive injustice than to do it, he
said. tin shears, he said, places, he said, the placelessness, grasping, he said,
one winter morning almost without twilight, he said.

what torments us, he said, what strikes us, he said, what touches us, on my windowsill today, he said, even in december the roses bloom here, he said, on my windowsill, in a rundown neighborhood, on my windowsill i have a rose today, that my wife picked for me this morning, he said, even in december the roses bloom, he said, in a rundown neighborhood, he said, i don't have much more time either, he said.

SOJOURNS IN BORMIO

ANGELIKA MECHTEL
translated by Gary A. Smith

FOR THREE WEEKS, ONLY HEAT.

Scorched landscapes on the ocean. And then the downpours in the Ligurian Mountains. The earth was black with moisture.

Dripping olive slopes.

We could have drowned in the torrents of rain. Our windshield wipers no longer carried the water away.

Later, the sultry Po plain.

We drove by way of Milan and shortly after Bergamo turned off toward Lago d'Iseo. There we stopped for gasoline again. I stopped the car at the gasoline pump. While the attendant filled the tank with premium, I went across the street. An ice cream sign was hanging there on the wall. I took pistachio with vanilla.

It was midday, but no longer so hot. Since we had been in the mountains, the heat had let up.

Then I get in and start the car.

In the late afternoon, I say: How beautiful the Adda Valley is!

We drive from Tirano to Bormio. I sit at the wheel and he beside me. He holds the map on his knees.

We know the route from before.

What has changed? I ask.

What can change in twelve years?

He tells about new hotels.

At times, I know that he is looking at me.

We do not speak about ourselves. He talks with me. And when I want to smoke a cigarette, he lights it for me.

At that time, he was twenty-three. He has put on weight. Because I like it that way, he wears sideburns and glasses with gold rims. He looks good. Even better, when he is brown. And he will get black as a Negro, if they only lay him in the sun long enough.

I am fond of him.

When we reach Bormio, he puts a new cigarette in my mouth. For a moment, I take my right hand from the wheel and grasp his hand, which is warm and soft and very broad.

We take the same room as before, the one with the bidet. It is not bad. We know the old hotel in Bormio. Twelve years ago it was no better.

Even the building has hardly changed. Still old and magnificent. Under the wild vine on the wall the stucco is peeling off. The hotel does not look as if it could change.

It was the same then as today.

For three weeks there has been no more rain, only clouds at times, which rose up darkly behind the coastal hills and blew over the beach out to sea. Heat and the smell of suntan oil.

Later the return trip and then this hotel, the smell of the kitchen, the sounds of dishes and pots.

The window with the view into the interior court stood open, the other, which looked onto the street, was closed. After a day's drive, we were in the heart of the mountains. The coast lay behind us.

The room is not bad.

Only the flushing mechanism of the bidet is leaky. Again and again a stream of water rushes through.

When I squat on the bed, opposite the bidet, I see the water coming.

The light is miserable. The bedframe looks as if it were made of wood. Inadvertently I bump it with my elbow and hear the metal.

Linoleum on the floor and a scrap of carpet.

Tomorrow we will drive on, because the vacation is over. We have spent it together.

I turn to him.

He has stretched out on the bed, his arms under his neck and his legs crossed.

Are you hungry? he asks.

I just might be, I answer.

Downstairs on the ground floor they are frying meat. I can smell it. The smell penetrates upward through the light shaft.

The signora in the black dress, who showed us the room, asked us whether we wanted to eat something.

No thank you, I said, we have already.

We hadn't. But first we wanted to see the room price.

We can pay that, I now say.

He nods.

And there will still be something for the rest of the trip home. After all, we can't be on the road without anything.

He has brought up the transistor radio from the car and is searching for a German station.

Time for the news, he says, and looks at his watch.

In the bidet the water rushes through again, and I feel that it is too great an effort to reach my hand out toward him, to touch his hair or his skin.

I am so tired.

Close the window, he says.

Are you hungry? I ask, because I am conscious of my stomach.

He is still searching for the radio station. He is stubborn.

I get up from the bed, go past the bidet to the window. Before closing both casements, I lean out. We are lodged on the second floor. The interior court is not narrow. Below on the ground floor I can discern the kitchen, two large, bright windows. A woman moves about behind the windowpanes.

I need fresh air, I say. Then I turn the latch to the left and the window is locked.

Finally he has found the station.

He lies on the bed and listens, smokes his fifth cigarette without offering me one.

I ask him for one, but he does not hear, because he is listening to the news.

Please give me one too, I say.

He grabs the pack and pushes it over to my side of the bed. And he does not even turn his head.

Naturally he is furious because the car is broken down.

The clutch could have gone out somewhere else, I say. He does not answer.

He is too tall for Italian hotel beds. His head hits at the top and his feet at the bottom.

Surely we can spare two thousand five hundred lire for a night, I say.

I talk incessantly.

The transistor radio plays music.

I smoke the cigarette that I have taken from the pack.

Do you know which way we must drive if the car is fixed tomorrow? I ask.

He nods.

Don't you even want to check the map?

He crushes his cigarette in the ashtray on the nighttable and gets up from the bed. Then he starts to undress.

Back along the Adda Valley to Tirano, he says, and then over the Bernina Pass.

He does not look at me.

Why don't you want to talk to me? I ask.

Lay off, he says.

Can I help it, that the clutch is out?

He has opened his suitcase and is looking for his pajamas. He is gorgeously brown. His legs are long and slim like a woman's, his ankles very narrow.

He pulls his pyjamas on and takes off his watch. He always does it that way. On his hairy wrist I see now the white strip of skin.

I am fond of him.

But he does not even brush his teeth before he crawls under the covers.

He simply turns over, and I see his back.

The room price, I say, is not too high for one night.

Leave the window closed, he says.

I do not take hold of him.

With the window closed I cannot sleep. I need fresh air.

Turn off the radio, I say.

He leaves it on.

I could caress him. He would let me caress him a long time without turning over toward me.

Stelvio Pass, he says: That was your idea!

It is not so easy to divert him from his rage.

If you hadn't been wrong by a thousand meters, we would be almost home by now.

I defend myself: That can happen to anyone. The numbers on the map are printed too small.

And there also was no sign there.

Or did you see a sign? Did you discover something? They must have indicated somewhere that the pass is still blocked, that there's still snow up there.

Don't you think?

He does not move, has turned his back to me, and is quiet.

Are you asleep? I ask.

He says nothing more.

I get up, turn out the light, go to the window, this time the other one, and open it.

He says nothing.

I undress in the dark. Again a stream of water comes through the bidet.

What does one use these things for? I ask him. I have never done anything like that.

He does not move, even when I slip naked under the covers.

I do not understand anything about cars. I cannot even drive, since that is his concern. I have never even been interested in it.

Naturally, I can imagine that a man who controls 66 HP is strong.

He is a good driver. I have never doubted that.

I say: Sleep well.

He answers: You too.

But I cannot keep my eyes closed. Every time water flows through the bidet, I press the back of my head deep into the pillow.

And I think of the Stelvio Pass, an annoying business. As soon as we are home I will go to the eye doctor, because it distresses me. I really had trouble reading the given altitude of the Pass.

When we arrived at the Pass, it was blocked, and we had to go back to Bormio. The sun was setting already, and he wanted to be back in the valley before the fall of darkness.

Just beyond Bergamo we had turned from the Po plain into the mountains. In Iseo he stopped for gasoline again, and I ate some ice cream, green pistachio with yellow vanilla.

Every time, he says that I will get diarrhea from it.

We wanted to travel a new route. I had the map on my knees. As soon as we were in the mountains, the heat let up.

In the late afternoon I said: How beautiful the Adda Valley is.

We drove from Tirano to Bormio. Beyond Bormio he pushed the car up to the pass.

I sat next to him. At times I looked at him. The narrow face on the broad neck. He wears dark horn-rimmed glasses, which give a heavy and crude effect.

He looks good.

He is completely brown. The sun has dried out his skin.

I notice that he is afraid of the steep bends in the road. That makes me affectionate. I would like to take him in my arms like a small boy. But I don't say that.

The road is narrow, hardly any plants in the mass of rock.

As we again travel through one of the galleries, I can hardly make out his face in the shadow of the overhang, as if he had become remote.

I lay a hand on his leg and notice that the skin of his thigh is quite damp with perspiration.

He does not turn his head.

How far still? he asks, how high do we have to drive?

I look for the pass on the map with my index finger and we reach the first snowfields.

A thousand seven hundred, I say.

He holds the steering wheel so tightly with both hands that the knuckles appear white under the skin.

You're afraid, I say.

He asserts, You must have made a mistake. At the same time he motions with his head to the snowfields outside. The snowline is higher, he says.

I read out to him the number that I can recognize. To me this pass is no higher than seventeen hundred.

The air up here is cold and thin. I think of the beach. No rain for three weeks now. Scorched landscape.

When we arrived at the top, we had to turn around. An avalanche had blocked the pass. Only the pass hotel is in operation. Up here they still ski in June.

It is not passable until July, someone from the pass hotel says.

The altitude is given on a sign: Two thousand seven hundred.

At this altitude the snow stays for a long time. We were driving on summer tires.

It happened while driving back down. For the last thousand meters he kept the car under control only with the brake. Scrupulously he took hairpin curve after hairpin curve, and spoke not a word.

Just at the end of the gorge is the auto repair shop, the hotel across the street.

The young mechanic shows no surprise and is friendly.

They have to order replacement parts from the next city.

We ask about a hotel, since he says: Not before tomorrow afternoon.

He recommends to us the hotel across the street. The cases he carries over himself.

In high season a lot of work falls to him there. Cars and guests. We are actually too early. The Stelvio Pass will be opened only when there are no more sudden changes in the weather.

I have seen no guests in the hotel. Only the women. The younger one talked with the mechanic who put down our bags in the vestibule. She giggled when we went up the stairs with the old lady.

I mentioned it to him.

But he said it didn't mean anything.

Even at breakfast we are alone. Only two place settings on the terrace. The other chairs are leaning against the tables.

We are the only ones, I say.

It is nine a.m. We are breakfasting in the shadow of chestnut trees. It is cool.

He drinks his coffee with plenty of milk and sugar. I eat white bread incessantly. They have placed a basketful before us.

On the other end of the terrace the girl from yesterday evening leans over the balustrade and yells something across the street.

We do not speak their language.

I see the mechanic standing in front of the workshop. He is cheerful, answers and waves to the girl. They seem to understand each other well.

That's funny, I say.

He pays no attention to the two of them. He drinks his coffee and looks toward the building.

The hotel is very old and very magnificent. Under the wild vine on the wall the stucco is peeling off.

I have brought the highway map along to the breakfast table for him. He does not want to open it up. He is still furious. He can be furious for a long time. He thinks that's right, that's proper, because he is a man.

What's funny? he asks.

Only the street lies between the two of them, I answer.

Before we sat down at the table, he told the girl that we were leaving today. She nodded and smiled.

I do not like her smile. But he finds nothing wrong with it.

We could go sightseeing in the town, I suggest.

The car is supposed to be ready in the afternoon.

In the afternoon the young mechanic tells us that the bus that makes the short trip from Tirano to Bormio once a day has not brought along the replacement parts.

We return to the room.

He has the transistor radio along, and he searches for the station.

I'm hungry, I say.

In the kitchen they are frying meat in olive oil.

For whom are they cooking? I ask. There are no guests besides us.

He lies on the bed, smokes, and stares at the ceiling.

I undress. And then I stand next to the bidet and ask: How does one work this?

He does not even turn his head.

That's your problem, he answers and expels the cigarette smoke from his lungs.

All night long I can't sleep, I say, because of the water rushing.

When I lie down next to him, he gets up. I watch as he unbuckles his belt and opens his fly.

I make up my mind to take hold of him. That always helps. It must be a great effort for him to reach out his hand, to touch my hair or my skin.

For three weeks I have lain in the sun with him. Sometimes the ocean smelled of oil. We lay together in the midst of the sun.

All affection has dried up.

I talked because it would have been so lonely otherwise. And we did nothing to counteract it.

Now he closes the window before he comes to bed.

He acts very virile. He has learned to do that.

The next morning we again eat breakfast on the terrace.

Once more we wait for the bus from Tirano. But again the bus does not bring the replacement parts, and the girl smiles when he approaches her to reserve the room for the third time.

She nods and yells something across the street. The mechanic is relaxed and cheerful.

The two understand each other. We are outsiders.

Do you understand what they are saying? he asks me.

As if he didn't know how foreign their language is to me.

We no longer are sure of ourselves.

In the evening we go up to the room again, and we are afraid.

He carries the transistor radio. When we close the door behind us, a stream of water rushes through the bidet.

He says: We are powerless against them.

Tomorrow he will lodge a complaint at the carabinieri station.

Then we lie beside one another on the bed, with our arms crossed behind our necks and our elbows touching.

Only the contact of skin still gives us warmth. He turns his head toward me. And because we are looking at one another we feel secure.

Together we wait for the news on the transistor radio.

Later we make an attempt at affectionateness.

The bidet still makes a rushing sound. The signora has gotten older. The young girl has married the mechanic.

I lie on the bed, arms behind my neck, legs crossed, and think about the smell of suntan oil.

Downstairs in the kitchen they are frying meat. We have already eaten.

We have brought the transistor radio along to the room, and I search for the station.

While I turn the knob, I watch him get undresed. He has the beginnings of a paunch. But his legs are still long and slim.

To me he is beautiful.

How long are we staying? he asks.

I do not hear, because I am listening to the news. When they give the weather report, I ask: What did you say?

He brushes his teeth before he gets under the covers.

He is naked. I love his soft skin.

Three nights, I answer.

This time we have opened both windows wide. He has gotten used to fresh air.

The Stelvio Pass is open, I say.

Did you see the sign?

Aperto, I say, because I have learned their language.

This time I'll drive. I'll control 66 HP.

I'll be afraid, I say.

This mountain driving demands expertise. I look at him.

You are beautiful, I say.

For three weeks we have lain together in the sun.

I reach my hand out toward him and he moves nearer to me. We have learned how to deal with affectionateness.

No matter that I am driving the car up to an altitude of two thousand seven hundred meters.

He will sit beside me. My face will be lost in the shadow of the galleries, and he'll find it again.

I have practiced driving hairpin curves.

I am in complete control of the car.

Is that so important? I ask him.

On the transistor radio, music is playing.

I am happy that he is lying next to me.

The light in the room is miserable. The bedframe looks as if it were made of wood.

Only the price of the room has changed.

Are you hungry? he asks. I shake my head.

He takes off his watch and I see the white strip of skin on his wrist.

If they lay you in the sun long enough, I say, you will get black as a Negro.

He doesn't know whether he should smile at that.

Then I get up. After I have undressed, I use the bidet.

STRUGGLE

LUTZ RATHENOW
translated by George Peters

He was trying to drown the moth. The moth was trying to get away from him.

The whole time he was sitting on the pot, he was trying to drown the moth.

He was sitting next to the washbowl, without getting up—without being able to get up, because he was sitting on the pot.

With his left hand he turned on the water faucet, held his hand under the steadily growing stream, held his opened hand under it to increase the radius of the area sprayed by the running water.

The moth was to be sprinkled, was to be hit, was to drown. That same moth that had accidentally strayed onto the smooth white bottom of the washbowl, was scrambling upwards on the bright, slippery surface. Toward the rim.

He wanted to finish the moth off and was trying to squirt the moth. It was to be rendered incapable of flying. It was to be crushed. To be squashed, stomped—that's what ought to happen to these moths. They were everywhere, crouching in the cupboard, sitting in the kitchen, in the lamp. In the bread. When he started to brush his teeth in the morning and opened his mouth, a moth flew out.

He had to destroy them once and for all.

He wanted to drown the moth that had climbed into the washbowl to frighten him. He had to keep going, destroy the moth—keep going, this one stood for them all, even if it didn't work right away.

He tried to get closer to the washbowl without having to get up—he tried to edge closer to the bowl because in that way he could aim better.

He had to aim better because he hadn't hit the moth; he had to aim better because he wasn't hitting the moth. It evaded him, it trembled, clambered, crawled, evaded him, trembled—it made it to the top. Was gone.

He couldn't see the moth anymore, raised up, wiped himself, and pulled the chain.

He couldn't see it anymore.

As he inspected below and next to and behind and everywhere else around the bowl's rim, it became clear to him that the moth wasn't there anymore.

He could have flooded the bathroom, but the moth would fly up to the ceiling and the water wouldn't come up to the ceiling because the doors weren't watertight. If the doors were watertight, he would flood this room.

He wanted to drown the moth and had not drowned it.

Were the doors watertight, that would have been the way out. As it was, they were coming, ought really to come any minute, right away or almost right away they would come, the one will incite the others, stir them up; and then they will all come together, will fly at him, jump on him, eat up his things, eat up the furniture, eat up everything he has—the apartment, which has been in their hands for a long time now already, and with the mothflakes from the cupboard, long since useless, to which they have long since been addicted, with that they will come, shower him with the stuff, they'll impregnate him, turn him into a moth if he doesn't capitulate, assuming he hasn't already been one for a long time.

He had wanted to drown the moth. He could have drowned the moth.

He could burn down the house, or the block, or the whole city, as long as the house went. If the windows were sealed beforehand, there would be no chance for the moth to get out. If everything is properly doused with gasoline, the moth wouldn't be able to escape. Only he'd have to stay inside, so that nothing gets out the door, stay inside, so that nobody can come into the house to put out the fire. If he were to stay in the house, nobody would be able to break in a window or the door, he'd make sure of that. The house would burn right down to the ground, the moth wouldn't escape. But he didn't know where the matches were. Didn't know if he had any matches, had any gasoline. If he were to go and get matches, the moth could escape through the door when he opened the door to leave the house. He couldn't go get matches if he wanted to kill the moth.

He listened for sounds, listened carefully all around him and heard nothing except for the silence of the moth.

Because of the stench he pulled the chain a second time and waited until enough water had flowed back into the tank to pull the chain a third time.

He pulled the chain the third time and would pull it again if necessary.

Perhaps moths will soon become extinct, he hoped, perhaps they will quickly and totally die out.

He began to tremble. He began to sweat. He was beginning to catch a cold.

Surely it was waiting in ambush, lurking with the others, they were all waiting, that one with the others, waiting for him to keel over, cave in. The others, which he didn't see, which he felt, which were upon him, clinging to his back, covering his eyes.

He felt deaf.

He had wanted to kill it.

He was waiting until enough water had flowed into the tank and he could flush again. He still wanted to finish off the moth, this or another one, he still wanted to catch at least one, any one at all.

With great show he climbed into the bowl on which he had only recently been sitting and drew attention to himself. He waved his arms, sang a children's song, and hoped that the moth that was tormenting him would follow him.

He wanted to drown one, at least one.

And he was in the bowl and pulled the chain and he flushed himself away. He had taken off his shoes beforehand so as not to get stuck.

The moth that was trying to attack him. That had attacked him.

And he undressed completely in the bowl so he wouldn't get stuck on account of the buttons, so that nothing would jam, so that his things wouldn't clog up the pipe.

Undressed completely and pulled the chain again.

Nothing happened. Nothing happened.

He climbed out of the bowl. He lay down and cried.

THE SEX ATTRACTANT

W. E. RICHARTZ
translated by Johannes Vazulik

THE FOLLOWING IS AN ACCOUNT OF A TRIP WHICH THE AUTHOR AND A colleague made to the U.S.A. in the summer of this year. There we wanted to familiarize ourselves with the status of *pheromone* research. As is generally known, *pheromones* are the sex attractants of insects, i.e., specific chemical compounds of great volatility which are secreted by female insects and are perceived by the male of the same species over long distances. It is in this way that the sexes are brought together for the purpose of mating.

To date scientists have identified the sex attractants of more than twenty insect species; among them are those of the silkworm, the apollo butterfly, and the tropical butterfly, *Papilio paradisea*, as well as the pheromones of certain pests such as the cherry fruit fly, *Rhagoletis cerasi*, and the cutworm moth, *Polia pisi*.

Pheromones are materialized messages and, as such, are of great theoretical value. But they can also be of practical use, for example, in the elimination of pests. Once we possess the substance which is discharged by the animal, rather than lure the males to the females, we can lure them to another place where they can be destroyed. Reproduction is thus prevented, and the pest becomes extinct.

The United States has taken the lead in this scientific field.

It was our first visit to this country. To the European entomologist the New World at first appears a paradise: With joy he beholds its wealth of species and its large populations. The local people perceive it differently: For them this abundance is rather annoying and not infrequently threatening. This is particularly true in the Southern states, where the climate favors insect over man. The inhabitants have to be unrelenting in resisting the onrushing insect world. There is humming and buzzing among houses and trees; large flies or chitinous moths drone through the air—you have to be on the alert for them just as you would for falling rocks. Not a day, not a place without serious trouble, without crises or combat. Swarms of walnut-sized darkling ground beetles, *B. nigriferrus*, appear on the outskirts of the cities: Fogging machines move into position and stop the advance with caustic vapors. Ichneumon flies and ticks bore into the skin of human beings and other mammals: They have to be removed one by one and often leave painful inflammations. Dragonflies cover the land like thunderclouds. Airplanes drop incendiary bombs where they rest for the night along the Mississippi. You can see a yellow glow on the horizon. In the distance you can hear the crackling and rattling of the many dragonfly bodies bursting in the heat. Insofar as insects are concerned, the United States can be brutal.

As usual, we traveled long distances by air. On these occasions majestic views from great heights offer themselves to the entomologist. Here his science becomes all encompassing; it concerns everything that stirs.

Landing, on the other hand, had a sobering effect and was often very distressing. In Natchez, Louisiana, we were greeted by an insect phalanx, behind which the local entomologists could scarcely attract our attention. What splendor and variety as we were leaving the plane! The European specialist had to reorient himself here; to be sure, he was used to dealing with laboratory specimens, with specimens of moderate size. But here colonies of *Dynastides*—each one a half-foot long—fought their way up the boarding ramp! Then down below instead of stepping on the ordinary concrete walk, we stepped on a pavement of beetles that could be identified as the genus *Calosoma*—animals with garish salamander-like dorsal markings—not unlike the pattern on the ties of our hosts, who finally caught our eyes by furiously waving their arms.

We had to walk only a short distance from the foot of the boarding ramp to the cars. Every step required self-control. Not even the obvious abundance could dull our senses. The constant crunching, crackling, and splintering of countless chitin shells strained our nerves almost to the breaking point.

By contrast, the next stop on our trip, the Wood Products Laboratory in Gulfport, Mississippi, was like an oasis of peace. As are many important scientific research institutes in this country, it is a private foundation and is located on the property of its founder, on a one-time cotton plantation. The laboratories and part of the insectary had been set up in what was formerly the mansion, a temple-like structure with columns. One could see additional insect cages, like those in an apiary, scattered around the grounds.

Here we learned firsthand of many new, somewhat surprising research findings. Dr. Jack Smithson, a talented young colleague, demonstrated for us, among other things, the behavior of one termite species, *Reticulotermes flavipes* (*Koller*) vis à vis the ink of a certain ball-point pen. The ink trail of this pen—the pen in question being a cheap department store product with the trade name of TELLTALE—had a strong effect on these animals. If they were released at a distance of a few meters from such a line, they at first acted restless, running back and forth as if searching for something, and all the while moving their mandibles and drumming on each other with their feelers. At the same time, they came—unintentionally it seemed—closer and closer to the line. At a distance of about fifty centimeters they appeared to perceive it and ran straight to it. They stopped briefly in front of the line with signs of intense excitement. Then they began to move on top of it, rapidly, with lowered heads, straddling it between their limbs. They reacted to a broadening of the line by extending their legs.

The ink had the effect of a pheromone. Did it only affect one of the two sexes? Was it coincidence or a chemical deception? The novelty of these questions hadn't worn off in Gulfport either. They were discussed at length with the American experts and were tested in a great variety of experiments—even apart from the daily work at the research institute. In this way—occupied with this phenomenon—we spent many an evening behind the window and door screens of our colleagues' large, airy homes on the plantation grounds, with air-conditioners humming softly and with unobtrusive black attendance.

Screens are indispensable in the South. If a screen is missing from a door or window somewhere, or if it has a hole in it, one immediately gets a feeling of defenselessness, even before he is conscious of the reason for it. Not until the opening is closed do you again feel at ease. After a while you are barely aware of what is outside—incessant buzzing and crackling, many legs plucking and groping, furry limbs sticking through, dim reflections of compound eyes behind the mesh.

For the termites, of course, this was no obstacle. The test animals didn't even have to be brought to the laboratory. They seemed literally to be waiting for us. As soon as one of the aforementioned pens was activated, they appeared on the scene. The experiments were usually conducted on a large table in the middle of the parlor—or, if many spectators were present, on a specially designed, slanted, table-sized drawing board. The surface was well lit. In time, a large number of variations on the termite experiment had been devised, of which a few were especially popular and therefore often replicated. For example, the "Obstacle Derby"—using a broken line, or the frustration game with several figure eights. Aesthetically pleasing in particular was the behavior of the animals on certain filigree ball-point pen patterns, somewhat resembling Marc Tobey abstractions. There was spontaneous applause.

At such times socializing and professional activity combined—life and science became one. At this point we wish to gratefully acknowledge the generous hospitality of our friends. Our lodgings and meals were in a

Southern aristocratic style. We were taken to the most elegant eating establishments in the area and were served, for example, prime-quality steaks that had been delivered from nearby Texas cattle ranches. In addition to the customary charbroiled steaks we were offered sweet potatoes, cotton-white bread, spicy Mexican beans, and sweet gelatin on leafy green lettuce. To be sure, there were some rather curious-looking combinations, but one got used to them quickly.

Our generous hosts gave us a congenial and warm-hearted farewell. When we departed after a ten-day stay we were presented with, in addition to gifts related to our specialty, one of the aforementioned ball-point pens.

The remainder of our trip was dominated by this small instrument. Even though it wasn't our intention, its effect could be demonstrated at any time. Termites, of course, are everywhere—on trains, on planes, on the roofs of skyscrapers, on busy streets. As soon as you set down the tip of the pen, the animals began to appear on the spot. When you moved the tip on a surface, they lined up and followed one another at short intervals.

Our limited knowledge of the language was often compensated for by such demonstrations: Those who traveled with us were always well entertained—there was no need for words then. They laughed good-naturedly at the apparent difficulty the animals had in deciding what to do when the lines branched out or discontinued. They eagerly observed the nervousness or helplessness with which the animals raised up at the end of the line as if they were on the lookout, then started on their way back, collided with those coming toward them, exchanged messages with them, and in this way were perhaps again persuaded to turn back, and so forth.

From New York we started our homeward journey aboard the steamship "Berlin." After eight eventful weeks we arrived at the ship in an animated state of mind—even though we were in need of some rest. We had come away with some rich scientific prizes. In our baggage were movies and photographs, reports and reprints, and, in addition, a small collection of rare American beetles in transparent containers with miniature versions of their natural habitats, which had been given to us with high prices affixed to them to assure their careful handling.

Immediately after boarding, the author retired to his cabin in order to write a preliminary report on the most significant findings of his trip while they were still fresh in his mind. The "Berlin" cast off at midnight. At approximately 4 a.m.—the ship was well at sea more than fifty miles off the coast—we were awakened by the steward and asked to step outside. Without saying a word he pointed to a line of termites, which, for as far as the eye could see, was moving toward us through the corridor and disappearing into an air vent next to our cabin door. This vent opened into a closet drawer in which I had kept my writing case. By this time hundreds of animals had clustered around the pen and around my notebook and, if they hadn't already suffocated each other, were at once destroyed with an insecticide. But the stream of those following remained undiminished.

This discovery surprised us more than anything else up to that time. Even the specialist who knows the power of instinct would find it hard to believe that the American pen containing this attractant produced its effect on the reticulo termites in such a hostile environment as the ocean. But that's how it was, indisputable, a fact, hard and fast. The writing of this report—which, in consideration of life aboard ship, was moved in the meantime to the open rear deck directly above the ship's propellers—was followed by the animals without interruption. Even during the pauses. Even when I didn't write.

Brief reflection on the matter suggests that the ink trail—produced by the motion of the ship and the motion made while writing—can be conceived as a slightly wavy bridge extending from the port of embarkation to the ship. This bridge was used by the animals. A problem arises from this, namely, the question of the real reality (please forgive the pleonasm) of a transatlantic ball-point pen line—which also exists, although in reduced form, in the entries of my notebook (standard, lined, black binding)—an abysmal dilemma. It has something to do with relativity, with the incompatibility of the stationary and the moving observer . . . it is provoking . . . fascinating . . . engrossing. But we are dealing here with a mathematically, perhaps philosophically insoluble problem—as entomologists we can leave it at that.

Let's keep to the facts. Straightforward conclusions, common sense are the pillars of science. The behavior of the termites proved that the attractant pen had in fact been in motion during every part of our voyage. How could it have been otherwise? Even when I wasn't writing, and during the night, the tip of the pen was moving on a fixed surface. If it wasn't the paper, then it was the geographic location. The effect lasted as long as we traveled. But where and when was this trip to end, since the earth moves also?

The destination of our trip is in sight; were are halfway across the English Channel—and now (I have it admit it) my usual scientific objectivity forsakes me. My colleague, apparently not suspecting anything, is still asleep in his bunk, an open professional book at his side. But I have been awake since daybreak and have taken my place on the rear deck, where I write. On the one hand filled with dire misgivings, on the other titillated by a barely controllable fit of laughter, I observe the fidgeting of the animals in a single file on their invisible line; clinging to each other's legs, balancing and groping with their feelers, they are hanging one by one from my table to the rear deck railing, a glittering chain along which some animals, perhaps assigned to repair weak spots, are crawling, and extending into the air from the rear deck, a thin, knotted string arcing gently, as far as you can see, toward the surface of the water but not touching it; and I see the termites that are closest to me pattering around, piled up, several next to each other, waiting attentively to see whether I will continue to write and when I will finally reach the mainland while writing—or else while not writing—the difference is irrelevant now anyway—and I know only one solution, which, it is true, presents a sacrifice, almost a disgrace for a scientist, as if he believed in magic and in the demonic—but fear wells up; I no longer have any choice: *I throw the thing into the wind.*

GRAUFF

GEROLD SPÄTH
translated by James Feuge

MEANWHILE THE MORNING WAS ALREADY GETTING ON TOWARD SIX-THIRTY, the waking day was beginning for the others as well, it was early summer but weather as in bleak autumn, rain-gray for weeks, and the lake empty and leaden-looking; not a good water color. In his hip-high, wet-black rubber boots Hotz had been standing in the shoreline gravel since four o'clock, he still yawned occasionally and shivered, held the rod with damp fingers, cast out, reeled in; not a single catch had he made, torn the lure off twice and the second time at least fifteen meters of line.

He found the woman and sounded the alarm. Hotz always fished along the shoreline at the dredged-out holes. No reason not to on that morning, no one had thought of such a thing, only later did they all claim to have had their suspicions, and they recalled again, suddenly—GRAUFF? Strange name.

Two-and-a-half or three years ago he had moved here, about a half-dozen fellow workers knew him fairly well. Keller, for example, a mountain climber like himself. Since he had become acquainted with Keller, he had never again gone into the mountains alone, until that one time. A nut for the mountains, sure, such people exist. Hotz and more than a few others are nuts about fishing, then again others get excited about cars or flowers or stamps, rabbits, pigeons, and so on. He went into the mountains. But on that second weekend in September, Keller had not been able to make it, some kind of family occasion had to be celebrated, and Grauff, they say, had wanted to talk it over with his wife on Friday evening, casually, just to mention it, so to speak, but she observed immediately that he knew very well how she felt about that. He went alone anyway, on Saturday morning with his backpack full of rope and crampons, the stainless steel ice-axe with leather thongs attached on top. Take care, she might have said. And he: Sure. You don't really mind? Thereupon she could perhaps have replied: I don't have to tell you.

A wife and two children, at that time still six months and two years old; but he was said to know a lot about mountain climbing and was always careful, hardly ever one step off the safe trails, and when on that Sunday after six o'clock in the evening she pushed the baby buggy homeward alone and a bit later, after the little ones had been tended and were asleep, she rushed back to the train station and then around eight o'clock telephoned, already nervous and tearful, Keller was supposedly not yet at all uneasy, quite possibly because of the just-ended family celebration—since one's mood won't switch over to gloom instantly. Besides, Keller knew better than anyone that Grauff really did always know what he was doing and what he enjoyed at any given moment. But then Monday forenoon suddenly: excitement, and his wife supposedly could not stop weeping, and Keller brought a bundle of maps with trails penciled in in red, and in the afternoon the first rescue party is said to have been sent into the Glärnisch area, more or less at random, they knew nothing, were just guessing.

No! the woman sobbed, No! again and again, as often as she was asked, No! he did not know himself exactly, on Friday evening the whole question had been whether he should set out in the first place, without him, and then he only said he wanted to take the first train to Glarnerland; and sobbed again, for they had not argued, they had never argued; whereupon Keller tried to calm her. "And you? Do you believe Friday passed without a fracas at the Grauffs' . . . I mean, your mentioning the possibility of an argument shows that . . ."

But no, no one knew anything definite. The people north of the massif, such as the innkeeper in Klöntal, and his wife, had had a lot to do and had not paid attention to each individual. Certainly, they knew him from earlier hikes into the mountains, even if they didn't know the name right away, but they recognized him again: Grauff was the name of the man in the wedding picture. Yes, in the autumn of last year or the year before he had indeed spent the night with them and in the darkness of the early morning had gone up along the ridgetop trail to the Eggstöcken; in the fall two years before they found the entry in the register, and Keller suddenly remembered, too, and there were their names, of course; Erich Grauff and Robert Keller, from the tenth to the eleventh of September a few hours of sleep in the dormitory, then on up to the Eggstöcken, 2,500 meters above sea level; Keller supposedly even remembered details, even though that had been only one of many outings they had gone on together.

The wife of the innkeeper mentioned the possibility that Grauff, for instance, might have had a drink of beer in the garden, but they would have to ask her sister-in-law, on nice Sundays it was always crowded and then she came up from Glarus to help out, she took over the garden during those times. They said that the sister-in-law had not been able to say anything with certainty either, and so the search parties searched all the possible trails in the entire region, but after five days they gave up, the weather had turned bad, in the last two days pockets of fog had often partially or even entirely blocked visibility. Then, on Friday, it was in the paper, and then everyone knew about it. From that day on his wife supposedly did not leave the house for weeks. Keller took two weeks off work, he checked off every mountain systematically for fourteen days and often in wretched weather, every mountain from the Großer Aubrig to the Clariden, to the Scherhorn, also the Tödi range and the Bifertenstöcke, all of them over 3,000 meters high, interrogated all the Alpine cowherds, all the hut caretakers, all the mountain dwellers, he gave them photographs: Erich Grauff eight months ago, in climbing clothes, with backpack and complete equipment, black and white, postcard size, and always on the back the telephone number of the nearest police station.

"And?"

Only a certain Kurt Seiler, approximately fifty years old, who sought peace and quiet and who was at that time responsible for the management of the Fridolin Hut way back in the Glarner country, recognized him at first glance, but from a much earlier time; Seiler had worked on the Rhine at the beginning of the sixties, and if he wasn't badly mistaken, Grauff had worked in Basel with the customs at that time. That was correct. But, in the meantime, Grauff had turned thirty-four and had a family and hadn't been with the customs for five years, and besides even before his marriage had changed his residence, had moved away from Muttenz near Basel.

"It could be, he simply took off. Hasn't the thought occurred to anyone, that for some reason or other Grauff was waiting for the right opportunity, in order to . . ."

Certainly. In such cases the police must at least think of this possibility. And they did search, and they did it at home and abroad. The radio carried the bulletin, precise description, also in the newspapers and on television, age and so forth, missing since such and such a time, last seen at such and such a place, namely, at the train ticket office in Rapperswil; he lived in Rapperswil on Lake Zurich around thirty kilometers from Zurich. Whenever they hiked into the mountains, he and Keller had always left the car at home. But his wife did not want to admit such a thing, impossible, how could they ever get such an idea, he was dead, she knew it, she already knew on that Sunday evening, that he was dead, that he had fallen over the edge, she should not have let him go. Some say they hardly knew what to do, she was completely beside herself, and even though they all tried to persuade her to take her children and visit her parents at least for a few weeks, none of them had considered that she could harm herself. However: She did not want to go, she stayed, and she appeared then to some extent even to get hold of herself with time, although she still isolated herself and didn't associate with anyone anymore nor want to associate with anybody, when she finally tended to her affairs again herself and was seen on the street maybe two or three times during the week, though usually only in the early morning, when only a few women are out with their shopping bags, especially in winter, when it is as cold as that December. And then there were long since certainly other things to gossip about, too, life goes on. The rumor that he had perhaps feigned an accident in the mountains but cleared out instead, to South America, for instance, never really got started good, they considered him dead, eventually she even received a widow's and orphans' pension, she was pitied, but other women become widows, too, and she wasn't even thirty yet and wasn't bad looking, could even get married again.

"Yes, and why not?"

Keller left in the spring; transferred, they maintain, others say he requested it. At first, that is, in the weeks right after his fruitless searches, he supposedly visited her almost daily, he was considered to be serious, and because he was single and Grauff's best friend, soon for once everyone mused on what was finally obvious to everyone; but in January he was certainly not seen as frequently on the stairs on his way to or from her apartment, in February once or twice more, as far as people still observed this affair at all anymore, and then, of course, it was also known that during carnival he said in the Swan, the best place on the square, if it really came down to it, he would want to make his own children. In April he moved away, into the neighborhood of Bern, the report was; at that time there was weather such as usually does not come until May, March had already been surprisingly sunny. But then those who had said that too much sun too early was not good, for it would take its revenge, you'd soon see, were proven right, and when May not only was unpleasant but even brought freezing nights, so that the farmers community was reduced from its usual complaining to loud lamentations, naturally everybody claimed to have foreseen all this, the freeze and the frozen buds and new shoots and that now everything would be even more expensive. The cool, gray weather hung on, Pentecost was a holiday for people who like, for instance, to wander in the woods during generous and widespread rains, there are always the die-hards. Hotz was one of them. He fished every morning in spite of drizzle, steady rain, or downpour, with two poles at the dredged-out holes in the man-made inlets near the mouth of the Jona east of Rapperswil. With one pole he used a heavy weight, baiting the hook with earthworms or partially boiled bits of potato to the left side of the estuary, where, in his experience, barbel and carp are to be found, and with the other he cast a spoon or lure a bit further to the left; in all those years he had caught not a few pike there, because of that thought at first he had God knows how many pounds of live weight when he hooked her that morning.

Around nine o'clock, it was probably raining again by this time, the divers from the lake patrol found the baby buggy and still before noon the two children also. When Grauff's widow, together with her two children, had left the apartment, nobody in the building could say, and that she had not come home that evening, they also did not notice. Then the doctor also established that the bodies of the children had not been in the water for more than twelve hours, the woman ten at most, and further, the autopsy had shown that she was pregnant, beginning of the sixth month, it was said.

"But Grauff had been missing over eight months already by that time!"

Officially authorized investigations supposedly established beyond a doubt that Keller had nothing to do with it.

"But then who else?"

It is certain that after a few years there will seldom be anything heard about the Grauffs and then at most pure conjecture.

SIGN LANGUAGE

WOLFGANG WEYRAUCH
translated by Earl N. Lewis

•WHAT IS THAT? A DOT, OBVIOUSLY. OR IS IT SOMETHING ELSE? AN EYE? Only one eye? Where is the second one? Why is it missing? Anyway, on Friday night it was not yet there, but since Saturday morning it has been in plain sight. The dot, or eye, or whatever it stands for, can be seen on a ferryboat where the passenger cars are parked for the ferry trip. The ferry-boat attendant tries to remove the symbol, just in case it is a symbol. He cannot do it. The thing is neither large nor small, and it is composed of something neither soap nor water will remove. No broom will help either, nor any brush, gasoline, detergent, even spit, not even rain, not a thing.

•••••• And what is that? A series of dots, no doubt. A series of dots that produces a line, if it is connected by dashes, a straight line interrupted by, yet held together by dots, a dotted line, as such a thing is called. Why that way exactly and not different? Why seven dots and not six or eight? Why horizontal and not vertical? Presumably the dotted line produces a continu-ity for the first dot encountered, although on the other hand that could be doubtful because the dot and the dots are separated about one and a half kilometers from each other. The dotted line, or whatever it is, can be found right in the middle of the Darmstadt "Kreuz." A milkman was the first to see the symbol early Saturday; at least he was the first to report it. Because this symbol stuck to the asphalt as stubbornly as that dot did on the wood of the ferry, and defied all attempts to remove it, the Commission is almost certain that the second symbol is composed of the same substance as the first sym-bol. The Commission convened as expeditiously as possible, from which it may be concluded that it was already in existence. Why it had already been formed cannot be stated. Naturally, careful deliberation will be made as to whether or not it is merely a dotted line. And whether it is a dotted line or a track, the thing must have some sort of significance. But what? And whose track can it be, just in case it is a track? Where does it come from? Where is it headed? How could whatever left the track not form a track at first, then form one, then leave no more behind? Maybe it is not a track. Maybe it's a signal. But from whom? For whom?

• Now what is *that*? A colon, that is clear. But what else can it signify? A traffic light? A U-boat periscope? The mercury in a thermometer that has been dropped so that the mercury column has been separated. Eyes of a spider, located one below the other, that is waiting for an already stupefied fly? A military signal known to others but not to us? But who can the opponent be? Is he living right out in the open among us without our recognizing him as a opponent? Is he one of us who is secretly against us? Is he some individual, or rather some group of foreigners pretending to be natives, or maybe even natives whose intentions toward us are good? We do not know what the colon in front of the rebuilt Civic Theater means. We are also not doing all this as a secret attempt to deceive any enemies. Everyone should rest assured we are merely groping around in the dark.

❙ Even a blind man can make that out to be a vertical line. Yet it could also be a tree, a metal pole, a wooden post, a worm, a snake, a stick, something nobody can hit upon even after having given it a lot of thought. Anyway, there is a connection between this fourth symbol and the three others; yes, one could even say that the second one can be formed from the first one, the third from the second, the fourth from the third. A dot, a series of dots, horizonal instead of vertical because the vertical series proceeds in the form of a colon, and this sequence was used·to make possible the vertical stages. We can expect a frequently interrupted vertical line to result. Our search parties are on their way. We are waiting for their reports. Moreover, the vertical line has appeared at the intersection of Rhine and Neckar Streets.

❙ This time a straight vertical line, twice interrupted, so that three smaller vertical lines plunge down. A symbol for bombs? If so, where was the plane? If it was a jet, it's a thousand miles away by now. But it could also be the track of something going from north to south. What can it be? An animal? What sort of animal? A person? A person on skis? But in the middle of summer? One must not make the mistake of confusing the actual symbol of something with whatever it actually symbolizes. This symbol can be found on the sidewalk in front of the administration building of the FIDC bank.

━ ━ ━ Three horizontal lines follow three vertical ones. This new symbol is also consistent. It is a variation of the preceding one. Is that all? Certainly. But what is it? A new track? Of what, then? It would be easy to bet that the next symbol will connect the three horizontal lines to form one line so that some sort of boundary will prevent any possible escape. But why first one way and then the other? Why allow something and then turn around and forbid it? A warning, a threat, a promise. The three horizontal lines are painted on the traffic lane leading to the main train station.

+ A cross, also at the train station. Likewise this asterisk:✳. Likewise this wheel; ⊛ . Likewise a laybrinth: ◎ . Simultaneously announcements from all parts of the city that appear as ⊙ and ⊘ and ○ . Additional announcements: the symbols cease to be symbols. They arise from the street and from the sidewalk and from you name it. They become three dimensional. They appear simultaneously in front of the National Museum, the old theater, the entrance to the underground garage, the White Tower, the new Main Auditorium, the indoor swimming pool, and most notably on the slopes of Mathilda Heights. By doubling, tripling or multiplying, they link together like a chain. Whoever tries to sever, crawl under, or jump over the chain will be paralyzed, making it seem as if the figures, which are no longer symbols (apparently because they had not been scrutinized enough, had not been recognized for what they actually are), were capable of incapacitating. Announcements from adjacent areas indicate that no place is free of these phenomena.

Reports about the last mentioned symbols are especially prevalent from the Odenwald, Spessart, and Taunus districts. It is no longer so important to interpret the symbols as it is to face thoroughly, radically whatever arose, is arising, and will arise, even to the risk of losing life and property.

Consequently, we here and now inquire whether or not you might know of or at least express an opinion about any ways and means wherewith the symbols can be eliminated. No matter if you are convinced your ideas are either unsuitable or even absurd, please share them with us. Absolute discretion and a generous reward are not only promised but also assured. We do not wish to make the amount of the reward public, owing to immediate circumstances. In any case the amount will not be small. Should anyone from our municipality, from its immediate or distant environs, and especially from the mountain forests, provide us with symbols from those areas and voluntarily and completely share his information with us, we shall guarantee that person immunity from penalty. Strictest confidence concerning all such evidence goes without saying. Even the minutest detail can be important.

( ) ◡ ◠   The four final symbols, which at first glance resemble paren-
theses, parenthesis open, parenthesis closed, parenthesis opened facing up,
parenthesis facing down open, appear to be wings of birds, half-wings of
birds. Because a fifth, that is, all told the eighteenth symbol, ◠◠   , indisputably represents a bird in flight. This symbol is strictly limited to the
suburban areas of the city, above all to Cranestone. Cranestone? Here there
is a definite relationship. But one could imagine that we are supposed to
make such an association. At any rate a deception is not to be ruled out.
Final announcement: The phenomena, which also include   ◡◡   and
◠◠◠◠   and ∧∧∧∧   , and ultimately a triangle, △   , (obviously
intended to imprison us), have been explained. For that reason we implore
all female and male residents of this municipality immediately to cease sending all suggestions to us lest their lives be in peril. Let everyone remain
exactly where he is this very moment and await new orders from the Ants,
Badgers, Magpies, Hedgehogs, Screech Owls and Goats, from Cinnamon,
Lamb's Lettuce, Mushroom, Lupine, Hazelnut and Thistle.
God have mercy upon us!

                                              The Municipal Council

SLAUGHTER

GABRIELE WOHMANN
translated by Ingeborg McCoy

As far as Elsa was concerned, she was completely against their taking the child along. But she could not get anywhere with the father, because the child himself pleaded to go, with an obstinate earnestness which repelled her.

—Butcher, the father said. It's in his blood. Besides, it's a question of his future trade.

Against the forcefulness of the father, her lord and lover, she could not do anything, especially since she admired it and since she was enthralled not only by his smooth-oily voice but also by the ingratiatingly portentous words which it was accustomed to employ.

—Poor, motherless creature, she said, before she released the child out of the pressure of her hug into the delivery truck, where the child, wedged between father and assistant, found a place on the driver's seat, timidly avoiding the handle of the gearshift. But she said that mainly because it showered her with a similarly devout thrill as the utterances of the father; nevertheless, she was altogether against it, without having a feeling for the pigs which would have surpassed normal affection for animals, without wanting to object in the least to the process of slaughtering as such; only she did not like it as an exhibition and then especially not for a child.

The child did not look back at Elsa. He looked straight ahead with the men through the light brown specks on the windshield. During the unloading he kept close to his pig. He remembered how he had fed it the last meal at noon the day before, his thorough, enlightening actions at the occupation. Now he felt something which resembled gloating, as he noticed the expression of offended fear in the snorty face of his pig—because why had the animal yesterday tried to deny with inattentive gluttony, without any understanding for ritual, the present fateful hour?

He kept close to his pig. Among hundreds of them he would have recognized his pig. Filled with compassionate contempt he watched how it let itself be turned into something guilty through the butcher's coarseness, how it remained defenseless, as if it had committed a crime. It put up with the loop around the left hind leg, trotted to the butchering room. It did not start up in anger against being tied to the iron ring and having the shooting device placed against its sweating forehead. The child felt disappointment when his pig, hit by the projectile, dropped stunned and silent; the breathing hardly moved its pale belly. But he did not linger over prolonged emotions; he paid attention so as not to miss anything. Later they told how he had never stood around aimlessly, had not been in anybody's way. He remained with supple stamina within the closest circle of the events surrounding his pig; he paid attention to nothing else. He watched the butcher, who had dug his left knee into the animal's chest; while he was tightening his left hand around the left hoof, his knife hacked the jugular vein at the side of the throat. Now the blood shot in a fat stream into the bowl which an apprentice was holding; more bowls, buckets; the blood from his pig could be directed to the left and to the right. The smeary wounded belly floated meanwhile on a set of pulleys into the big tub and there, bedded on its back, kept a peace almost of contentment. Powder of pitch produced a rash over the underside of the belly, formed a frightening mask around the head, wrapped dark socks around the hocks. Steaming water splashed against the hide; the pig looked depraved in its coating of black pitch. With a chain which was lying across the vat the butcher and his assistants turned the pig; it rolled over on its belly lazily and now had its scarred back powdered and scalded.

The child stood close to the assistant who was plucking the bristles off the ears and the tail, but he didn't stretch out his hand to help. The bell razor was scraping heels, belly, and back: The child had kind of liked the name of this tool for a long time, and now he liked it very much, how easily the bell was doing its job; he liked watching it. The butcher pulled the pig, which was now almost naked, onto the huge wooden table, splashed cold water on it, shaved off the remaining fuzz: The blade grazed in a sharp angle across the skin. A thorough, conscientious preparation, undisturbed by any nervousness. The child felt great calm contentedness. After the humiliation of the opening scene he now seemed to be concerned rather with release. Dignity and redemption were growing in bloody passionate intensification towards final disintegration. The assistants tore sallow strips of sinew from the slit legs; the hanging pig seemed extremely anxious to have its belly cut open, so that the motley commotion of the intestines, the whole damp bother of the innards could gush out; with relief it spit away its gullet and its small wet heart.

Only when the hacking-apart started were the child's arms caught by the desire for action. He grabbed an ax and struck into the strongly aromatic, shiny mass; he paid such little attention to the others, was so much occupied with taking care of his pig, that he would not believe them later, when they were telling the shuddering Elsa that he all alone had hacked apart the animal; all of them had been standing around it, smitten and amused by this angry urge which did not aim, however, at planless destruction.

—Good work, butcher's sense, the father said.

The child left the kitchen, went across the yard into the barn, walked up and down the passage between the pig pens, and took a long time with the choice of the pig whose road to liberation he would pay special attention to, this time from the very beginning.

CHANGE OF PERSPECTIVE

CHRISTA WOLF
translated by A. Leslie Willson

1

I have forgotten what my grandmother was wearing when the bad word *Asia* brought her back onto her feet. I don't know why she should be the first to come to my mind's eye. She never stood out while she was alive. I know all her clothes: the brown dress with the crocheted collar that she put on for Christmas and for all the family birthdays, her black silk blouse, her large-checked kitchen apron, and the black mottled knitted jacket in which she sat in the winter next to the stove while poring over the *Landsberg General-Anzeiger*. She had nothing suitable to wear for the journey—my memory is not at fault. She could use her high-buttoned shoes—they always hung on her too-short, slightly bowed legs a half-inch above the floor, even when my grandmother was sitting on an air raid shelter cot, even when the floor was trodden-down earth, like that day in April that I'm talking about. The bomber squadrons, that now were passing over us in broad daylight on their way to Berlin, could no longer be heard. Someone had pushed open the door of the air raid shelter, and in the bright triangle of sunlight, three paces away from my grandmother's dangling, high-buttoned shoes, stood a couple of black high-topped boots worn by an officer of the Waffen-SS who had made a mental note of every single word my grandmother said during the long air raid: No, no, you're not getting me away from here, let 'em kill me, an old woman like me is no loss.—What? said the SS officer, tired of living? You want to fall into the hands of those Asiatic hordes? The Russians slice the breasts off of all the women!

That brought my grandmother with a groan to her feet again. Oh God, she said, what did humankind do to deserve this? My grandfather lit into her: The things you say! and now I see them precisely, how they go out into the yard and how each takes his place beside our hand cart: Grandmother, in her black cloth coat and her light- and dark-brown striped kerchief that my children still used for a scarf, supports her right hand on the rear haft of the cart, grandfather in a cap with earflaps and a herring-bone jacket takes up a position next to the shaft. Haste is advisable. Night is near, and the enemy, too. Except that the two are coming from different directions: night from the west and the enemy from the east. Toward the south, where they meet and where the small town Nauen lies, fire flares skyward. We think we can understand that fiery script—Menetekel seems unequivocal to us, and reads: Go west!

But first we have to look for my mother. She frequently disappears when it's a matter of moving on. She wants to go back and has to go on. Both urges are often equally imperative. Then she invents excuses and runs away. She says: I'm going to hang myself. And my brother and I, the two of us, still live in the realm where words are to be taken literally. We run into the small bit of woods where my mother has no business going, and where we don't want to have any business going. We each catch one another throwing glances into the crowns of trees. We avoid looking at one another—we couldn't possibly speak about unspeakable suppositions. We also remain silent when my mother, who week by week gets bonier and skinnier, comes up from the village, tosses a small sack of meal on the hand cart and reproaches us: Running all over the place and worrying people, what got into you? And who's going to pry those farmers loose from this stuff, if I don't?

She harnesses herself to the cart, my brother and I shove, the sky contributes uncanny fireworks, and I again hear the low sound with which the commonplace train *Reality* jumps the tracks and speeds in a wild dash right into the densest, most unbelievable irreality, so that I vent a laugh whose impropriety I feel strongly.

Except that I can't make it plain to anyone that I'm not laughing at us, God forbid, not at us settled, ordinary people in the two-story house next to the poplar tree, at us motley peep-show people in hot water: Manche, manche Timpete, Buttje, Buttje in de See; mine Fru, de Ilsebill, will mich so, as ik woll will. But none of us wanted to be emperor or even pope, and certainly not the Lord God. Quite content, one sold meal and butterfat and sour pickles and malt coffee downstairs in the shop, and the other learned the sounds of English at a black oilcloth and now and then looked out of the window over the city and the river that lay there quite peaceful and proper, and neither ever inspired me with the desire to abandon them. My brother persisted in screwing together ever-new curiosities from his erector set and then insisted on setting them into some senseless motion or other with strings and rollers, while upstairs in her kitchen my grandmother is cooking a variety of fried potatoes with onions and majoram that with her death vanished from the world, and my grandfather is hanging his cobbler's thread on the window latch and untying his blue cobbler's apron so that on his small wooden block on the kitchen table he can slice every piece of bread crust into a dozen fine chips so that his toothless mouth can chew the bread.

No, I don't know why they got us into hot water, and no way in the world do I know why I have to laugh about it, even when my uncle, who guides the second cart in our tiny procession, asks suspiciously again and again: I'd just like to know what's so funny here! Even when I realize how disappointing it is that the fear of being laughed at doesn't even stop when finally the proxy is in your pocket, even though I would gladly have done him the favor of assuring him that I was laughing at myself: I couldn't lie easily, and I felt clearly that I wasn't here, although one of the figures that leaned in the darkness against the wind could easily have been confused with me. You can't see yourself when you're in yourself. But I saw all of us, as I see us today, as though someone had lifted me out of my skin and set me aside with the command: Look there!

I did look, but it wasn't enjoyable. I saw us coming down from the highway, fumbling around on side roads in the darkness, and finally coming onto an avenue that led us to a gate, to a remote estate and to a bent, slightly wobbly man who was hobbling in the middle of the night to the stalls, to whom it was not given to be surprised at anything, so that in his way he greeted the desperate, exhausted little troop: Well, Sodom and Gomorrha? Doesn't matter. There's room in the smallest hut for a truly loving pair.

That man isn't all there, my mother said depressed, as we followed Kalle across the yard, and my grandfather, who spoke little, declared with satisfaction: He's really crazy in the head.—And so it no doubt was. Kalle called my grandfather maestro, and the highest ranks of service in his life had been a private in an imperial infantry regiment, a shoemaker journeyman with Herr Lebuse in Bromberg, and a linesman with the German Railway, Frankfurt/Oder inspection sector. Maestro, said Kalle, you'd best take that shack back there in the corner. Whereupon he disappeared and piped: Just take a drop, just take a drop . . . But the sleepers in the bunkbeds had their allotment of tea behind them already, even the unavoidable leberwurst sandwiches had been handed them—you could smell it. I tried to hold my nose shut with my arm while I slept. My grandfather, who was almost deaf, began to say the Lord's Prayer as every evening, but at "and forgive us our debts" my grandmother yelled in his ear that he was bothering people, and they got into a fight about that. The whole room could listen to them, whereas earlier only their old, creaking wooden beds had been witness, and the black-framed picture of an angel with the axiom: Even though the last anchor of hope should break, do not despair!

At the crack of dawn Kalle woke us. I suppose you can drive a wagon, he asked my uncle. You see, Herr Volk—that's the owner of the estate—wants to leave with bag and baggage, but who'll drive the ox cart with the feed sacks? —I will, said my uncle, and he stuck to it, even when my aunt whispered into his ear that oxen were dangerous animals and that he didn't have to risk his hide for these strangers. . . . Shut your mouth! he snorted. And how else are you gonna get your junk away from here? —We were all allowed to sit on top, and our hand cart was tied fast to the back side of the wagon. That's fine, said Kalle, just don't think that the oxen are faster than your hand cart. Herr Volk came in person to seal the engagement of his new driver with a handshake. He was wearing a hunting cap, a loden coat and knickers, and Frau Volk came to greet the women, who now belonged one way or another to her domestic staff, with a gracious, cultured word. But I couldn't stand her because she addressed me in a familiar way without ceremony and let her dachsund bitch, Sweety, sniff at our legs, which presumably smelled of leberwurst sandwiches. Then my aunt saw that elegant people were involved. My uncle wouldn't have hired himself out to just any Prussian. Then there was shooting right behind us, and we moved off at an accelerated pace. The Good Lord won't abandon his own, said my grandmother.

But in the night, I had for the last time dreamed the dream a child dreams: that I was not the child of my parents. I was a changeling and belonged to the merchant Rambow in Friedrichsstadt, who however is much too sly to announce his claim openly, although he has seen through everything and reserves measures for himself, so that finally I was forced to avoid the street in which he was lurking in his shop door for me with jawbreakers. Now on this night I was able to inform him conclusively in the dream that I had lost all fear, even the memory of the fear of him, that this was the end of his power over me, and from now on I would come by his place every day and get two bars of Borken chocolate. The merchant Rambow had accepted my terms meekly.

There was no doubt about it, he was finished, for he was no longer needed. I wasn't a changeling, but I was no longer myself either. I never forgot when this stranger entered me, who had meanwhile grabbed me and did with me as she would. It was that cold morning in January, when I left my town on a van for Küstrin in great haste, and when I was really very surprised how gray this town was, in which I had always found all the light and all the color I needed. Then someone in me said slowly and distinctly: You'll never see it again.

My fright can't be described. There was no appeal to this judgment. All I could do was keep to myself truly and honestly what I knew, watch the ebb and flow of rumors and hopes rise and fall again, for the moment go on doing everything that I owed others, say what they wanted to hear from me. But the stranger in me gnawed about and grew, and possibly she would refuse to obey in my place. Already she poked me sometimes, so that they looked at me askance: Now she's laughing again. If we just knew about what!

2

I'm supposed to report about *liberation*, the hour of liberation, and I thought: Nothing easier than that. All the years since, this hour stands sharply etched before my eyes; it lies ready and able in my memory, and in case there were reasons not to disturb it to this very day, then twenty-five years should have effaced those reasons, or at least have attenuated them. I only needed the word to go at it, and the machine would start, and everything would appear by itself on paper, a series of exact, readily visible pictures. But time, even though it effaces reasons, still produces new ones incessantly, and makes the designation of a specific hour even harder. I want to tell clearly what I was liberated from, and if I'm conscientious, perhaps for what reason: The end of my fear of the low-flying planes. If you make your bed, you have to lie in it, Kalle would say, if he were still alive, but I assume he is dead, like many of the persons involved (death *does* efface reasons).

As dead as the foreman Wilhelm Grund after the strafing planes had shot him in the stomach. So at sixteen I saw my first dead man, and I must say: pretty late for that time. (I can't count the babe that I handed in a stiff, wrapped-up bundle from a truck to a refugee woman—I didn't see it, I only heard its mother cry out and run away.)

As chance would have it, the foreman Wilhelm Grund lay there in place of me, for nothing but pure chance had kept my uncle in the shed that morning with a sick horse, instead of our preceding the others together on the road with Grund's ox cart as usual. We should have been here, too, I had to tell myself, and not there where we were safe, although we heard the shots, and the fifteen horses shied. Since then I've been afraid of horses. But since that moment I've been even more afraid of the faces of people who had to see what no human being should see. The farmboy Gerhard Grund had such a face when he threw open the shed door, managed a couple of steps more, and then collapsed: Herr Volk, what have they done to my father!

He was my age. His father was lying at the edge of the road in the dust next to his oxen, staring up vacantly—anyone who insisted might even say— into Heaven. I saw that nothing more could retrieve that stare, not the wailing of his wife, not the whimpering of the three children. That time we were not told that it was no sight for us. Quick, said Herr Volk, we've got to get away from here. They'd have grabbed me and dragged me to the edge of the woods like they grabbed the dead man by his shoulders and legs. For any one of us, even for me, the tarpaulin from the manorial feed floor would have become a coffin as it did for him. Without a song or a prayer I would have gone to my grave too, as did the farmhand Wilhelm Grund. They would have sent their wails after me, and then they would have gone on as we did, because we could not stay.

For a long time, like us, they would have had no desire to talk, just as we remained silent, and then they would have had to wonder what they could do to stay alive themselves and—just like us now—they would have ripped off large birch boughs and stuck them on our cart, as though the alien pilots would have let themselves be deceived by the wandering birch grove. Every- thing, everything would be as now, only I would no longer be there. And the difference that was everything to me meant practically nothing to most of the others here. Gerhard Grund was already sitting in his father's seat, driving on the oxen with his whip, and Herr Volk was nodding to him: Good boy. Your father died like a soldier.

I didn't really believe that. A soldier's death was not depicted like that in school readers and newspapers, and I informed the court of last resort with which I kept a steady contact and which—even though with scruples and reservations—I designated with the name God, that no husband and father of four children, and, in accordance with my conviction, no other human be- ing, should have to perish in this way. Well, it's war, said Herr Volk, and of course it was, and had to be, but I could maintain that this was a departure from the ideal of death for Führer and Reich, and I did not ask whom my mother meant when she embraced Frau Grund and said loudly: Those damned people. Those damned criminals.

Because I happened to have the watch, it fell to me to signal with a trill the next attack wave, two American fighters. Everybody who could move sprang from the carts and threw themselves into the roadside ditches. Me too. Except that this time I did not bury my face in the sand, but lay on my back and kept on eating my buttered bread. I didn't want to die, and I was certainly not resolute in the face of death, and I knew what fear is better than I liked. But you don't die twice on the same day. I wanted to see the ones who were shooting at me, because I had the surprising thought that in every plane a couple of particular people were sitting. First I saw the white stars under the wings, but then, when they nosed down for a new approach, I saw the heads of the pilots in their flight helmets very close, finally even the bare white specks of their faces. I knew war prisoners, but this was the attacking enemy, face to face. I knew that I should hate him. And it seemed unnatural to me that I wondered for a split second whether they enjoyed what they were doing. Anyway, they soon broke off.

When we returned to the carts, one of our oxen, the one they called Heinrich, sank before us to its knees. Blood was gushing from its throat. My uncle and my grandfather unharnessed it. My grandfather, who had stood without a word next to the dead Wilhelm Grund, now expelled oaths from his toothless mouth: The innocent thing, he said hoarsely, those damned blackguards, all cursed s.o.b.s, one and all. I was afraid he was about to cry, and I wished he could get it all off his chest. I forced myself to look at the animal for the length of a minute. There could not be reproach in its gaze, but why did I feel guilty? Herr Volk gave my uncle his hunting rifle and pointed to a spot behind the ear of the ox. We were sent off. When the shot cracked, I whirled around. The ox fell heavily onto its side. The women were busy all evening working up the meat. By the time when we were eating the broth in the straw, it was already dark. Kalle, who had complained bitterly that he was hungry, greedily slurped his bowl empty, wiped his mouth with his sleeve, and began to sing with relish: Alle Möpse bellen, alle Möpse bellen, bloß der kleine Rollmops nicht . . . Go to the devil, you crazy guy, my grandfather let loose at him. Kalle let himself drop into the straw and stuck his head under his jacket.

3

You mustn't be afraid when everybody's afraid. Knowing this is definitely liberating, but liberation came only later, and I want to record what my

memory is willing to hand over about it today. It was the morning of the fifth
of May, a beautiful day. Again panic broke out when the rumor came that
Soviet tank vanguards had encircled us. Then came the word: Forced march
to Schwerin—the Americans are there. And whoever might have wondered
would have found it really remarkable how everybody hurried toward the
enemy who had for days been after our very lives. Of everything that was
still possible, nothing seemed desirable or even endurable to me—but the
world stubbornly refused to collapse, and we weren't prepared to adapt ourselves to a bungled end-of-the-world. So I understood the ghastly remarks
that a woman uttered when someone remonstrated her that the long desired
miracle weapon of the Führer could now annihilate everybody, foe and Germans alike. Let it go ahead, the woman said.

We went past the last houses of the village up a sandy lane. Next to a red
Mecklenburg farm house a soldier was washing himself at the pump. He had
rolled up the sleeves of his white undergarment, stood there spraddle-legged,
and yelled out at us: The Führer is dead, like one shouts: Nice weather today.

More than the realization that the man was speaking the truth, his tone
dismayed me.

I trotted on next to our cart, heard the hoarse giddyups of the driver, the
groans of the exhaused horses, saw the small fires at the edge of the road, saw
piles of rifles and anti-tank weapons grow spectrally in the ditches, saw type-
writers, suitcases, radios, and all kinds of expensive technical war materiel
bordering our way senselessly, and I could not quit recalling within me again
and again the tone of that sentence which, instead of being one ordinary sentence among many, according to my notion should have reverberated fright-
fully between heaven and earth.

Then paper came. Suddenly the road was flooded with paper. They were
still throwing it in a wild fury from the Wehrmacht vehicles: forms, mobiliza-
tion orders, files, proceedings, depositions of a war zone detachment, banal
routine scribblings as well as secret command matters, and the statistics of
the casualties from double-locked armored safes, in whose contents—now
that they were cast at our feet—no one was any longer interested. As though
there were something repulsive in the heap of paper, I too did not look at a
single sheet, which I later regretted, but I did catch the canned food that a
truck driver tossed to me. The arc of his arm reminded me of the oft-repeated
arc with which in the summer of 1939 I had thrown packs of cigarettes to the

dusty columns of vehicles that rolled past our house eastward day and night. In the six years that had intervened, I had stopped being a child, and now another summer was coming—but I had no intimation of what I should do with it.

The supply column of an army unit had been abandoned on a side lane by its escort troops. Everyone who passed it took for himself whatever could be carried. The orderliness of our procession came unraveled. Many lost control of themselves with greed, as once they had with terror. Only Kalle laughed. He lugged a large hunk of butter to our cart, clapped his hands, and yelled happily; Oh you fat little devil! It's enough to make you kick up your heels in sheer madness.

Then we saw the concentration camp inmates. Like a ghost the rumor had been weighing on our minds that the inmates of Oranienburg were being herded along behind us. I never suspected, at the time, that we were also fleeing from them. They were standing at the edge of the woods, and they scented us from there. We could have given them a sign that the way was clear, but nobody did. Cautiously they approached the road. They looked different from any other people I had seen up to then, and I was not surprised that we involuntarily retreated before them. But this retreat also betrayed to us—it indicated, in spite of everything—what we affirmed to one another and to ourselves: We did know what had gone on. All of us, we unfortunates who had been driven from hearth and home, from farm yards and manors, from merchant shops and musty bedrooms and polished parlors with the Führer's portrait on the wall—we knew: Those before us, who had been declared animals and who were now slowly coming towards us to avenge themselves: We had discarded them. Now the ragamuffins would don our clothes, stick their bloody feet in our shoes; now the starving would snatch the butter and the flour and the sausage that we had just looted. And with horror I felt: That is just, and I knew for the fraction of a second that we were to blame. I forgot again.

The concentration camp inmates did not rush for the bread, but for the weapons in the roadway ditch. They loaded themselves with them; without taking regard of us they crossed the road, laboriously scaled the slope beyond, and took posts above, weapons at the ready. Silently they gazed down at us. I could not keep on looking at them. Let them scream, I thought, or blast into the air, or blast into us, for God's sake! But they stood there peacefully. I saw that many were reeling, and that they could barely force themselves to hold their weapons and stand there. Perhaps they had been wishing for this, day and night. I could not help them, nor they me. I did not understand them, and I did not need them, and everything about them was totally alien to me.

From ahead came the cry that everyone but the drivers should get down: It was a command. A deep breath went through the trekking column, for this could mean but one thing: Just ahead lay our last steps in freedom. Before we could put ourselves in motion the Polish drivers sprang down, slung their reins around the wagon uprights, laid the whip on the seat, gathered in a small troop, and set off and away, back, to the east. Herr Volk, who immediately turned purple, barred their way. At first he spoke softly with them, but quickly started yelling: Conspiracy and a put-up job and refusal to work, he yelled. Then I saw a Polish foreign worker push aside a German landowner. Now truly the bottom side of the world had risen to the top. But Herr Volk knew nothing of this. As usual he reached for his whip, but his blow did not fall—someone held his arm fast. The whip fell to the ground, and the Poles went on. Herr Volk pressed his hand against his heart, leaned heavily against a cart, and was comforted by his purse-lipped wife and the stupid female dachshund Sweety, while from above Kalle shouted down abusively: Trash! Trash! The Frenchmen, who stayed with us, called farewells after the departing Poles, which they understood no more than I did, but they did understand the tone, as did I, and it hurt me a little that I was excluded from their calls and waves of hands and tossing of hats, from their joy and their language. But it had to be that way. The world was made up of victors and the vanquished. The former wanted to give free rein to their emotions. The others—we—henceforth had to bottle up ours. The enemy would not see us weak.

Then he came: A fire-breathing dragon would have been more preferable to me than the light jeep with the gum-chewing driver and the three indolent officers, who in their boundless scorn had not even unbuttoned their pistol holsters. I tried to look through them with an expressionless face, and I told myself that their unconstrained laughter, their clean uniforms, their indifferent glances, their whole damned victorious demeanor was surely dictated to them for our particular humiliation.

The people around me began to hide their watches and rings, and I too removed my watch from my wrist and stuck it casually in my coat pocket. The guard at the end of the defile, a strapping lanky fellow beneath his impossible steel helmet—about which we had always laughed loudly at the newsreels—that guard, for the benefit of the few armed men, pointed to where they were supposed to throw their weapons, and another frisked us civilians with some sure, practiced police moves. Stony with indignation I let myself be frisked, secretly proud that they expected a weapon even of me.

Then my overworked guard asked businesslike: Your watch? The victor
wanted my watch. But he didn't get it, because I succeded in duping him with
the assertion that the other guy—Your comrade—his comrade, had already
collected it. I got away unscathed, as far as the watch was concerned. Then
my sharpened ears signaled again the swelling sound of an airplane motor. Of
course, it didn't concern me any longer, but from habit I kept an eye on the
flight path. Under the force of a reflex I threw myself down when it dove;
once again the nauseous dark shadow, which swept swiftly over grass and
trees, once again the repulsive sound of bullets striking the ground. Even
now, I thought, astonished, and I noted that from one second to the next you
can get used to being out of danger. With wicked malevolence I saw
American artillerymen bring an American gun into place, and fire it at the
American plane, which pulled up urgently and disappeared behind the
woods.

Now one ought to be able to tell how it was when it became still. I remained lying behind the tree for a while. I think it didn't matter to me that
from this minute on perhaps a bomb or a machinegun burst would never
more fall upon me. I wasn't curious about what would happen now. I didn't
know what a dragon is good for when it stops breathing fire. I had no notion
how the horned Siegfried was supposed to behave when the dragon asked him
for his watch instead of devouring him hide and hair. I had no desire at all to
see how Mr. Dragon and Herr Siegfried would get along as civilians. I hadn't
the slightest desire to ask for every bucket of water from the Americans in the
occupied villa, and by no means to get involved in an argument with the
black-haired Lieutenant Davidson from Ohio, at the end of which I saw
myself forced to declare to him that my pride bade me now particularly to
hate him. And I had certainly no desire for a conversation with the concentration camp inmate who sat at our fire in the evening, who was wearing a
bent pair of metal-rimmed glasses, and who uttered the unheard-of word
Communist as though it were a permissible everyday word like *hate* and *war*
and *destruction*. No. Least of all did I want to know about the gloom and
consternation with which he asked: Where *did* you live all these years?

I had no desire for liberation. I lay under my tree, and it was quiet. I was
lost, and I thought I would watch the branches of the tree against the very
beautiful May sky. Then my strapping sergeant came up the slope after his
tour of duty, and a chirping German girl had hooked herself on each of his
arms. All together they moved off in the direction of the villas, and I finally
had reason to turn away a bit and to bawl.

GERMAN LESSON

WOLF WONDRATSCHEK

translated by A. Leslie Willson

For example.

Whenever an Italian soccer team wins in a big, international game, the German sports writers find out right away whether one of the Italian players is of German descent. Besides, they point out again and again that various German soccer players in Italy play a very good game of soccer.

We are famous for knowing exactly what Paradise looks like. It's just possible that this is because we never learned how to eat breakfast right.

For example.

German men's choirs have their songs. Adolf Hitler owned a German shepherd. Even in times of peace we like to talk about the readiness of our soldiers.

As was announced in Bonn, Berlin lies on the Rhine.

We believe firmly that everything had to happen as it had to happen. And we're proud of that, for we still have no idea of our fears.

German innkeepers are pleased when their guests discuss the Second World War. That promotes business. After the third beer the foreigners are homesick for Heidelberg.

On a map we show the tourists where Heidelberg lies; even in rainy weather Heidelberg looks exactly the way the foreigners have pictured Heidelberg in the sun.

For example.

The German national anthem has three stanzas. Sometimes it begins with the first stanza anyway. We recognize the melody by the trumpets.

At the rest areas on the autobahns Germany is very beautiful.

Most German highways are planned so that even at top speed you can see the church in the village. Order is a must.

The dread of Communists is still a part of our education. In school the teachers tell about Russia. They say that many Russians understand our language.

Parents cause children great concern.

In Germany, it seems only the wrong people keep running into each other.

We've had practice at that. Our laws see to it. We have never profited from our reason. We prefer black clothes.

The Christian Democratic Union. The lawn in front of the building is mowed. Prosperity for all. Whiter than white. That's the main thing.

We are forgetful. Only in our mistakes is there a parcel of truth. But nobody wants to admit that. We believe in proper relationships, but not in political ones.

Humor is a matter for experts. On TV they have to persuade us to be amused. But then we laugh till we cry, because we want to be taken seriously in any event.

That the whole thing can't be half that bad—this always figures. One of the funniest words in the German language is "revolution."

For example.

Anyone who wants to get to know this country ought also to strike up conversations with barbers. In a passionate way they are typical of this country. Their training includes a lot of fury.

The queen mother is fine. The queen is fine. The king is fine. And the children of the royal pair are fine. German newspapers report that normal conditions prevail once again in Greece.

Anyone who doesn't belong to a party or a sport club is considered a rabble-rouser hereabouts. In the Black Forest the strollers greet one another. The neighbors have a dog, too. Among other things we read a newspaper. In the confessional the priests are enlightened. A German woman is not a naked woman. Exceptions prove the moral.

In the front yards of one-family houses little garden dwarfs bloom. Our cabinet members look likable. It is said that we are living in a democracy.

In the future Germany doesn't want to have any past. Since we have had too much past, and since we haven't come to terms with the past, we have gotten rid of the past altogether. Now we are getting along better.

For example.

We have enough federal presidents. The Mediterranean is again a German swimming pool. Nothing else is in the air.

We act as though everybody in Germany understood something about physics, but otherwise our indifference is almost a historical condition.

A single refugee is sufficient to justify our lack of political originality. The equation of Germany and German Federal Republic is more than simply an error in translation.

Because simple reflections are so difficult for us, we simplify the difficulties.

For example.

Misfortune remains the privilege of the misfortunate. Labor remains the privilege of laborers. Politics ought to remain the privilege of politicians, they say in Bonn. But this continuation has consequences. The pessimists criticize the optimists. And the optimists check on the pessimists. What we understand by political dialogue functions in this way here. But I hope that will be much clearer some day than it has been up to now.

Germans no longer look like they might be named Maier and Müller today. We have gotten that far meanwhile. And we call this illusion progress.

That is typical. A nice funeral is more important than convalescent leave in Switzerland. The little man in the street has not grown taller, of course, but instead fatter.

For example: Goethe, Adenauer, made in Germany.

We are all extraordinarily capable of being influenced optically. Anyone who speaks into more than six microphones here naturally has more to say than anyone else. Better arguments correspond to better clothes. We have learned these permutations. We are not politicking. We want to make an impression.

We never get tired of trying to prove to one another that we aren't actually at all the way we actually are.

In Germany shortcomings are getting rotund. We can't take a joke. The police help out their friends. Youth is a risk that the German populace doesn't intend to let itself in for anymore. That's why our government talked about natural catastrophe and passed the emergency laws.

We wear our destiny like a uniform. We applaud lies. Even the wrong track is made of German oak here. We recognize Jews again at a glance.

DETLEV

HUBERT FICHTE
translated by A. Leslie Willson

IT IS SATURDAY NIGHT.

The grandparents dressed in their best and at eight o'clock went to the air defense demonstration in the Koppelstrasse. Grandpa took along his good walking cane.

An arbor is supposed to be set afire for the drill and be extinguished by a new procedure according to directions.

Mama gets the house in order.

She checks whether Grandpa propped the broom handle hard enough against the doorknob and door frame in case of burglars.

Detlev is being bathed.

He hopes that the gas boiler will set his mother's hair on fire again and that in the spotless house in Lokstedt she will burn like a Catholic saint—between the mouthwash and the hand cream.

But the bath takes place without incident and Mama wipes everything dry and shiny.

Nobody can go into the parlor. It is already vacuumed and dusted there for Sunday. The parlor is closed off.

Mama wiped the tile in the kitchen, waxed the floor, and polished the tiles on the grandmother's kitchen stove. She takes the cheese cake out of the oven and sets it to cool on the crystal plate in the guest room. She lowers the blackout curtains and closes off the guest room.

Nobody can go in the kitchen anymore either.

Detlev is supposed to stick his arms under the bedcovers so that he won't catch cold after his bath.

The grandparents' bedroom has been aired enough.

The mother closes the ventilator and lowers the blackout curtains. She reads to Detlev for a while about the goose and the dwarf that fly over Sweden.

—Hermann Goering is married to a Swedish lady.

Then the mother fills the room half full of angels with her prayers, two to my right, above, below, in front, behind.

The mother sits down in the little room next door and waits for her parents.

The house is all ready for Sunday.

Mama doesn't want to mess it up again unnecessarily, and she hardly stirs.

Is she reading? Is she dreaming? Is she thinking? Is she remembering my father? Is she afraid? Is she content?

Later, when Detlev is already asleep, she will lie down in the other bed and be near to him all through the night.

He doesn't have to sleep alone in the little room anymore. He cried there. He wouldn't lie down. Falling asleep he slid down the wall. When his head touched the pillow, he cried again and sat up straight.

Outside the birds are singing.

It is still light. Detlev sees it through the star-shaped holes in the black-out curtains.

The monkeys in the Hagenbeck Zoo are getting their supper.

All the houses in Hamburg are now spic and span for Sunday, and the children lie bathed in fresh linens—their arms under the covers—and smell like mouthwash and hand cream.

The grownups sit on the fringes of cleaned rooms and rinse out the juice glass right after they use it.

An arbor burns and is extinguished quickly before the laughing residents in their light summer clothes.

Now everything is different.

The sky is black.

The sun is red.

The bathroom windows are lying in the rhododendrons.

Zebras are running down the Karlstrasse.

In the vegetable gardens hang poisonous spiders from the Hagenbeck Zoo. Elephants and water buffalo on the Kaiser-Friedrich-Strasse.

—My mahogany furniture! yells Frau Malchow.

—Poor woman, says Grandma.

Frau Wichmann has to be dug out. She loses an ear and a part of her leg. Cherry sauce.

Selge's flowerbeds are a yellow crater.

Silvery black strips of tinfoil flutter on the roof tiles, gooseberry bushes, quince boughs. The ash-hardened paths are full of silvery black strips of tinfoil.

Duds in the rabbit pens?

Grandpa takes the party membership book, the handcart, and four suitcases.

He doesn't look back at the light gray house against the black sky—like it says in Schiller's "Bell."

Grandpa, Grandma, Mama, Detlev are evacuating.

They leave behind Grandma's trousseau, Mama's writing desk, the leghorns, Jesus at Golgotha, and the little flasks full of booze.

—Christmas we'll be back.
—Christmas.
—Chrismus.
The words feel much too thick in the mouth.
Now the word "Christmas" has been ruined, too.
A Christmas tree is something that is thrown down and flames up to illuminate bombing targets.
—It will all pass.
It will all pass.
After every December
There follows a May.
—Will a December follow this May?

The Home for Cripples was here.
—A bomb fell on it.
—Cripples, and then killed by an aerial bomb to boot.

On the Chrismus in the mouth lies the taste left behind by the air about the decaying crippled limbs.
The combination of this taste and the sounds of celebration and the odor of the limbs of the crippled means for Detlev that it's all over, that there will never again be anything.

For hours pink. Rothenburgsort. Hamm. Horn.
No more buildings. No children's playgrounds.
No house was sturdy enough.
The camouflage that scared Detlev at the entrance to Hamburg has dissolved into planes of chalky, bloody pink that thrust against the horizon.

The woman is crying again.
The soldiers are still singing:
—Didadadada
Dadididada
Dadadadadadidada!

The window panes have already fallen out of the train.
Soon there will be no more railroad trains.
During the night trip the second raid of terror on Hamburg.
It doesn't matter.
It looks like the inside of an oven.
In Mölln at morning.
That excites Grandma:
—Mölln!
—We've traveled in a circle! After twelve hours just in Mölln!
Where is Mölln located?
That Mölln still exists!
Now the cattle car is standing ready for them.
The injured.
Also the burned.
Some can already no longer move.
It is already difficult to get to the restroom. The injured shit already in agony into tin cans, next to those who are eating. Finally they travel in cattle cars.

Changing trains they are put into a first-class compartment. Because everything is over now, they can travel in first class for a stretch.
Grandma with unkempt hair.
Grandpa doesn't know what to do with his hands because here he doesn't dare to trim his nails with his pocketknife. Mama sooty, and a diplomat in a snazzy gray suit says to her:
—You're exaggerating!
Finally, in the upholstered compartment, Mama understands that it hasn't gotten that far here yet, that you can't say everything again here for the last time yet, that the war is still being won here, and you can get turned in for spreading defeatist enemy propaganda, and that she gives the effect of vulgar excitement in the elegant atmosphere of the first-class compartment.
Mama's anxiety is larger than her horror and, after she has stifled her voice, she makes a little joke again to relieve the tension.

On the return to Hamburg Detlev sings:
—Homeland, thy stars
Like diamonds they shine on me.
In a wide circle a thousand stars.
All snugly da-dum turned to thee!

Martin, the plumber, comes and repairs the drainpipe.

And the drainpipe is made of lead and already melts when you hold even a match against it.

He wonders if Detlev doesn't want to learn to solder. Detlev laughs at the plumber. But the next time the plumber brings Detlev a soldering iron and solder and muriatic acid, and he shows him how you've got to hold the copper tip of the soldering iron against the bar of tin. The acid steams from the pot, the hole of which Detlev is supposed to solder up. The tin melts. Detlev feels happy. He would never have thought that soldering could keep you so occupied.

Grandpa takes Detlev along to Herr Martin in the Tornquiststrasse.

—Are all the pots in Lokstedt soldered?

Detlev finds this conversation boring.

—Later he can learn to be a fitter with me.

—Later.

Finally Detlev can go outside.

On this street the houses are still intact and decorated with muscular men.

Detlev strikes the wall with his hand. The paint doesn't even flake off— and if an aerial bomb comes, everything will easily break apart, and Herr Martin will have soldered in vain.

—Make it whole, make it whole is the weirdest thing.

—You shouldn't talk so precociously.

—What do you mean precociously. I've matured early.

Fifty years ago Grandma ran around here with four petticoats and crinoline, and eggs cost twenty pfennig a dozen.

—There's even a bookstore in operation here still.

—I wonder if I'll be arrested, if as a nine-year-old I buy a book?

—What do you have in the way of the classics?

The saleslady is also astonished and offers him an ugly yellow cheap-paper edition of "Iphigeneia on Tauris" and "Torquato Tasso."

Mama already has "Iphigeneia."

That doesn't matter.

Detlev has enough pocket money.

Grandpa and Herr Martin just don't know what to say.

Grandma is proud of Detlev.

But Mama, when she comes home from the employment bureau, is completely exhausted and has a migraine.

She takes Detlev into her bed for a moment and tells him how a woman who dreaded to work tried to slice her arteries in the restroom when she was led in at the Raboisen employment bureau.

—It isn't the first time that somebody has tried to commit suicide in the employment bureau. A week ago a shirker hanged himself with his tie. The things that happen: The youngsters are letting their hair grow long and dance English dances and call themselves "Swingers"—just to look like Germany's enemies. And an honest-to-goodness halfbreed was there, too. You certainly wouldn't do anything like that, would you?

—Grandpa is patching his garden together again and I'm allowed to pull up chickpeas and transplant them.

—A philosopher thinks everything all over again, as though no one ever had a thought before him.

—Grandpa doesn't listen to me. It wouldn't be hard to transform the garden into the Island of Death by Böcklin or into the not exactly Hanging Gardens of Semiramis.

—Philosophy has dug its own grave, says Grandpa. He must know, if he says so.

—I'm supposed to learn how to dig. It's stupid to dig the garden again for the bombs.

—He's repairing the chicken wire for the leghorns.

—My Heraclitus! Unfortunately the earthworm is cut in two now.

—I'm thinking about the shovel, about the soil, the shovel thrust and the importance of digging, and about the juice,

Which is running out of that halved thing, the earthworm.

—I'm supposed to put the earthworm into the can for the chickens.

—The can is rusted, and Vatel-Paul-Grandpa uses it,

When he goes behind the balls of peat to piss.

—You're a true friend, the leghorns eat even the half of an earthworm,

Both halves of which go on squirming,

While it's running out.

—Fat chickens burn better.

—So I want to quick write poems and sing my songs.

And be a philosopher.

—Lots of digging makes the shovel shiny.

—Why does half an earthworm squirm?

—The boiled worm in the cherry sauce spoils the appetite.

—Till I die, Heraclitus,

So, soon now,

I will nevermore eat cherry sauce.

—Though the diligent grandfather repaired the cracks behind the bed.

And fastened the laminated woodfiber sheets under the plaster in the parlor.

Nothing holds. Nothing holds. The next attack will come soon!

—Like a fanfare!

—But no soul shall be lost!

—I want to try everything, be everything!

—But you're forgetting the worm again.

To put it in the rusty can.

—But everything is too late. I will never take up a profession.

—I want to experiment.

—You chickens, stop it,

Don't bother my shovel.

—I want to try everything now: Be a poet and thinker. Peasant and hero.

—Get lost! You fowl!

How quickly it happens, to become so immeasurably much.

Until it's all over, geniuses!

And the chicken tribe at the Last Judgment

Groans under the fire bomb.

But perhaps I

Would be this, and that, too.

Until there finally is nothing more at all.

Not God and not anything else. Not nothing.

Everything

Is what I want to be, you Greeks—

As much as possible.

—Aunt Frieda was taken away this morning! They were all sitting in the Schwarz's cellar, and Aunt Frieda couldn't keep quiet again, and she said that the Führer . . . Or something about the war. And the Möller woman went to the district bureau and reported Frieda, and this morning Aunt Frieda was taken away. Just don't say anything. We'll probably never see her again. Whoever gets in now will never get out again. Into prison or how do I know where. Grandma doesn't say anything. Grandpa doesn't say anything. Mama is quiet again, too.

The end of the Thousand Year Reich:

Run back and forth between Schuhmann's Volks-Radio and Schwarz's Volks-Radio.

—Will Hamburg be razed? Even more than razed?

—The Armistice is signed.

—The thousand enemy planes are leaving again because Hamburg has been surrendered without a fight.

The victors, Stalin, Churchill, and Roosevelt, are playing "Hail to Thee with Victor's Wreath!"

Mama starts to cry.

Willi Schwarz, who is too fat and because of his glandular disturbance was supposed to be drafted into the Volkssturm only at the last minute and who broke something doing calisthenics on the horizontal bar so that he receives a war-injury pension now, takes Mama by the arm obligingly and goes out with her.

The enemy tanks are already clanking down the Kaiser-Friedrich-Strasse. Mama says:

—Willi was so tactful.

—Why?

—Because he didn't ask anything.

—Why is that tactful?

—Don't ask so many questions today, not on this day.

—But why were you crying?

—Who wouldn't cry, when his homeland is being defeated?!

Two old people in a slate house in the garden settlement of Maiglöckchen froze to death.

They woke up in the morning and were already completely stiff and speechless. They couldn't rise and could no longer move their mouths. Then their eyes froze. The Red Cross nurses, who themselves have nothing to eat and get very cold at night, had to carry them carefully out of the slate house.

When something breaks off and falls to the ground it shatters into a thousand pieces, and the blood lies like red ice on the garden beds.

—Rabindranath Tagore, says the woman director before all the participants at the blocking rehearsal.

—A poet of the Indic subcontinent. The most important thing, the thing we must never forget, not during rehearsals and not a second during the performances: The Indians step first with their toes and roll the soles of their feet behind, back to the ball of the heel!

In "The Trojan War Doesn't Take Place" Detlev plays Peace.

It is meant symbolically.

Almost naked, bony and pallid, Detlev has to appear before Cassandra and Helen.

He must drag along an artificial palm frond.

The make-up girl blows gold dust into his hair.

Curtain up!

Spotlights on!

America, the land of unlimited possibilities.

Johnny Sonnyboy is sitting in the sun.

—What shall I do with my strength?

Jump! Do cartwheels! Stand on my head! Hup! Happy! Lucky!

That's how the writer Saroyan imagined it.

Detlev tries it out.

The color-swallowing spotlights of the rehearsal light. At the blocking rehearsal the entrances were blocked out.

—You from the right! You from the left! In a wide curve around the father's chair, to the left. Look. Stop. Look. Exit front right.

The colorless stage floor is covered with loops and knots, the fixed steps are scored for scene after scene—the Indians step first with their toes—into sewing patterns that Detlev steps out in imitation, stumbling, remaining cramped.

Then come the play rehearsals.

Not only are Detlev's steps led with loops—supporting leg, leg with no weight on it—the height of his arm motions are also determined, the breadth of the gesture of a hand, the extent of open eyes, the duration of a smile.

The cube of the stage accrues hair-thin, thread-like algae, not discernible to the eye, in which Detlev gets as muddled as a waterbeetle.

Headstand.

Detlev can't do a headstand.

But in the script the poet wrote:

Headstand!

So the producer and the woman director and the dramatic coach and the stocky hero, who is already miffed as it is because in the program he is second, behind Detlev, and the lady stage manager, and the prompter all demand a headstand.

Expression of exuberant joy of life.

Detlev can do a shoulderstand or the polka.

Dances joy of life. Forgets that it's the stage and for a rehearsal. He forgets the thread-like algae as the camouflage for the whole world, dances his honest-to-goodness halfbreed dance of emancipation, and it is so painfully embarrassing that all of them would rather not watch, but then do watch because it is so gigantically painful, Detlev, the giddy lanky kid who bubbles his frightful joy of life over the slimy sewing pattern.

That has nothing to do with Johnny.

Headstand it says in the script, because everything is supposed to have the effect of lightness and easiness.

His mother goes with Detlev to the Lola Rogge School of Dance. There his body is rhythmically relaxed, and two weeks before the premiere Detlev can twirl expressively and call out Abraham a Santa Clara—but he can't do an American headstand.

Detlev goes to Käte Kahl's School of Gymnastics.

There his abdominal muscles were strengthened. His calves are freed of spasms. A headstand is built from the bottom up!

One week before the premiere Käte Kahl has tried everything and, so to speak, has transmitted to Detlev a new consciousness of his body—but he can't do an American headstand.

Detlev is laced up, rinsed thoroughly, another head is crammed onto his head. His eyelids, his rainbow skin coalesce with the eyelids and the rainbow skin of the American youth.

The camouflage has become frayed. Detlev stumbles over wires. Sticky threads get caught in his mouth.

The dress rehearsals begin.

Detlev, a forgetful, rattling monster, drags himself through the whole play in costume and mask.

The prop man wants to hold Detlev's legs up, if he can only get his legs up.

On Johnny's legs hang two bells from the Liebfrauen Church in Scheyern, hang the hanged men in the restrooms of the employment bureau, oatmeal broth, chilblains, Creon's cock, Grandpa's axe, the seating plan of the secondary school of the arts, and a battered chest and photos with groups of children and two ladies' shoes with high heels.

These dress rehearsals, however, are only one of Detlev's attempts among many—it could be otherwise; there could be no more attempts—to kill time in the most suspenseful and novel way before total destruction.

At the dress rehearsals, when all the pieces of the piece are put together, the producer yells at the stocky hero, the stocky hero yells at the prompter, the prompter yells at the lighting man, the lighting man yells at the assistant director, the assistant director collapses, the lady stage manager cries, the stagehand quits, the lady director comes with a sack of sweets.

Detlev begins to eat his way through the sticky algae. Detlev's head on the

cushion and both of his arms in front of the cushion prop Detlev's complicated legs—involved is the attempt to play the leading role in Germany's
best theater.

—How would we live without the money I earn from it?

—I want to try it, even if I have to go through the whole play on my head.

Everything gets going again.

The stocky hero didn't crush me to death and carries me for dead from
the stage.

The father has shut his mouth now, and Detlev says what Johnny must say.

The prompter in her box is enthusiastic that she never has to give him
anything.

I forgot what Detlev just barely didn't forget. My name stands as the first,
before that of the father on the program. Now I can casually die.

Nothing. Imageless. Nameless. Unconscious.

I can never be forgotten again. One person will know to all infinity, too,
that I played Johnny in "My Heart's in the Highlands."

Applause.

Because Detlev is playing the leading role, he may take his bow alone. It
is a success and so everybody is smiling.

Someone yells:

—Bravo!

down from the balcony.

The first one to yell "Bravo!" always stands in the balcony and looks
around proudly.

I get older. I soon change my type-casting. I can no longer be so selective.
I must also accept roles that do not fulfill me artistically. People are buying
frying pans and no longer go to "Iphigeneia." I can still earn a bit with film-
dubbing, although I am fundamentally opposed to let my talent be exploited
through purely mechanical and commercial activities. You must think of it
this way: The English film is cut into small strips by Eagle Lion and they run
off again and again right in front of your nose. You speak into the mute
mouth movements of James Mason and Stewart Granger until it's right. It's
irritating to the nerves. But the pay is sensational—if you have a name. It

does, of course, happen that completely unknown and moderately talented actors are the purest geniuses at film-dubbing and can demand the top salaries because they always get it right quickly. The most painful thing is that you have to negotiate the honorarium with the recording director. —Well now, say what you're thinking, he'll tell you. After that there can be a great variety of courses of negotiation. If you mention something and mention too little, he has made a deal. Not he, Eagle Lion, he is actually only an employee, but he gets a good reputation because he's thrifty. If you mention too much, he can say: —But that's completely out of the question! And you have to be ashamed, and he really puts the pressure on you, because otherwise the next time he will give preference to someone else. If you let him speak first, you can keep the lead. With the first sum he mentions, he lays himself wide open. Now you can say: —But that's completely out of the question! Besides, you have found out about how high his budget is. Naturally, whoever's got the dough also has the power, and you can at best prevent the recording director from cheating you out of another hundred marks.

You won't get him up to four thousand, if he has the intention of paying a hundred and fifty. But remember this: In a negotiation never mention the first sum! He must lay himself wide open. And even if it takes half an hour: Never mention the first sum! —Why you're nothing but a half-Jew, says Jürgen Rühl.

Writers must: —in 1944 come from the East and go back to the East, be mowed down by violent death like a full ear of grain, listen into the quietness, store up quietly, be laconic and quiet, grow ever higher in the memory of descendants, and finally hold out the wreath of life to the people as its most sacred inheritance,—1945—not only lead the Germans in the direction of the future but help them attain it, despair in torment when no one gives them a pencil, choke down hoarsely a hot feeling, string pearls and cultivate their handwriting,—1946—throw others a light on the path, turn against calligraphers and begin to plow under the slave language, as clearers start from the beginning in language, substance, conception,—1949—serve the reduction of the evil in man, put a truth into every sentence, circle and circle through their hawkishness,—1950—tear off the mask of man, hold up the mask to us,—1951—lay out existential backgrounds or have them lacking, assemble montages in fascination,—1952—steal bibliophile editions from their friends, be good seismographs of spiritual catastrophes,—1955— be in form, like a sprinter at his starting blocks, let the paradox of human existence come forth, work suggestively on prerational planes, but also alienate, deform, cause the secret zones of concepts to vibrate,—1957—set in motion the process of continuing, ceaseless attempts at interpretation that liberate, state insights that can only have been attained by walkers on thin ice, take up into contents the technical civilization and its areas of problems, —1959—give whole generations of philologists nuts to crack,—1960— confront the spectator with the lack of understanding, with the questionability of life,—1961—plead for the positive, find that a cold is more difficult to describe than cancer,—1962—be mistrustful of words, change into the twenty-first century,—1963—control the Second Thermodynamic Theorem, require argumentative series of principles, record the situation, investigate grandfathers in efficiency apartments, try out standpoints,—1964—be precise, solve partial tasks according to definite requirements, consider hunger the proper mealtime for a writer, continue the report, bring language to the point of expressing itself, like to be kitschy,—1966—labor not without an overt political stance, destroy political theater, take language at its word,— 1967—fix a possible end-point to literary development, write badly in order to be really good, make language itself the point of focus,—be chasms of integrity, shoot their critics, at every reading call the listeners assholes, prepare their contribution to the achievement of basic positions,—1969—be at the forefront,—1970—produce wares, be works of art, not get uptight.

FRAGMENT FROM A STORY

MAX FRISCH
translated by A. Leslie Willson

FOR A WEEK NOT A DAY WITHOUT THUNDERSTORMS AND DOWNPOURS, THAT is the truth, and since Sunday the road has been closed. A slope had slipped, a part of the road blocked by rubble—

No honking from the valley.

You have been standing at the open window for an hour or longer, Herr Geiser, no one is contradicting you, you are alone at home.

There is just a gurgling.

A fieldglass (army model) is of no help at all these days, one screws it back and forth and screws it without finding any outline at all that could be brought into focus. The trusted instrument only enlarges the fog. If one holds it reversed before the eyes, then one's own eaves appear deceptively distant.

Today is Tuesday.

Lavender blooms even in the fog. As in a color film, without fragrance. One wonders what the bees do in such a summer.

If one trudges out into the countryside to look around in spite of dampness and fog, after a hundred steps one can't see one's own house anymore, only ferns in the fog. There have always been gullies and small landslides during long rains. For a time only the trees go on dripping, while the lightning flashes. Without thunder in the valley. A small wall in the garden (rock wall) has slid: pebbles in the lettuce, patties of gray clay under the tomatoes. Nothing else can be seen. Not one bird in the countryside. A telephone pole close by in the fog, the slowly sliding drops on two wires, the stakes for tomatoes in the fog. Perhaps it happened only yesterday or days ago—

Herr Geiser, what are you thinking?

When the rain lets up some, not completely stops, but thins out, so that it cannot be seen even against the darkness of the nearby pines, only felt on the skin if one holds out one's hand, there is no quiet: Only now does one hear the rushing sound in the valley. It must be brooks, many brooks, that otherwise don't exist: a steady rushing from the whole valley.

It is night, Herr Geiser, it is night. You have forgotten that it is night. No reason to be terrified. It is dark because it is night.

No landslide.

It ought to be possible to build a pagoda out of graham crackers without a thought in one's head and without hearing thunder or rain; perhaps it won't be a pagoda, but time passes anyway and one forgets what could happen.

You see, Herr Geiser, it works—

Well, it almost worked.

Nature knows no catastrophes, only man knows catastrophes (insofar as he survives them)—

The morning is already dawning, there is a gurgling around the house; you forgot that it's raining, and all the graham crackers are there still, it didn't get to be a pagoda, Herr Geiser, but Wednesday.

Or Thursday?

No honking in the valley.

In the winter, when it snowed, it was a black valley. Black the asphalt between the fields of snow. Black the footprints in the wet snow as it thawed, and black the granite. Snow plopped down from the wires, the wires were black. Snow in the woods, snow on the ground, but the trunks were black. Snow lay on the roofs too: black the chimneys. Only the post bus stayed yellow; it drove with chains, their tracks were black. Now and then a reddish willow, almost fox red, the ferns as though rusted, and when the brooks were not iced over: black the water between snow-covered rocks. The sky like ashes or lead; even the snow-covered mountains over the black woods did not look white, just pale. All the birds were black. Beneath the gutters it turned black from the dripping. Pine branches stayed green; black the pine cones in the snow. The nearby telephone pole (concrete) remained gray. The crosses in the small cemetery were black. Not even the sheep in the countryside were white, but dirty. A white snowman, built for the grandchildren, stood on black moss. Both shoes, set by the heater later, were black with dampness—

Herr Geiser, why are you thinking of that now?

Marriage with Elizabeth was happy.

Chop up kindling with the ax, fire in the fireplace, then carry up pail after pail, without stumbling on the stairs with the boiling water, pour pail after pail into the big tub, which isn't full even in half an hour, not even half-full, so that the water cools off continually, in the end it isn't even luke-warm, and other unpleasantnesses—

A salamander, once, in the bathtub.

On the other hand it makes sense to tidy up the drawers in case the whole mountain doesn't start sliding and bury the whole village; one can also clean out the medicine cabinet for once, throw away everything about which one no longer knows whether it is meant to be for itching or for uric acid, for mosquito bites, for weak heart, for migraines, for neurovegetative disturbances, etc.; no remedy for fog in the valley.

Why are you wearing a hat, Herr Geiser?

The federation and the canton (it can be assumed) do everything to restore the road, the only one in the valley.

Herr Geiser, you are wearing a hat.

Once before, in 1968, a piece of the road below the village slid away; the next morning the iron railing hung down crookedly into the gorge; a barrier was erected, ropes with red pennants on them, and for a whole summer traffic was held up by construction, though not interrupted. There have always been slides of that kind in this region.

Picking up the black receiver again and again in passing by in order then, as expected, not to hear even a dial tone, that's no way to occupy one's time either, as senseles as writing letters when there is no mail delivery.

Today is Wednesday.

By the way, it isn't true that no honking can be heard in the valley. There is only less honking. No post bus comes three times a day. The noisy trucks, which usually come into the valley with granite or wood, aren't on the road. Whoever has a car or a motorcycle above the place where the road has been blocked since Sunday can drive up as far as Spruga; he just can't get out of the valley.

There was a honk just now.

The salamander in the bathtub must have fallen in through the window, and it is still lying there: helpless, since it can't climb up the slick sides, on the slick bottom also almost helpless. Then it simply sits. Only when one threatens it a little with one's shoe does it thrash about as though out of duty; shortly thereafter it sits again, head lifted high. As though of stone; but yet it is alive, black with yellow spots, scaly skin, slimy.

What do you plan to do, Herr Geiser?

Of course, it could be that no one will call any more because one hasn't called anyone oneself for two weeks: then relief every time when after a bit of hesitation (what news is there after all to report) one picked up the black receiver and confirmed that it's just an interruption in the telephone service.

Herr Geiser, you were planning to do something.

The small landslide in the garden (pebbles in the lettuce) has not grown larger, and despite new downpours there haven't been any more slides. Perhaps here and there a single tree has fallen over, a pine or an old chestnut: Then its trunk lies down the slope with splintered crown, the black roots spread out in the air, the cliff lies naked to the day, shale or gneiss or a yellowish nail-shaped stratum, and when the roots no longer hold the brown earth, the rain washes it down the hill.

Kitty, the cat, won't touch the salamander.

A German summer visitor, professor of astronomy, knows a lot about his field, especially regarding the sun. Even if as a layman one doesn't understand most of it: A human life is nothing at all. Afterwards one carries out the empty glasses, grateful for the visit: one knows now approximately what protuberances are, and the wife of the solar scientist has brought a pot full of soup, minestrone, to warm up. Above all one knows, afterwards, that one's not crazy: other people, too, find that it's raining and raining.

Autumnal crocus already in August.

In winter, when it didn't snow, one could often go without a coat, it was so warm at noon, sky like that over the Mediterranean, no foliage, one saw more cliffs than in summer, the grapevines bare, the slopes brown with withered fern, the white trunks of the birches; only the nights would get cold, through the day the ground remained frozen under the rustling autumn leaves, but there were Christmases where one could sit out in the sun. The glaciers, that once stretched to Milan, were retreating everywhere, at the time there wasn't even perpetual snow in this region. The last patches of dirty snow in the shadows melted even on the heights, in August at the latest. All in all a green valley. When the canton came with a yellow bulldozer to widen the road, one saw moraines, debris from the big glaciers, in some places so hard that it had to be blasted; then they blew three times on a small horn and displayed a red flag, shortly afterwards there was a shower of gravel and detritus from the ice age.

Herr Geiser, why aren't you warming up the soup?

There never were volcanoes in the Tessin.

It still hasn't come to the point that one talks to the cat. Now and then a curse that one hardly hears oneself. One hears one's own steps in the house. It's enough to get up from the lexicon and pick up the cat so that she isn't always rubbing against one's pants legs. Without a word. Cats always fall on their feet. Of course, now she's yowling at the front door. Perhaps on the threshold one said: Get out! but then not another word in the house.

You were thinking of something, Herr Geiser:

In the winter one could go without a coat—

There never were volcanoes in the Tessin—

Today (Wednesday) the salamander is lying on the carpet in the living room, but it can be picked up with the shovel and tossed into the garden.

You remember, Herr Geiser:

One summer (1970?) the woodpeckers got an idea: They did not pick with their beaks on the bark of the old chestnuts, many chestnuts have cancer, the woodpeckers picked on the windowpanes, and more and more came, all obsessed with the glass. It became a fad. Even strips of glittering tinfoil did not scare them away for long. It became a nuisance. If one went to the window to scare them away, they simply chose another window; one couldn't stand everywhere and clap one's hands. It was more effective if one hit the granite table with a stick so that there was a loud pop; then they fled and waited in the branches all around. Shortly thereafter there were sounds again at this or that window; they flew up and could not hold on to the slick pane so that in their fluttering they picked only two or three times, in exceptional cases four times. The following summer they had forgotten all about it.

You often remember the same things, Herr Geiser.

Not a ladder in the house, but the spider webs over the steps must be removed, Elizabeth never manages to do it, no ordinary broom can reach. That requires a procedure that reveals the engineer: by screwing off the hand rail of the balustrade (not easy to do, with the rusted screws, but accomplished in two hours) and then (one has to have ideas) having tied a small broom on the long hand rail with wire—

Herr Geiser, that wasn't smart:

The spider webs are gone, but the balustrade remains without a hand rail, the old screws won't go back into the rust, and Elizabeth will be surprised: nothing but staves without a hand rail.

One can't read all day long.

A man remains a layman.

Everything is breaking, yesterday the thermometer, today chopping wood the glasses fell on the stone floor and broke, fortunately not the reading glasses; it makes one dizzy to look at everything through reading glasses, and without glasses one can hardly see the eaves of one's own house, the nearby pine in the fog, the slowly gliding drops on every wire or branch, everything else only in the memory.

Yes, Herr Geiser, the soup—

Loss of memory would be bad.

The salamander on the carpet in the living room must have been a different one; the other one is still lying in the bathtub: black with yellow spots, scaly skin, slimy. If it is put under the magnifying glass: a monster, legs splayed and the oversized head lifted high, the black eyes without gleam or gaze. No reaction to sound. Then suddenly, without a visible cause, the monster does move. Its awkward gait a kind of push-up, it's black tail remains motionless. It stomps stubbornly in a direction in which it never makes progress, and then it stops, head held high. As though of stone, although its pulse is throbbing. A monster—under the magnifying glass it reminds you of saurians (JARDIN DES PLANTES, Paris), a horrifying stupidity in all its limbs.

What would you like to know, Herr Geiser?

There never were saurians in the Tessin.

If one oneself knows, for example, about air conditioners or about Baghdad and vicinity: oh, all the things a lexicon doesn't know.

No thunder, just a gurgling.

Yesterday the sun almost shone, for minutes one could believe there **were** shadows under the pines, and that the sun could suddenly break through did not seem beyond the realm of possibility. It was still steaming out of the gorges, curtains of fog, suddenly the nearby pine could no longer be seen. Then one again surmised where the sun was located behind the drifting cloud cover; there were still occasional showers, but the rain glistened. That was yesterday. At night one saw occasional stars. In the early morning the birds around the house were noisy—

Now there is a gurgling again.

No idea why one has the pliers in one's left hand; later in the day, when one sees the crooked nail in the wall, no idea where one laid the pliers down. One forgets why one went to the cellar. One remembers only that during the night, sleepless with eyes open in the darkness, one knew for hours what it was one absolutely had to check on. Instead of that, suddenly the pliers appear. What now? Water in the cellar as always with long rains, but that wasn't what one had to check on. That one knows, that's not bad. It has nothing to do with the pliers that one nevertheless keeps in one's hand just in case.

Herr Geiser, what is bad?

A salamander doesn't hurt anything.

You are alone at home, Herr Geiser, nobody will notice you looking for a word and not finding it, a foreign word.

Once toward evening a stray dog in the countryside, a mutt sniffing around the house again. Finds nothing and lifts its leg here and there anyway—

Coherence was the word.

You see, Herr Geiser, you know without a lexicon what that means, and you don't need to get annoyed at your son-in-law who lives in Basel and is such a know-it-all.

Coherence, the coherence factor.

The dog interrupted you.

Coherence, the coherence factor.

The dog belongs to no one in the village, not even to those Dutchmen who walk through the rain in bluish rain slickers; nobody wants it, still it comes often into the countryside and looks for scent marks in the streaming rain.

Today is Wednesday.

The tank was filled in July. That's what one was going to check on in the cellar. One remembers tipping the men in gray overalls. 5000 liters. But heating oil is no good if the electric current is off—

You know that, Herr Geiser.

In winter one could often go without a coat, but the nights got cold, in winter one saw more cliffs than in summer, the federation and the canton did everything to keep the roads in shape, all in all a poor valley, panning gold in the streams never had paid off, there were woodcutters, there were quarries, in August there were shooting stars or one heard a screech owl, a reservoir was not planned, twice a week a blond butcherwoman drove up through the valley, many stalls abandoned and collapsed, the fern high as a man, there were lizards and salamanders, but even when it rained for weeks they never grew larger than lizards and salamanders.

Herr Geiser, what worries you?

It isn't the stray dog in the countryside that interrupted you; it must have been the pliers.

Elizabeth would know.

It was something else, Herr Geiser, that you want to find in the lexicon that is lying on the table.

You stand at the open window, you're not crazy, Herr Geiser, you don't see any saurians in the countryside—

Why are you throwing dishes?

The doorbell rang, many times, even yesterday. Perhaps good news. Anyway the electricity is on again, otherwise the doorbell wouldn't ring.

Herr Geiser, why don't you open the door?

In the village they'll be saying that Herr Geiser wears a hat in the house and throws dishes out the window when the doorbell rings, Herr Geiser is crazy.

Now the doorbell isn't ringing any more.

They're worried about you, Herr Geiser, because you don't turn on the light at night—

The electricity is on again.

Why, Herr Geiser, don't you turn on the light?

Sometimes (like yesterday), with fog in the lower valley, when the moon is shining down on it, it can look like a whitish lake, a fjord between black mountains, a jagged ocean bay; the only thing missing then would be a ship lying at anchor below the village, a cutter, a whaling ship—

The village stands unscathed.

Herr Geiser, they saw you at the window.

That wasn't today but yesterday. It was during the night, otherwise they wouldn't have come with flashlights when the sun is shining, and the sun is shining today.

Everything is back again.

What are you going to do, then, Herr Geiser, when they come back and break down the door to see what is wrong with you?

The oil burner is humming again too.

Herr Geiser, someone is talking to you.

. . .

(1974)

THE MORNING STAR
Excerpt

EBERHARD HILSCHER
translated by David J. Ward

Perils and Peregrinations

WALTHER AND YOUNG DIETRICH WERE RIDING FOR THEIR LIVES. ALL THE while, it seemed as if life were just a game to Sir Walther; although their pursuers were close behind, he held his steed at somewhat less than a full gallop. Quite calmly he kept abreast of his page, whose dun gave its utmost and still did not advance with sufficient speed.

With their golden trimmings and bulging sacks they had attracted the attention of seven robber knights. The bandits entertained hopes of rich bounty and redoubled their exertions to overtake the strapping black steed. Muted cries rang out, hooves beat at a presto. The distress of the pursued grew mightily. Oh, if only the celestial cloud-gatherer would blow a blanket of fog across the highway, or part the waves of the Danube's flow.

In a terrible panic, Dietrich turned off through a narrow opening in the wood, caught hold of a low-hanging branch, and clambered up into a tree. His dun loped on a few paces, then drew up, much relieved.

Sir Walther swore. He found himself in the unusual predicament of being able to slip away on a fleet mount, yet not being permitted to do so for reasons of social prestige, for he was compelled to set an example of manly courage for his page high in the foliage. But was it not foolhardy, alone and lacking sufficient armor, to attempt to defy a superior force of many swords and steeds? Of what use was his "knightly honor" in the face of death?

Our poet, meanwhile, had little time for such ponderings: Even now the first of his opponents had set his lance and was bearing down on him at a gallop. Walther raised his spear as well, rode forward, and emerged from the cover of an elm. In the course of his brief advance, he gained no particular speed, while the bandit flew at him like the blade of an ax. A violent collision and fatal fall seemed inevitable. At the last instant, however, the shining black steed responded to a nudge by its master's knee and dodged to the side. The robber knight rammed into the trunk of the elm full force and fell senseless to the ground.

After this little exercise in agility, Walther found himself in much the same situation as Hercules of Alcaeus doing battle with the Hydra of Ler-

na: In the place of the one monster he had done away with, there immediately appeared two more. The highwaymen could not pass through the
narrow opening in a broad front to encircle our undaunted hero, but even
against their columns of two there was little hope of success for a single
combatant. All he could do was to harass those who blocked his path by
swinging his spear like a scythe and compensate for his steed's lack of
weight with maneuverability, until he had to take on one of his attackers
in single combat. A mighty crash, and Walther saw lances splintering—all
was lost, for before he could draw his sword, the third bandit drew back
for a thrust upon his exposed flank . . .

When our poet looked up hesitantly a moment later, he did not believe
his eyes. Both the robber knights lay motionless on the gravel of the sylvan
path. A bit farther on he made out a gigantic figure, which sent another of
his opponents flying from his saddle with a blunt spear shaft and drove the
remaining trio across to the river. At that moment, the page, Dietrich,
slipped from his tree and cried out: "Victory is ours, milord! Just look
how the scoundrels flee before us!"

Indeed, their enemies were quitting the field of battle. They were being
pursued by the unknown warrior who pressed them ever closer to the river
bank. Suddenly two horses crumpled, slipped down the bank, and tumbled,
along with their heavily armored riders, into the stream, from which they
did not again emerge. The last of the bandits made an effort to flee into a
thicket, but he felt the slash of a sword upon the harness supporting his
iron chain mail and suddenly found himself standing on the Nibelungen
highway in his underbreeches.

While the triumphant hero forced the remaining rascals to cast all their
weapons into the water, Walther discovered black half-moons and flecks
of gold on the giant's blue shield. Now he knew whom he and Dietrich had
to thank for their rescue. And much like the bold Hadmar von Kuenring
in days of yore, Walther felt inclined to see in the celestial swordsman a
hero from extraterrestrial realms. Fortunate is he who enjoys such pa-
tronage!

As he strode toward them, the irresistible warrior said: "Well, what do
you know, the singer from Vienna. Your mount there bears nearly as much
gold as the crowned head of Alexander of old. Have you been named lord
treasurer, or are you on the trail of the Queen of Sheba?"

"I am in your debt," remarked the poet softly. "How may I repay you
for your assistance?"

The celestial swordsman laughed. In a curiously melodic voice, he answered. "Add the horses of these vanquished to your treasures, but keep
the means by which you came to them a secret. Travel on to the court on
the Rhine, and if, perchance, you should encounter milady Alayta—give
her my regards."

Walther and young Dietrich, who now sat upon a fleet mount taken from the day's spoils, and who led the spare nags along on a tether, spoke for a long while about their patron and protector from mysterious realms.

Toward noon, the sky brightened. The high road between Krems and Bechlaren grew lively with traffic in both directions. Students and minstrels in colorful outfits passed by, conversing and singing. Pilgrims with *chapérons*, long cloaks, and staffs streamed past. And in their midst maneuvered riders: heroes in search of adventure, scurrying messengers, and elegantly clad gentlemen of state. The pace of all this traffic was slowed by a train of covered wagons, in front of which horses, draped with pennons, bearing sacks of grain, ambled along. Several merchants in green caps and red shoes hurried to and fro.

This company of traders was escorted by men at arms; this caused many travelers to adjust their pace to its slow trot. Sir Walther decided to do so as well, although the company of noisy troubadours from districts of Vienna soon began to annoy him. These wandering musicians recognized him, of course, and made a point of mocking him. For example, they told of a poet who harped upon the locks of a lady's hair, while she connived against him, or they warbled the sarcastic ditty: "The veils about her form I see / fall quickly to the ground. / From her hammy little cheeks / to her lovely knees so round / a paradise she offered me / —breasts in which I'd drown."

Before the poet had time to grow angry at them, a merchant approached him to ask whether the horses he was leading were available for a reasonable price. The transaction, which was accomplished without difficulty, induced the two traders to continue their conversation. Their new companion was one Volkmar Dusentherz, who introduced himself as a dealer in linens and wines from Frankfurt, whereupon Walther inquired with some interest about the rights of the citizens there. "You must know, of course, that I encouraged Austrian aldermen to restrict several areas of their duke's authority, and to think first of the good of their city."

"That I call astonishing," declared the merchant, "for if I am not mistaken, you are yourself of the nobility, attached to a princely court."

"My lord is the greatest bard in the world!" interjected Dietrich.

"Wilt thou hold thy tongue, boy!" Walther concealed a touch of embarrassment, then explained: "These pages always feel compelled to exaggerate. Just between the two of us, I did achieve some modest notoriety because of my efforts at the court to engage my gift of song in the cause of freedom."

Dusentherz remarked: "That is equally astonishing. And you met with success?"

"Not enough, unfortunately."

"Perhaps you had set your goal too high. Would you permit me to ask what meaning freedom has for you?"

"The very highest: I want to be able to speak out truths and appeals to reason without fear of harm and to be able to do what I wish, although it is clear that my wishing cannot be absolutely free."

"Do you take into account the limitations imposed by Christian teachings?"

"No, only other people's need for freedom. Although if I were wealthy like yourself, young man, I would cast my words about without restraint, like lances."

The fifty-year-"young" man smiled. This bold speech pleased him, and he himself now began to speak of the efforts of the citizenry of Frankfurt to exploit the presence of the head of the Hohenstaufen family to acquire duty and market authority for the surrounding countryside in return for their hospitality. Obviously, it appeared advisable, in accordance with English and French precedents, to ally with the crown in order to keep the nobility off their backs.

This made sense to the poet. He offered his services in advocating this sort of idea at the royal court on the Main, whereupon Volkmar Dusentherz invited him to lodge with him in Frankfurt.

That evening the company of travelers reached Bechlaren. After their meal, the guests called for the coarse refrains of the minstrels and not for the artful chansons of courtly love. A downcast Sir Walther soon departed for his chamber. Even so, the strains of some stupid refrain about "hours of love" and "breasts billowing beneath her blouse" reached him from the taproom for quite a while longer.

These fools, thought the poet. As if a woman's bosom constituted the very navel of the world!

Of Wealthy Poverty

That same day, two gentlemen wended their way along the Nibelungen road in the direction of Bechlaren. They were wearing long cowls with broad sleeves, and on their feet, sandals. Both this attire and this form of locomotion seemed to be unfamiliar to the man on the right; he tugged cautiously at his robe from time to time and with each step set his foot upon the ground much as a prowler would. And he slipped his hood on and off over his bare rounded pate, which was surrounded at the temples and in back by bushy brown hair.

This domed head, with its mane, was—just as much as the St. Stephen's cathedral with its pointed cap—among the major sights of the city of Vienna. But is a landmark allowed to change its location? Of course! In fact, it *must* do so, if the powers that be find it "decayed" or "dangerous." And precisely that is what had happened to the luminary of sciences in the Babenbergian lands. Duke Leopold mistrusted a man who offered hospitality to conspirators, dared to perform dark experiments, and could at any time serve his regent a poisoned potion. For this reason, he had discharged his cup-bearer from the court.

The wise minister did not regard this all too tragically. In accordance with the Biblical exhortation, he sold all his useful goods, distributed the proceeds among the poor, and joined the company of an itinerant Catharist preacher whose teachings came from far away and led far away. Not by any chance into the countryside of Bulgaria, in which Pater Bogomil founded his churchless congregation three hundred years ago? Now first of all, the two wayfarers set their steps to the west and not to the south and in their conversation competed with one another in exceeding the heresies of the aforementioned forefather.

Haimo: "It distresses me that the founder of our brotherhood shunned wine. It is particularly the juice of the vine that causes to rise, in a double sense, that which lies in the depths, for which reason prophets and creative spirits knew how to value it highly. Fortunately, an ampulla beneath my robe conceals a modest supply of this gift of the gods."

Preacher: "It is Satan's gift, Brother. Even back in Paradise, Adam was tempted by strong drink to fornicate with the Mother of Man and fall into sin."

Haimo: "The things you say! You convert the famous apple into grapes, make the one into the many, and the many into the one bestower of knowledge. Conclusion: Lo, he saw her private parts and she whispered: 'Private! Depart . . .' I find the garden of Venus more appealing when Bacchus hasn't spat upon my members."

Preacher: "How can you make a laughing stock of such evil things! Our Pater Bogomil battled with demons and commanded that evil must be hunted down wherever it opens its jowls. It appears in abysmal baseness, deceit, and savagery, vilifies the pure and whips the sea of passions like the serpent of Midgard."

Haimo: "Poison, my dear Brother, is at work in all things. Only the dosage determines whether a thing is poisonous or not."

Preacher: "The foulest of poison is spewed forth by the clergy. The stones of their churches are clad with gold, while the faithful go around in rags; the rich feast upon the splendor of their altars, while the poor starve. In the houses of God there dwells no god."

Haimo: "In the name of Heaven, Hell, and the Body of Our Lord! You would restrict the Almighty's rights to residence?"

Preacher: "And you pronounce oaths?"

Haimo: "Forgive me! It was done only in the belief that coarse speech is becoming to the German tongue. It is likely that even God used this language when he wanted to drive Adam and Eve with strong words of condemnation from Paradise following their wanton revelry."

Preacher: "It was the voice of the Devil that spoke there, teaches Pater Bogomil. The Eternal revealed itself only in the Gospels."

Haimo: "That may be so, although litanies from the Old Testament reappear in the New. Would the Savior recite from the words of Beelzebub? To come to your assistance, Brother, I should compare the Biblical lyre with the stream of breath that serves both to warm and to cool us. By the way, I fail to understand your denial of the God of the Patriarchs."

Preacher: "I am miserable because of the imperfect Creation, and I refuse to place blame for it on any god. We must believe in a Creation by Lucifer."

Haimo: "I believe what I know. And I know of a world that is beautiful in its imperfection, because it challenges mortals to strive for completeness. This task is given unto us: to discover the secrets of Nature, to learn the fairy-tale languages of the fish and birds, to penetrate the veils of the Mystery of the Universe and, in doing so, not to scorn the power of wine to give us wings."

Preacher: "And now you jest, while I mourn over the existence of Existence."

Haimo (drawing forth from his cloak a goblet): "Why? Even the Apostle John commanded us to be joyful. Just drink, Brother, and sing with me the Psalm: 'In poverty through life we pass / wealth comes in the hereafter. / From time to time, though, raise your glass / and bring forth Heaven's laughter.' "

Two gentlemen journeyed along the road in the direction of Bechlaren.

experiments in immersion

i too journey. without wine. a fine pair of hypocrites, those two in their robes, who in the above assert that they are poor. treasured more than spirits, dearer than they, are few things to the black marketeers in the resselpark, vienna, fourth district. threatened am i, although i've made off with no treasures on the shoemaker's shining steed.

query: why am i walking? because i gave up, when something came up that i wasn't able to get up. my desire to see the girl's body once again just like when we went swimming in the danube. will she laugh at me? ah, me, if only i might paint her as danae having seen her as venus!

i may. she arrives, undresses, invoking shades of correggio, rembrandt, titian. valerian would be required in veritable streams to extinguish the flames within me and the thought of danae's lap beneath jupiter's golden showers. now there's a stirring of the corpora cavernosa, which is why my brush executes a drachm-dance in a blond rhombus on the canvas. meanwhile, i declaim bright phrases. heine: "the body of woman is a poem"; mörike: "for such is love"; kästner: "don't get all worked up over every little thing that comes down the drain." the girl responds pertly: "i'm your next victim, cupido!" and makes inviting gestures.

ovid! the memory disturbs me. if what the roman poet describes in the seventh book of the "amores" were to take place now: inability to partake of the available, passion in love's position. anxiety brings about downfall, in the middle of an embrace. it rubs me the wrong way that there's nothing there to rub her.

"weak worm," remarks the girl. "quid me ludis? your painting here is like egg with mustard sauce on it. you give me dead stumps and call them timeless blossoms. there you go, skulking off with your tail between your legs. what *can* you do, anyway? you have to have something to offer."

"i'll get over it," i say.

i rue my ineptitude. my trek to the north is dreary beyond measure. realities: damaged roads, blown-up bridges, workers dismantling factories, harsh food rationing. illusions: pâté de foie gras, omelette with champignons, meringue pie, poached trout. —stout blows had to be administered just outside bechlaren, where bandits demand my shoes of me. with karate chops i propel them into muddy ditches under some elms, singing the twenty-third psalm as i resume my journey, and receive alms from charitable brethren.

crossing the danube, elbe, and spree within a month. suffering from hunger, nausea, lack of shelter, only expressible in last words. country-pastor conversations about partition plans of victorious allied powers. what's ahead? stern supervision of german reparations, the fixing of fluid borders. especially the franks, etymologically bound to freedom, demand separation of the areas left of the rhine and organization of spheres of influence.

spears of wheat were ripening in the fields when they concluded, in paragraph fourteen of the potsdam agreement, to look upon germany during the duration of the occupation as a "single economic entity." singularly insightful people look toward more widespread democracy and the assertion of proletarian sound thinking. council bringing regional leaders together in munich brings up east-german proposal of a central government, a matter, however, which west-german delegates would rather not discuss.

rumblings in the allied command central. blindness in the lightning bolt on the western horizon. mighty oak transformed into tiny motes. we have been splinters for over seven-hundred-fifty years, ring-pored, coarse-barked chunks, tinder for the fires of war. why the battle cries again so soon? the recent deaths were not enough? acknowledgment of desperation: the chaos-dragon could not be tamed with peace.

to attain a bit of peace, i leap into the river. yearning for death and security in the elemental, whose depths no longer contain anything mysterious. resolution through dissolution, eternal calm, timelessness . . .

uplifting revelations while sinking, shade-like perceptions into bio-synthetic processes that began two billion years ago in the slimy global bouillon. skittering sunlight, a dancing atom-quadrillion, in each ten grams of moisture, experimental arrangement: 6000-volt sparks agitate $CH_4 + NH_3 + H_2O$. concretely speaking: ultra-violet radiation caresses the primeval mixture of methane, ammonia, water. starter stage is activated for chemical transformations and swings into the organic. run-off of amino and nucleic acids, lipo- and polysaccharides, energies cause clustering into droplets of albumen, microstructures of the life's-procession. ionic nature-philosophers, sixth century b.c., honor the sea even then as giver of life.

which stage of development shall i choose? sponge, coral, shrimp, star-fish? since no wine-god appears to remodel me into a dolphin, i snap open penknife and define myself as fish with spiked dorsal fin. awakening to the adventure of weightlessness in fluid space, hovering, free of pressure. refreshed by gliding through the shadow of the water plants, swirls of pebbles, limestone mountains of mussels, that lift like angels' wings in chagall watercolors. brief stretch of boredom in green undergrowth, above which rounded reflection of sky glimmers with edges the colors of the spectrum.

somebody flapping around over there? naiad or triton? thoughts must be perceivable here. skin vibrates and hears signals from the fish world: barking, growling, rumbling, croaking, peeping, bleating, peu à peu, i begin to discern the high-frequency alphabet and to understand it, when companions approach. modern hydro-myths.

tufted-fin: "hurry, hurry! high roads to humanity, that's my hobby."

sword-fin: "reading freud gives rise to desire for masculinity. with awareness comes success. organ of reproduction grows, female becomes male."

baby-blue carp: "mimicry happens without witchcraft. push nerve-buttons, squeeze pigment cells out and in to produce any color you could wish for. o no, with awareness comes failure!"

while cyprinodont pales, disappears, i blush bright red. female turns up. "careful how you use those colors," she hums at 25,000 hertz, "ultrasonic vibes wash everything out to white!" —in courting-carousel, i turn circles around her. circumspect silence brings acceptance, excesses of potency in the fertility-fluid of the species. synchronized fanning of fins, symbolic posturings, ritualistic dances. development of artistic grace, rhythm, beauty in affectionate play, that renders me tipsy. tenderly dip we, creatures, into the sediment that creates new life.

o happy metamorphosis, beyond the sorrows of mankind! myriads of fishes swirl around me, bestowing a sense of physical immenseness. since silurian ages we've been streaming along.

i am the stream.

Frankfurt Potpourri

There was the stream! In a graceful curve the Main flowed by at the foot of the hill where the fortress stood. The water did not feel aroused by wind or melting snow, did without surface ripples, just lay there, leisurely, basking in the sun. Clear reflections of towers, piers, and bowers of Würzburg appeared in the running wetness. This peaceful, friendly panorama pleased Sir Walther such that he was moved to speak of eternal calm.

"In the name of Heaven!" cried Volkmar Dusentherz. "We need fresh breezes. You see my two sailing vessels there? At midday we plan to hoist anchor."

During the journey downstream the poet could not get his fill of looking out over the ship's prow. Several times the river seemed to disappear at the horizon; but it was just changing direction and offered up surprising vistas over cliff-ridden terrains with stands of trees, sloping vineyards, cliffside bastions, and villages. Along the channel numerous craft approached and slipped away again. Nearly every one was resplendent with colorful, billowing square sails, although from on board the calls of the oarsmen echoed across the water. Aside pot-bellied cogs bearing fortress-like structures, dinghies and cutters dipped and coasted, their prows displaying decorative woodwork.

The next day, as the ship traffic grew more and more congested, the battlements of Frankfurt appeared on the right bank. Dusentherz had his freighter steered up to a mooring below the Mainzer Gasse, where he supervised the unloading and once again surveyed his acquisitions: cloth, skins, spices, and horses. A little later on, he rode with Sir Walther to his abode on the Hirschgraben.

The poet was quartered in a room off the garden, from which he could see past city wall and fortifications and far out onto the plains beyond. The afternoon sun shimmered through small, amber-colored windows, illuminating climbing plants on the sill, an expansive bed, lamps, and chests. There were still logs in the fireplace from the previous winter. Maidens brought in a tub, attended the guest during his bath, and offered their services for any "courtesy" he might desire. Things were starting off quite well indeed!

The following morning Walther complimented his host on the care he had provided, whereupon Dusentherz explained with a chuckle that, though he was lord over a thousand ladies' hearts, he had no influence at the Duke's court. For this reason he considered himself fortunate to be permitted to offer a place under his roof to an artistic minstel, to whom the greatest of princes gladly lent an ear.

The merchant continued chattily: "Do you know which form gives me the most pleasure? The most useful one. I care little for love songs—after all, what does one accomplish with them? Of course, you can turn the heads of young girls, who can be won just as easily with money. Verses for the persuasion of the simple and mighty, on the other hand, are more than worth their weight in precious stones. The value of a verse grows with its practical utility; which is why you should present truly pithy maxims to Milord Philipp."

This was more easily said than done. In the court all was a-bustle: Emissaries arrived from all corners of the globe, carried on urgent conversations in the palace, and then waited weeks for some event that was always postponed. From inns and courtyards resounded the sounds of foreign tongues, bringing about confusion and misunderstanding, until people resorted finally to grotesque gesticulations. Moods were understood better than meanings.

In spite of the demand for artists to entertain at the court, Walther von der Vogelweide received, upon visiting the antechamber of the Great Hall, the suggestion that he first go to the ducal chancery, and there place his request to perform through the proper channels. He declared this to be the very pinnacle of effrontery, swore, demanded, threatened—and finally had to content himself with submitting a written request.

While young Dietrich inquired of the clerk each day, whether a concert by his master had been scheduled, the latter ambled through the city, trying to forget his rage. He heard the crescendo of the boatmen along the banks of the Main, listened to refrain-like commendations of the shopkeepers and the fishwives in the market square, or observed women in a workshop on the Snarrgasse processing threads of flax, wool, and gold. On occasion he would also make his way to the Imperial tournament grounds and watch knightly contests, because he hoped to meet influential acquaintances of his there.

This involuntary inactivity vexed the poet and made him conscious of how unfree he was in his new-found freedom. At the same time, his will grew firm to fight doggedly for recognition. But only when he pondered upon the spiritual needs of secular dignitaries did Fortuna tug at his coattails.

In the vestibule of the little Salvator Chapel he discovered Prince Philipp, the papal legate and bishop of Sutri, and—hallelujah—the shepherd of the diocese of Passau, the Honorable Wolfger, all partaking of the mass. What a happy coincidence! Walther could not wait for the service to end. He hurried to the portal and placed himself such that the black-cloaked man with the white hair would, without a doubt, have to notice him.

"Ah, there he is, the man whose lips give comfort to so many!" said Wolfger. "The heart alone knows its sorrows, nor should any man meddle in its joys. This excellent troubador wishes to serve you, Philipp."

The duke stopped, raised his eyebrows, and remarked: "How? He won't delay doomsday."

"Try him anyway," advised the cleric. "Our knight is skilled at dealing with women, and composes songs according to Ovid's requirement: 'Quam volui, nota fit arte mea.' And that is saying a great deal!"

Now Lord Philipp smiled. He looked the artist over more attentively and said: "You are welcome in the castle this evening."

Walther bowed and rejoiced as he watched the group depart. This double favor gave wings to his feet. He whistled between his fingers like a boy and ran to the Hirschgraben. In his garden room he threw himself onto the bed, drank two goblets of Magyar wine, and began to croon in a high-spirited singsong: "High and higher! Rank and melody! The proud shall kiss the dust. My psalm is my salvation." As he was enjoying expressing his thoughts aloud thus, he went on: "This day by the waters I sat and / I heard what all the fishes were saying. Coarse scales' creations / their high-pitched vibrations. / They squeaked about life being blatant / destructive curiosity: It mixes / its poison with wellsprings of goodness. / Although each man finds that the cosmos / is chaotic, the one who preserves us / from a worse fate is often the art-boss. /

"The simplest of minds understands / when someone says: 'It is I who commands!' / But what mankind has truly a lack of / is reason. The Germans will follow / only rulers and never just regents. / —Philipp, we call on you now to take up / the crown. Bring an end to our sorrow!" /

The poet fell silent, astonished. The playfully spun sentences had a sense to them; they could be arranged in strophes and set to music! He reached for his harp and composed—strumming, plucking, and humming—the lyrical

Reichsmelodie.

That evening he performed the canto in the Hall of Banners of the Imperial Court at Frankfurt. Seldom had a song received such applause in these chambers. The word was a call and the hour and time for this call had come. Lord Philipp appointed the author First Singer of the Court and entrusted him (upon the recommendation of Bishop Wolfger) with an important mission.

A PART OF NEW YORK

UWE JOHNSON
translated by A. Leslie Willson

THE UPPER WEST SIDE IS A PART OF MANHATTAN IN NEW YORK, BUT NOT a part with a charisma. A quarter like Greenwich Village at least has its myth, just as such names as Trastevere in Rome, Montmartre in Paris, and Pöseldorf in Hamburg are at once known from a legend, from an image formed by memory and fantasy, which allows a general familiarity. A part of a city need not be famous for this to happen. Ordinary city neighborhoods can be represented by a trait; they are characterized; their reputation gives a vague idea of their social climate. The Upper West Side in New York, in Manhattan, presents no such concept. The surrounding neighborhoods furnish many facets for description: To the north Morningside Heights is named after a park and after a street which overlooks Harlem. In Morningside Heights are Columbia University—which is buying up one block after another and is becoming a city in the city—famous churches, and a hospital which not only determine the features of the neighborhood but also life in it. The area south of the Upper West Side offers the Lincoln Center—the opera, the philharmonic orchestra, a theater—rising land costs, urban renewal, an enormous complex of apartment buildings, modern and multi-storied. But the Upper West Side can be introduced only by its location. It is located in the northwest part of the island of Manhattan, between 70th and 110th Streets, bordered on the east by Central Park, on the west by the Hudson River. North and south the streets run along Central Park: Columbus Avenue, Amsterdam Avenue, West End Avenue, Riverside Drive, and obliquely through the pattern of squares runs Broadway. General particulars about the area are as valid as their opposite: In the side streets are slums. In the side streets are middle-class residences, polished as gems. Seen from the air the high-rise buildings along Central Park and the river seem to dam up the area, an irregular combination of towers and huts. How many blocks does that make? Not quite two hundred. How many people are there on a block? Almost a thousand, more than is usual in the world. What kind of people live there, does the area belong to one group more than to another? In the majority are whites of various extractions. Not counting the Jews they make up a half, the Jews furnish a fourth, the Latin Americans are a sixth, the Negroes an eighth, the remainder are composed of Japanese and Chinese and others. All are Americans, but all the groups cling fast to their languages, to their cultures. They do not associate with one another, and the confusing mixture is not settled; its individual parts come and go, do not endure as if at home. The Upper West Side does not even have a name. Once Dutchmen founded a village here. It was called Bloomingdale, "Valley of Flowers," but it is no longer a valley of flowers, rather it is a residential city built up as closely as possible, and left over is only the insipid description from the geography. The language proves that the neighborhood lacks an independent identity, not to mention the coherence of a community, for when the inhabitants speak of the neighborhood among themselves they call it "The Area," as though it were undeveloped and uninhabited or else was only an accidental collection of houses, an accidental juxtaposition of people, not a neighborhood but a place of diversities.

The obvious difference is between riches and poverty, the pleasant life and a difficult life. The life of affluence is represented by the streets Central Park West, West End Avenue, and Riverside Drive, old-fashioned, respectable, tenaciously defended heirlooms. Central Park West looks upon a carefully cultivated landscape, artificial lakes, mirrored clouds, hilly greens, outcropping rocks, meadows, paths winding under open sky to the even better address of Fifth Avenue, which languishes radiantly under its watering cans. West End Avenue, right next to the Hudson, is a deep, almost gloomy canyon between brick monstrosities and it bares the essence of riches: the canopies before the portals, the liveried doormen who whistle at taxis for their employers, the clean-swept sidewalks, the composed quiet which wishes it could prevent heavy truck traffic. The third of these streets, Riverside Drive, is counted among the famous streets of the world, but it also is not a symbol of the Upper West Side; it is joined to the neighborhood, but did not grow up with it.

Riverside Drive, along the Hudson River, the "street on the river," laid out in the 80's of the last century, is the inner edge of an extended artificial landscape, beginning with a promenade on the river and extending landward with an expressway with divided lanes and really garden-like approaches, then with a broad, hilly park forty blocks long (a railroad line passes under the park), with monuments, playgrounds, playing fields, fields for lounging on, and bench-bordered walking paths. Only then is the park framed by the real street, which is curved in many places, swings over attractive rises, toward the houses stretches out narrow exit fingers behind more green islands, a unique thing in Manhattan, an exhibition of the art of gardening, a street that looks upon trees, water, scenery. It all revolved around the view. It was the view that was appropriated. Because the residences along Riverside Drive, hardly one under ten stories, most of them more than that, were built for the new aristocracy of the nineteenth century, for the new money, railroad money, mining money, oil money, speculative money, the money of the industrial explosion. Riverside Drive was to surpass Fifth Avenue as a residential area, with copiously decorated façades, Oriental, Italian, Egyptian, in an always magnificent style, the eight-room suites, the servants' quarters, concealed delivery entrances, the solemn foyers, employees in uniform, along with the exclusive view of nature. On all of Riverside Drive there is not a single shop, no stores, only two or three hotels, and those, of course, residences for permanent guests. Where business resided it wanted to be of noble birth. Here there lived such figures as William Randolph Hearst, the Axel Springer of the U.S.A., the true inventor of yellow journalism. And it is true that he lived at first on three floors which he later rebuilt into a three-storied room. He had his own private elevator, then even more floors until he finally bought all twelve in 1913. An address on Riverside Drive signified in those days wealth and credit, power and princely rank. It was a street for white, Anglo-Saxon protestants. They were joined after World War I by those Jews to whom the once exclusive quarters of Harlem no longer seemed equal to their social level and by immigrants from the Lower East Side whose incomes had in the meantime become adequate for the prestige of this address, emigrants who had "arrived." In the 1930's came the Jews from Germany, in the beginning with their possessions in boxes, then without luggage, then from the German-occupied countries of Europe, and after the war came the survivors of the concentration camps and citizens of the state of Israel, unchangeable Europeans who had not come to terms with the deprivations, the climate, the siege of Israel, so that on Riverside Drive and on West End Avenue a Jewish colony was assembled, bound together not only by family and religion but also by the memory of a lost Europe. (A woman, an emigrant from Karlovy Vary, whose memory of her homeland is utterly spoiled, speaks of homesickness for Karlovy Vary, of homesickness for Europe, of the taste of the bread of her homeland. She has been living on Riverside Drive for fifteen years.) Then also the younger and better situated Jews moved into the suburbs north of the city, for the sake of the children.

250   UWE JOHNSON

Riverside Drive, however, did not surpass Fifth Avenue as a residential
area—the widow of President Kennedy does not live here. Here live the
pensioners, people of modest incomes, the employed class, intellectuals,
student groups. (A butcher's apprentice refuses to move here—he believes
in his own lawn in front of his own home.) Most apartment buildings are
still too fine to have dark-skinned citizens as tenants; Negroes may manage
them, keep them up, operate the elevator, polish the brass. The grandiose
architectural hulks still seem fortresses of prosperity, made even more respectable by weathering, but the age of neglect abides in them, too. Many
of the manorial suites of rooms have been divided into frugal efficiency
apartments. The steam heat is leaky, there is knocking in the plumbing,
all kinds of interrelated defects, and in the foyers that smooth layer of
dirt over the marble paneling and the aging furniture against which water
and brooms are no longer effective. In some buildings the rents have been
frozen by law since the war. The doormen, who are not only supposed to
greet the tenants but also to keep away burglars and kidnappers, can meanwhile seldom be found, and very often the manned elevators have been
exchanged for automatic ones, in which the riders examine a stranger
cautiously. However it is not easy to find an empty apartment in these
buildings, for reasons other than skin color and income. The ceilings are
high, the floor plan old-fashioned, the walls muffle noise; the management
takes care of trash and repairs. The street is considered practically safe
(suspicion greets the homosexuals who wait for one another in the summer
at the Soldiers and Sailors Monument and call it the Wedding Cake). And
the street is one of the quiet ones. At the most it witnesses two parades
a year. To be sure, the almost uniform sound of motors encroaches from
the express highway on the river, in ocean-like waves, filtered two
seasons of the year by the greenery in the park, but except for rush hours
(and the weekends before and after national holidays) Riverside Drive
itself is a street with local traffic, at night empty and silent, until 6 a.m.
when the first people head for work and the hollow whistles of the train
beneath the bulge in the park penetrate lighter sleep. But the view is un-
assailable.

The view is nothing more than another river bank, a piece of the State
of New Jersey, but the bank rises steeply and loftily, and the width of the
river can blur the architectural wasteland on the other side into a landscape mirage, into the illusion of openness and distance. The river under
the unpretentious sky moves on to the ocean close by, presents slowly
passing ships, at night foghorns, green, gray, blue colors framed by those
of the park, a festive view. But the river is so poisoned by industrial refuse

and wastes that the fish die even far to the north, and a swim is perilous for human beings, though not because of the current. The river collects the light of the sky and dyes the clouds overhead with its vapors, but the air is thickly saturated with sulphur dioxide, carbon monoxide, and solid smoke particles, which after all assist in coloring sunsets immensely. The early morning sun reddens the opposite shore, and in a line with the prospect of nature manufacturers plant unavoidable letters which are supposed to impress the dreamers even on this street with who doubtless offers the Best for Baking. (One peace-loving and composed lady has announced that some night with her husband's gun she is going to blow up that host of red neon which crazily, unceasingly yells ALCOA, ALCOA into her window. She does not even know how to hold a gun, but her husband owns one.) The roofs of Riverside Drive do not return a light signal to the shrieks of Alcoa. Over the blinking light terraces of New Jersey, over the tangled colors of the amusement park on the Palisades, over the gray river—a wide gate to the north—white bulbs are lined on shallow arcs of cable, headlights and reflectors grope across the two-storied surface between the two piers of the George Washington Bridge, and the travel guides of the world recommend the view.

The park is part of the view, the broad green grounds made of gentle slopes, paths for strolling, retaining walls, highway approaches, tunnels to the river, old trees. On the lower floors it colors the light in the rooms. At night the leaves hug the lantern light to themselves in radiant hollows. The park can be used, for the police are partial to it. Their patrol cars drive up there for a break and a little masculine conversation, and in the warm season the mounted policemen sit their horses in the deep shadows of the shrubbery. In the summer the park seems to be the setting for a perpetual folk festival. The benches on the riverbank promenade are crowded with excursionists from the poorer sections, tennis games are in progress, men with fishing lines hope for fish of considerable physical proportions, chess players sit straddling the benches and issue instructions to kibitzers, people with day-before-yesterday's newspaper over their faces sleep as though in their own apartments—which the park may be—strollers with dogs encounter one another and gladly stop for a talk about their animals, picnics are spread out on the grass, half-naked children jump and shriek under the flashing cool fountains on the playgrounds, chase after the swings, crowd around the ice cream vendor, and parents on the benches speaking all the while aim their conversation at one another. The picture seems to present a peaceful existence, and actually many residents on Riverside Drive do feel a togetherness. They have a modicum of education in common, their incomes are comparable, they are only occasionally not rosy-complected, they send their children to the same schools, they have residential conditions in common to defend, and appear as a group at political and parents' meetings. Whoever waits mornings for the bus with a child by the hand can almost certainly count on being taken along by a stranger to school or kindergarten, or even perhaps will let the child get into the strange car alone; and the bus driver, having escaped from the crush of city traffic into the fleet stream of Riverside Drive, speaks with those who climb on here as though with a family that is nicer than the others. But the dark-skinned Sunday excursionists come from neighborhoods where parks are not provided or are less favored by the police and are now ruined, the grass withered and worn away, the benches smashed, the sparse trees damaged, and the ground densely strewn with pieces of glass which was smashed there in purgative, constant anger; there every step crunches. In Riverside Park the dark-skinned children are in a minority on a weekday, they play in groups by themselves, and the Negro woman in the white smock, who keeps her eye on a pack of wildly running children, is not watching out for her own youngster but for the one belonging to her rosy-complected employer. On the baseball diamonds the Puerto Ricans are by themselves, on the basketball courts the Negroes practice all alone, and the West Indians play soccer together. People on Riverside Drive warn the foreign tourist about the side streets around the corner, and advise him not to walk on them at night without at least, but not more than, eight dollars in his pocket, the approximate price of a heroin injection, so that an assailant will at least let his knife alone. Around the corner are the slums, socially alien territory seen from here.

The word *slum* is accepted, it no longer requires a translation into German. Its derivation cannot be traced. Originally it is supposed to have been a deprecative expression for a room. The corresponding expression in German is usually the "poor quarter." But the slums of the Upper West Side are not quarters made expressly for the poor, they are different from the workers' blocks knocked together by housing speculators in German metropolises, different from a Bidonville in Paris, or a barracks village for refugees. The slums in New York were not built as slums. These brownstones, so-called after the façade of reddish-brown sandstone, were actually the sign of middle-class prosperity after the Civil War. The roomy staircases were created for elegant events. The four stories were meant for a single family with servants, richly outfitted inside with hardwood paneling, oak parquet floors, marble fireplaces, carven doors, turned stair newels. They were luxury buildings, and the grime on the fronts, the de-

caying pieces of furniture and mattresses, the uncovered garbage cans
and the scattered trash, the smeared windows do not suit them. They are
forsaken houses. They were erected for whites, protestants, Anglo-Saxons.
The Irish, who came here in bright hordes in the 70's of the last century,
gathered in the rent houses along Columbus and Amsterdam Avenues, but
many saved up for such a brown house in the latest style and profited by
their ownership through subletting. The Irish were the most powerful
political group in the quarter before the Jews wandered in from Harlem.
After World War II great waves of Negroes from the New York ghettos
and Puerto Ricans moved in, and the white-skinned immigrants, long used
to the scale of values they had found there, surrendered one street after
the other. Not entirely, to be sure. From one such single-family house the
owner can first of all make four apartments, one per floor, and make up for
the loss in property value with the increased rent incomes. The landlord
can further divide these small apartments into single rooms. Meanwhile
he has multiplied his old rents. Since his tenants, who come from Harlem,
must look upon even such apartment conditions as an improvement, and
the Spanish-speaking residents at first are not capable of resistance, the
landlord is free to put off repairs to the future, to save on the heating, to
forgo a superintendent. The law provides fines for all such neglect, but
people without formal education and an adequate knowledge of the language recoil from bureaucratic red tape, and the courts are gently inclined
toward the slum landlord, for he represents the concepts of business and
property. It is such enterprise which produces the slum: the ugliness and
permeability of the walls, the unrepaired window panes, the defective door
locks, the broken letter boxes, the slippery encrusted dirt even in the halls,
the closet kitchens, the repulsive condition of the sanitary installations, the
infestation of the compartments by insects, and of course a behavior of
the slum dwellers which corresponds to their social situation.

Conservative whites, when they wish to keep Negro families out of their
apartment houses, point to the slums and believe they have proven that
the Negroes simply do not understand how to live in civilization, as though
that were a natural trait. Idiotic as all arguments are which try to put an
obstacle in the way of an equitable distribution of social wealth, this one
too overlooks the fact that not all Negroes live in slums, and that not only
Negroes live in slums. The prejudice of the American people against a
long established one-tenth of the citizens may be incomprehensible; the
things which are defended with the help of this prejudice are clear. It is
a matter of jobs as a means of income, of education as a means of better
income, of equal rights as a guarantee of income. No group has had to

fight so long for these rights as the Negro. The runaway and freed slaves who invaded the progressive North in the last century were there isolated in segregated areas, exploited by white landlords and merchants, excluded from equal education and training, always fired first, always hired last, and they saw group after group move in from outside, take a foothold, become equal citizens, the Irish, the Italians, the Jews, and in the 1950's the Puerto Ricans. In 1960, as today, their condition can be summed up in classic statistics: "The Negro child has . . . aside from his talent, statistically . . . half as much a prospect of finishing high school as the white child, a third as much a prospect of graduating from college, a fourth as much a prospect of working in a profession, and four times the prospect of being without work" (John F. Kennedy, in a campaign speech). Whatever the root cause may be for their traumatic exclusion by the whites, the Negro group must for this reason endure the highest casualties in the competition for jobs. As a consequence they represent the majority of those citizens who have given up hope of work, who were never in a position to have this hope, who let themselves drop into the slum. The slum is a prison to which society sends those whom it has itself crippled. Those are apartments out of which the bedbugs cannot be driven with the most patient efforts, in which the most important function of the refrigerator is not the cooling of foodstuffs but that of a safe which the insects cannot crack. Children in the slums have learned to recognize a dope addict, a homosexual, an alcoholic on the street and to expect him as an everyday resident of the neighborhood; the dogs bark at the staggering figure with the bottle and scarcely have the chance to settle down. These children are at a loss for games, they stand around like the jobless, watching, bored, hostile. The Negroes in the slums feel neglected by the police, their streets are sparsely patrolled, burglaries of their homes are more negligently investigated, in a fight the dark-skinned participant is more likely to be arrested than the light-skinned; nevertheless the Negroes still want more policemen, better protection (whereas the whites can afford to demand a civil supervisory board for the law officers). Two-thirds of the Negroes on the Upper West Side are unmarried men, perhaps not least of all because a family abandoned by its bread winner can claim relief, but also complete families live here in a single room. The children who are supposed to do homework there, who are necessarily witnesses of inevitable scenes of argument, come tired and troubled to school; their performances must lag behind the requirements; they leave school as early as possible and begin to work in the lower occupations which will die out with the development of electronics, and they are trained for poverty. The city administration tries through its welfare agencies to assist needy cases with patches, tatters, and crumbs at least; it offers premature school dropouts trade courses; it promotes desegregated school attendance by light and dark children. These programs are decorative, palliatives, treatment of the symptom, they have no influence on the economic situation of the injured group, do not support its family structure, do not relieve the isolation. Where tidyness no longer matters, trash flies out the window, and if it lands in a white backyard it could be the mail; as a matter of fact, the procedure is called "airmail." The whites do not hear as a group; perhaps the white passerby hears something when a bottle shatters next to him on the sidewalk. Since this reality does not contain a way to a life worth living, why not escape life in the illusions and sicknesses of narcotics. Since the whites as a group refuse to help, why not put a knife to the chest of the individual white man and take succor from his wallet, his cash register, his apartment. Since society has erected a wall around this life, why observe the standards of society, why treat the welfare lady differently than the bearer of an installment payment, why not send the children begging, why live under a roof? Since the lines of communication with society are broken, why not rip out the wires of the public telephones; why leave a forwarding address when you move away? The word *slum* exists also as a verb, with the meaning of strolling in run-down and dangerous streets, and the New York police have just ordered 5000 more protective helmets for the coming riots.

The behavior of the Puerto Ricans under slum conditions differs from that of the Negro, to be sure, and they more easily escape from the slum. Of course, their mass immigration after World War II at first really cramped the housing conditions on the Upper West Side, but they came from the island conscious of being equal citizens, and their reaction to over-priced apartments and joblessness was resistance, not the hundred-year-old resignation of the American Negro. They were held together as a group by their independent culture, by stable bonds of family and kin, and by their religion. (The Puerto Rican mothers go with their children to the park.) They made use of the influence of the churches, their officials, their organizations for better accommodations, more playgrounds, more police protection; and since the light-skinned among them were less susceptible to racial prejudice, they found work more easily, and steady work. They are now a powerful political group within the quarter and have also changed its exterior, with Spanish signs, Spanish religious services, their own newspapers, a movie theater which shows films only in their language, and with shops which not only display a Spanish sign but also belong to them.

An example of the disorganized relations between the city administration and the poor of the quarter is the renovation program which began here ten years ago. The authorities surveyed an area between 87th and 97th Streets, bordered by the street along Central Park and by Amsterdam Avenue, and at the cost of a quarter of a million dollars found out that between 1950 and 1956 no new buildings had been constructed here, though the number of residents had increased by one-fourth. One-sixth of the households lived each in a single room. But the rent per square foot was twice as high as in a protected and well-tended apartment house on West End Avenue or on Riverside Drive. The average income was at a minimum, and the characteristics of the area had become poverty, constant crime, and the misuse of drugs. The authorities proposed to produce about 3000 luxury apartments by repairing some buildings, however to raze the largest part of the brownstones and old rental buildings and to erect high-rises in their place. These skyscrapers were supposed to contain about 5000 more luxury apartments, almost 2500 apartments for families with median incomes, and about 400 low-income apartments, thus a share of about 4 per cent for the low-income group which formed the majority of the residents. True, citizens' protests brought about the increase of the planned low-income apartments to 2500, but it remained evident that these twenty blocks were not to be restored in favor of their current residents. The goal of the authorities was, rather, to increase the property values drastically, to improve tax incomes fourfold, and thereby, if possible, to gain a showpiece, a showhorse of city construction. The city took administrative possession of the buildings to be razed, but to the astonishment of the tenants the restoration was by no means punctually carried out, the fire and police regulations by no means implemented more strictly. The tenants who had found accommodations in other parts of New York were provided with assistance in moving, and the remainder, too weak or because of their skin color incapable of such initiative, were temporarily housed in city-owned buildings south of the renewal area, often under conditions which were similar to those of the slum or tended in that direction. The Irish resisted to the last. Certainly their well-preserved and roomy apartments along Columbus and Amsterdam Avenues could not be replaced in quality and at the old costs of construction, but the age of a building—however solid it might be—marks it for the role of the victim in the dialogue with city planning, and these buildings too collapsed under the swinging balls and the air hammers. The Irish colony took its children out of school, gave up most of its stores, and has since scarcely been felt in the life of the quarter. The renewal required a ridiculous amount of time from the planning through the eviction and the razing to the new structures; the condemned houses, without windows, without doors, were for a long time places of play for children, sanctuary for dope circles, prostitutes, the homeless, and rats as fat as cats. The enterprise brought with it the customary scandals. Once the city turned over to a construction firm for razing one block which was still densely settled, and the business firm for years pocketed the rents, which could not be obtained at such levels anywhere else—and built nothing. Another time a construction firm filled in the excavations of an entire razed block and used the surface gained as a profitable parking lot; even today such areas lie behind neat fences, unbuilt-on for years. The high-rise structures meanwhile, gigantic, rectangular boxes, stand in large part in the midst of the low surroundings, and they have not become a showpiece of city planning ingenuity. Those which produce full taxes, the imported luxury apartments, are provided with horticultural embellishments, balconies, and caretakers; the others, in the construction of which the city had a part, must be content with the decoration of a bronze plaque at the bottom, where the social accomplishment is proclaimed in a solemn way and the names of those responsible are included. The monoform boxes are surrounded still by half-destroyed brownstones and by the abandoned rental buildings on Amsterdam Avenue, the relinquished, nailed-up stores, bars, snack-shops, workshops. Three-fourths of the former residents of these streets had wanted to stay in this area, but most of the Negroes and Puerto Ricans did not fulfill the qualifications for a low-income apartment and were crowded off into other poverty-stricken quarters of New York and into the remaining side streets. The slum which was supposed to be wiped off the face of the earth was moved around the corner.

The various front groups, the separate parties, income groups, and races of the quarter meet on Broadway, the old highway between the village of Bloomingdale and the settlement of New Amsterdam in southern Manhattan. But the Broadway which runs obliquely through the Upper West Side has little in common with its legendary stretch above Times Square, which is hung with enormous illuminated canvases fluttering under movie marquees, under the impure colors of neon gas, running bands of letters, under searchlights, and the spinning, leaping, bursting lighted signs. On the Upper West Side the lights are fewer, and they hang lower.

Another Broadway begins at 72nd Street, where it meets Amsterdam Avenue and cuts it off from Verdi Park. Here a spacious median, studded at intersections with diagonal benches and occasionally with shrubbery, divides it into two broad traffic lanes. On both sides patterns of the Renaissance tower up in elefantine masses, and far into the north the many-windowed boxes testify under their sentimental cornices to the feverish trust in the construction market which began to gallop in 1900 with the building of the subway under Broadway. They are hotels, apartment houses, movie theaters, from the time when profits were invested, with artistry in construction. The demand did not suffice for an exclusive colony of these decorated monsters; between them squat, four-storied and pitiful, the more cheaply planned rental buildings, which took less pains to camouflage their fire escapes, and now their age compromises them. Few hotels have been able to keep their prosperous clientel and preserve the reputations which their façades promise; principally they now domicile permanent guests, poverty-stricken pensioners, cases on welfare, and often the kind of guests who are more in need of medical treatment than hotel service which does not go much beyond pocketing the rent. The apart-ment houses are still reckoned among the more desirable in the quarter, less because of the address than because of the proximity of shopping areas and means of transportation. The movie houses, with names such as "Embassy," "Symphony," "Riverside," and "Riviera," have survived as memorials of a majestically planned new culture, with art nouveau or Italian scrollwork on their fronts, the foyers of plush and marble, living-room carpets between the multitudes of stuffed seats, and the celestial ceiling vaults; and stubbornly they defend their endangered splendor with prices which are twice as high as those on Times Square; two of them, the less pompous ones, are known for their continual reruns. And the park in which Verdi stands with pigeons on his head is nowadays called the "Park of Needles," the hypodermic needle. For forty years nothing new has been built on this street, and in spite of the swarm of lights at the bottom of weathered and sooty expansive façades, Broadway is remini-scent of a photograph of the age when horses still trotted before carriages and one spoke of the "Boulevard."

Broadway is the marketplace, the Main Street of the quarter. The ground floors are crammed with shops in a dense, unbroken chain, with delicat-essens and supermarkets, with launderettes, hairdressing salons, cafeterias, vegetable stalls, bars, shoe repair shops, laundry outlets, tax consulting firms, driving schools, and travel bureaus. Whoever wants to fetch the weekly load for his refrigerator need go hardly two blocks, even if he should get a hankering for Japanese beer, Kamchatka crabs, Irish honey, Düsseldorf mustard, or Dresden cakes. Here there are Chinese restaurants in which even the Chinese eat, Israeli restaurants and Spanish bars, and one establishment called "The Maharaja," Italian pizza parlors and ice cream shops; here there is displayed a *Novoye Slovo* and the West German newsmagazine—which shall be nameless—on Monday evening of the same date. A resident of the quarter hardly has to leave it to go shopping; around the corner he will find antiques as well as children's apparel and damson plums, even though the goods displayed are on occasion dusty, the textiles cheap in quality, and the shops not as spotless as on Fifth Avenue around Rockefeller Center. But anyway, hardly anyone here asks for those watches which the great of this world constantly wear. The battle for the favor of the customers is ruinous. Many of the small shops dislodge their lessors every few months and wait then dusty and full of rubbish for enterprising businessmen with longer-lived money.

Broadway is the promenade of the Upper West Side, comparable to the main street of a small town, a place for seeing and being seen. The passerby meets brown, yellow, black, white, red, and pink faces; he is callous enough never to look around at the matron in bermuda shorts or blue jeans, the Harlem resident in African costume, the Jewish habit of longcoat and black hat, the headscarf over hair curlers, the sari, the hat made of the finest vegetables, the coat of leather and the coat of rags— a clergyman's black and white collar is striking, and elegant attire would be sensational; along with the passersby go housewives who drag their shopping carts behind them over the cement squares, and delivery boys who will bring other housewives their purchases to the back door; there go average citizens, beggars, madmen, students, prostitutes, there police- men stand. The languages on this Broadway are manifold, the accents of all continents labor confusingly on versions of American English; pass- ing by one can hear the Spanish from Puerto Rico and Cuba, West-Indian French, Japanese, Chinese, Russian, Yiddish, and the secret language of the world of narcotics, and again and again the German that was spoken thirty years ago in East Prussia, Berlin, Franconia, Saxony, and Hesse. (Here there is a butchershop for Westphalian tastes, and both the Puerto Rican assistants of the butcher are able to express themselves in German with a Yiddish intonation.) Here a man goes around with a folding camera, looking for children who want to have themselves photographed on his aged pony. Here policemen stand. They stand in pairs on the corner and twirl their nightsticks on their wrists as they learned to do at the academy, they have the blunt and sweeping gaze of those who see everything, friends and helpers of the citizen, conversation-piece number two. Everybody, the residents of the side streets as well as the princes on Central Park, are agreed that the police are never found when they are needed. Here they stand, right in the midst of the lights, tall and mighty with their backs to the wall, waiting until they are needed. The man who turns his hotdog cart around the corner at the sight of them will not have "paid off." The residents of the quarter cling to the belief that the police are "paid off" by everybody, by the laundry as well as by the ice cream vendor and the newspaper stand, but they would find out for sure only from the guardians of order themselves, and obviously they do not expect the question. A policeman is to be addressed as "Sir." A policeman enters a bar and points with his gloved finger in the direction of the restroom door, and without a question the owner presses the buzzer which releases the snaplock. The apparatus is supposd to prevent robbery assaults in the restroom. On his way back the policeman passes people at the bar who to the uneducated eye belong in a hospital, in a withdrawal clinic, in jail, or in bed, but the glance of the policeman is directed at the football game on the television screen, where things have some sense to them. The answer to the question of whether conditions could be improved by generosity one must have promptly and clearly in mind; for the beggars are not always polite, they do not always make use of a religious formula, and a light-skinned person who evades them is to them a dirty Jew. (One midnight three friendly Negro children approached a passerby with fixed knives, and because he appealed to them for assistance and claimed to be a tourist from Iceland looking for a hotel room with his last four dollars, they gave him back his wallet with all four dollars and directed him to such a hotel and bade him good night. However, the man at the hotel desk suspected an emergency and demanded eight dollars, cash in advance.) Now the policemen move. Shoulder to shoulder, the revolver holsters on their hips, playful hands on their nightsticks, they go off through the mob, past a child dozing on a box with its head against the wall because none of them damned whites wants his shoes shined at eleven o'clock at night, the policemen go past a young woman in tight red slacks, the girl's makeup erupts suddenly in a wink, they go on, they go past an old man sleeping in his dandruffy beard and his tatters on a bench in the middle of Broadway, they go past a white-skinned matron bending down with a goodnatured smile over a dark-skinned baby in a stroller. Suddenly from the subway cavern a swarm of young nuns under hoods bustles–they fly across the intersection with the green light, and now the policemen are no longer to be seen.

THE SIXTH DAY
A Now-and-Then-Vision or Retropy

KARLHANS FRANK
translated by Ralph R. Read III

With

Michel Angel
Bob Loucembert   = Space travelers from another star
News Announcer = A Texan
Addy
Eva   = Robots with small defects

(*Constant sound field /shrill interference / a persistent interference signal changes the sound field / strenuous breathing*)

MICHEL: Come in, Bob.
BOB: No.
MICHEL: Hey, come on! You're getting spaced out.
BOB: Leave me alone.
MICHEL: Don't you want to have a look at the early news?
BOB: Guess I do. (*strenuous breathing*) This is the saddest moment of my life.
MICHEL: You say that every time.

(*Breathing / door squeaks and snaps shut / this breaks off the sound field / sounds of a space suit being taken off / TV screen is turned on*)

NEWS ANNOUNCER: Stella Seven from solar system eight x p three one transmittin early news for space travelers. Ariel Three with pilots Michel Angel and Bob Loucembert is approachin the Earth and'll land there this very day. The cordial best wishes uv owah Praisident Goddah, the revered an green sun of owah planit, accumpany the courageous pioneahs on theyah arduous earthly coase. Wunce agin, we'll show shots of Ariel Three's ass-cent. That's Michel Angel climbin intuh the space ship.

BOB: Look pretty good, don't I?

Here's Bob Loucembert standin in frunt uv the rack with the Knowlidge Ampules.

In othah news: The Science Counsul uv owah planit has succeeded in developin a new occupational therapy fur millyuns uv owah fella citizins. Yestiddy the project wuz re-ported to owah revered Praisident Goddah, the green sun uv owah ...

BOB: I'll turn the box off.
    (*Click* / NEWS ANNOUNCER *falls silent*)
MICHEL (*sighs*):—Well, then—let's land.
Bob: If we have to. I'll read off: 11 points port—13 full spherical

(*voice grows softer*)	ahead—at congruence X mix in 007 right away—
(*sound field begins*)	set at normal suds cycle— hard cut
(*voice even softer*)	18—20—2—passé—stir with left hand on the left
(*sound field louder*)	grip—hoist the flag—accelerate slowly—
(*interference*)	and switch from major to minor when light turns red—
(*voice dies away*)	recite rite proverbs 17 and 4
(*Crash!!!*)	

                (*Silence!!!*)
(*Birds twittering / door squeaks*)
BOB: We've made it.
    Nice place.
MICHEL: According to the plan, each of us has to drink one Knowledge Ampule dry, then hold our morning devotional, after which we check the area, if appropriate assemble Addy and Eva and start them up.
BOB: I'm ready for a swig. But we can skip the morning devotional.
MICHEL: Not as long as I'm here. We owe Goddah respect always and every-

where.

BOB: You're just afraid the old man's going to heave a slipper at you. Here, catch!

MICHEL: You shouldn't toss the Knowledge Ampules around so carelessly.

BOB: Won't you ever cut out the ideological drivel! Drink!

(*Pop of a cork / sounds of swallowing /
birds twittering*)

BOB: Listen! A lark.

MICHEL: That was a nightingale and not a lark. It's still early in the day.

BOB: True.

That stuff takes hold of you much faster than it does me.

MICHEL: You should pursue your devotional exercises more seriously. Now fetch the Holy Horsemudel, therewith to consecrate this star to Goddah to the end of time.

(*Steps moving away*)

MICHEL: That isn't the last trouble I'm going to have with this Loucembert.

(*Steps approaching*)

MICHEL: Set it up here.

(*Bright tone / clattering*)

MICHEL: Careful!

There. Now clamp the liturger.

BOB: Can I wind it up now?

MICHEL: Yes, please do. Turn it on.

(*Winding-up sound / devotional music begins / the litany is spoken
by* MICHEL *as high priest, ceremoniously, by* BOB *as congregation
compelled by convention, droning and dull.*)

MICHEL: We are waiting?

BOB: For what are we waiting?

MICHEL: Waiting for Goddah.

(*Devotional music grows louder / a fire siren is intermixed*)

MICHEL: Solúmno solúmno verdérre derbér

BOB: The ravens. The ravens.

MICHEL: Randóro andórra de láki derbér

BOB: The Jews. The Jews.

MICHEL: Hestára solúmno archcousin derbér

BOB: Love. Love.

MICHEL: O saána silsánnah zerköre derlör

BOB: Freedom and loneliness. Fidelity or opportunity.

MICHEL & BOB: Give us give—don't loot us—love us—Goddah

MICHEL: You'll wonder where the yellow went—
when you brush your teeth with Pepsodent

MICHEL & BOB: Prorate our debts—postpone our payments—
                rescue our schools—Goddah
BOB: Sly—slyer—Babo sly
MICHEL: Seek us not with the telo-eye—
                leach us not in truth's lye—Goddah
MICHEL & BOB: Babo-sly
MICHEL: For we drink Ovaltine
MICHEL & BOB: And what do you do?
NEWS ANNOUNCER: Y'all hurry, heah?
MICHEL & BOB: Olé guapa!
        (*Music breaks off*)
BOB: That's over with!
        Anyway, the telo-eye doesn't even reach into this solar system.
MICHEL: You can never be sure. And besides, it's on our schedule. What do
        you think of this Earth?
BOB: Pretty peaceful up to now.
MICHEL: We'll assemble Addy and Eva then. Come help me get the crate.
        (*Steps moving away /*
                                in the distance a tiger roars /
        panting / steps approaching)
MICHEL & BOB: Heave—ho—heave—ho—heave
BOB:—ho.   MICHEL: Ow! Be careful! Put
                                                    it down!
        (*Crash / noise of a crate being broken open /*
        clattering / assembly noises)
MICHEL: Don't bend the spine so much.
BOB: The what?
MICHEL: That tubing you've got in your hand there.
        (*more assembly noises*)
MICHEL: Here, pull on the radius a minute.
        Now hold the socket, so I can screw in the ball of the humerus.
        (*Squeaking / hammering*)
BOB: Dammit! My thumb!
MICHEL: You don't have to cram in his cerebrum so hard.
BOB: But it's too big for the receptacle.
MICHEL: Get the pump. Hurry up!
        (*Sound of the air pump / whistling / breathing / sound of heart
        beating*)
MICHEL: Addy's standing.   (BOB *laughs aloud*)
ADDY: Homm todderom tack   BOB (*laughs*): If that isn't the funniest robot
                                                    I ever saw.

MICHEL: The plasto-weld seams are still closing. True, they'll always become damp when warm, but we won't lose any sleep over that.

BOB (*still laughing*): Not over that. My nose isn't that sensitive, and anyway I've got Deodoknock in the nasal passages.

But he only has two eyes!

And look at the hair.

Michel, what kind of an eary monster is this?

(*can't stop laughing*)

MICHEL: That's Addy, the first Self-Made Man. A miracle of our technology. He's copied exactly from the so-called monkeys living here.

He'll serve us well in the cultivation of the Earth.

(*irritated*) Will you kindly stop your silly laughing?

And help me get Eva ready.

BOB (*chuckles a bit more, then stops laughing*): All right, all right.

Hey, what sleek balloons. What are they for?

MICHEL: Exit point of lactation installation. Later intended as the gear shift for erotic feelings. In the course of development the first gear is supposed to be here, the second gear here.

BOB: And reverse gear?

MICHEL: There's no way back.

Will you just hold her thighs even?

(*Smacking sound*)

MICHEL: Oh, it's run through!

BOB: A special juice?

MICHEL: Blood.

Get a hold of yourself. Now you've slopped some over.

Hm. Blood and earth. Nice isn't it?

Pump some more. That's it.

(*Sounds of air pump / whistling / syncopated heart beat*)

ADDY (*joyfully*): Pererish!

Ricke! Rerplerterterff.

MICHEL: Move, out of the way, Addy.

(*Squeaking and whistling / heartbeats grow more and more irregular / stop completely*)

ADDY (*mournfully*): Yowiyowiyauleubauleyauhuhuuuuuuuuuuu

BOB: A fine model!

MICHEL: Big-mouth! Can't you see she's leaky?

Something in her framework is out of order.

BOB: Hey! Don't grab her so roughly!

ADDY (*raging*): Hummefumm!

       Backeback!

       Tullekrrrrrrrrrrrr ...

BOB: Maybe she has a screw loose?

MICHEL: These models have no screw joints at all.

       Come here to me, Addy. Get up here on the testing stand. There.

       Turn around. Yes.

       Hm, a gland is plugged up here.

BOB: You mean, a jet?

MICHEL: Quiet! You're making Addy nervous!

       Addy, hold still. Hold your breath. Fine.

       Now breathe, very deep. In and out and in and out—

       Aha! Just as I thought! They put the rib that's missing from the Eva model into Addy's packing crate, and you installed it in him without thinking.

       Get me a drill and the cutting torch, Bob.

       Thanks.

       Don't be afraid, Addy. It won't hurt a bit.

       (*Drill buzzing / torch hissing*)

ADDY (*screams*): Chuhaaaaaaaaaaaaaaaaa ...

MICHEL: It's all over with, Addy. Didn't hurt at all.

       And now for Eva.

       (*Buzzing / hissing / hammering / air pumping / whistling / breathing / heartbeats*)

ADDY (*joyfully*): Hockadoodle terffterffterff

EVA (*jabbers uninterruptedly*):

       Oooooooh! Sillisillisilli stitirati

       sitirita mimikri kriminim dideldibs

                          BOB: What the heck?

       lovelov a labelab o love o plim

                              Won't she ever stop?

       ei songeson plim songeson so lala

                         MICHEL: Probably not.

       luse lust laugh loll hei bodybody

                           The jaw contacts

       bodybee hich killi tick i titi

                           are stuck.

       titi zizizizizizziiii hoi nigglishi

                           Now to work.

       rosebose rerseberse rififi die trili

                           Addy and Eva are machines for

       maine mein mimei meimi tickeltri

learning without the

friini friinei Ii i i nt nt

capacity for knowledge.

not but oft you I me nt she

They must be trained.

ne mi mone moni nomey money monmonmoney
yellabitmoneyy. . . .

(*For the time being* EVA *jabbers on—could also be a tape recorder
at high speed—a kind of Mickey Mouse voice on an endless reel*)

BOB: OK. I'll take Eva. You can coach Addy for now.

MICHEL: Agreed.

    Here's the program.

    But don't play with the buttons.

    And not out of hearing range!

BOB: Just over there behind the bushes.

    Come, Eva.

    (*Steps moving away* / EVA's *jabbering grows softer* /

leaves
rustle /

EVA *falls silent*)

MICHEL: There, Addy, listen to me.

    First Commandment: You may obey only those who are sent by Goddah.

    Understand?

ADDY: Knirch

MICHEL: The correct answer is:

    Yes sir!

    Say yes sir.

ADDY: Det-rir.

MICHEL: Try it again, my dear Addy.

    Yess—sirr.

ADDY: Yess—hir.

MICHEL: That'll do. A little louder and still faster. Yessir.

ADDY: Yes sirr.

MICHEL: Competent, Addy. Wholly competent. Just without the extra "r" at the end. Well, then?

ADDY: Yes sir!

MICHEL: Very good.

    A further commandment: You may not smash either someone sent by Goddah or another robot, even if he is much uglier than you. But whoever tries to pass himself off as sent by Goddah, him you must smash unless he has a sign like this. Take a look.

(*A clicking / then a music box playing "O Du lieber Augustine"*)

ADDY (*hums along a bit, then*): Yes sir.

MICHEL: In case of doubt, you must wait for Goddah.

ADDY: Yes sir.

MICHEL: There: Nothing without a directive from above, Addy.

ADDY: Yes sir.

MICHEL: But be skeptical.

It could happen that somebody impatient will proclaim prematurely that Goddah has come.

He'll be riding on the back of an ass, but don't depend on it, Addy. There are more asses than heroes.

Do you understand that?

ADDY: Yes sir!

MICHEL: You're a good pupil, Addy. Furthermore:

Every new Addy-Robot gets an Eva-Robot. You must keep your hands off, even if she's much prettier than your Eva-Robot. You mustn't touch strange robots at all, Addy. You mustn't touch our rocket, either.

You mustn't touch anything without an order, Addy.

An-y-thing.

Do you understand that?   (*Leaves rustling in the background* / EVA *giggles* / *more rustling* /

ADDY (*hesitating*): Yet—hir.   *more giggling from* EVA /

MICHEL: You're not paying attention,   EVA *giggles louder*)
        Addy.

ADDY: Grrrrrrrrrrr . . .

MICHEL: What's the matter with you?   EVA *giggles*)
        Bob is busy teaching the Eva-model
        always to subordinate herself to you.

ADDY: Yes sir?
        Yes sir.
        Yes sir! Yes sir!! Yes sir!!!

MICHEL: That's enough for today.
        (*calls*) Bob! Are you through?

BOB: As far as possible.

MICHEL: Then come out of the apple bush.

BOB: Those are strawberry bushes.

MICHEL: Tomatoes!

BOB: Olives!

MICHEL: Carrots! Oaks! Radishes!

BOB: Limes! Artichokes! Beans! Pineapples! Eggs!

MICHEL: Did you say eggs?

> Quick, Bob, we've got to take another Knowledge Ampule.
>
> (EVA *giggles / leaves rustle / steps approaching*)

BOB (*approaching*): Phialphialphialpillpill

> (EVA *giggles / corks popping / swallowing*)

MICHEL: It's lilac.

BOB (*dreamily*): Lilac.

> (EVA *giggles*)

MICHEL: She's not gabbling any more?

BOB: I soldered her a bit.

ADDY: Rrrrrrrrrr ...   MICHEL: Well.

> (EVA *giggles*)   At any rate, we have to celebrate the midday devotional now.

BOB: Leave me out.

MICHEL: Let's have no nonsense, Bob.

BOB: Nope. I'll instruct Eva now.   (EVA *giggles*)

> You can celebrate to your heart's content.   (EVA *giggles /*
>
> > *a tiger roars*)

MICHEL: Comrade Loucembert! I command you to celebrate the midday devotional together with me in honor of our President Goddah, the most illustrious and green sun of our planet, as is the duty of each and every devout inhabitant of the universe.

> In case of a refusal I will report you. You'll have only yourself to blame for the consequences.

ADDY: Yes sir.

BOB: Shut up, you cuckold.

> As you wish, Comrade Angel. Begin: the holy Horsemudel stands before you.
>
> (*Winding-up sound / devotional music begins*)

MICHEL: Are we waiting?

BOB: We are waiting.

MICHEL: For what are we waiting?

BOB: Waiting for Bordeaux.

> (*Music grows louder / Michel audibly angrier / Bob more cheerful /*
>
> > *the scene grows more and more turbulent*)

MICHEL: Racesrussiansrosesraul

BOB: Sex or seven. Seven or sex.

MICHEL: Helverbelverdorensaul

BOB: War or peace. Peace and war.

MICHEL: Reddybloodybagemaul.
BOB: And love. And lust.

(EVA giggles)

MICHEL: Ottermoddertrollenfaul
BOB: Eva. Only Eva.

(EVA giggles /
ADDY growls)

MICHEL & BOB: We await thy kingdom
            not now but soon
            Goddah
MICHEL: Today I bake
            tomorrow I brew
MICHEL & BOB: A thousand years
            blond hair
            blue eyes lurk about you
            Goddah
BOB: Day after tomorrow I'll take Eva away
            and what will you do?

(EVA giggles / ADDY growls /
music—furioso)

MICHEL (*screams*): I'm waiting!   ADDY: Yes sir!   NEWS ANNOUNCER: I'm
                                              waiting for
                                              the midday report

MICHEL & BOB: Olé guápa!   ADDY: Kwappa   the midday report
                                  Yes sir!   the midday report
                        (EVA screeches)   the midday report
      (*Music breaks off / pause, except for*   the midday report
      the NEWS ANNOUNCER)   the midday report
                                            NEWS ANNOUNCER: I'm
MICHEL: You've not had the last   waiting for
    word, Comrade Loucembert.   the midday report
    I'll transmit the midday report   the midday report
    to Stella 7 now.   the midday report
    (*Steps moving away / door squeaking /*   the midday report
                                slam—   the midday report
    silence—even the NEWS ANNOUNCER *cannot be heard*)
BOB: Come over here to me, Addy and Eva. I want to teach
    you something else.
    (*Steps*)
BOB: Now then:
    You may smash whatever you want.

You may put your hands on anything.

Only me you may not attack. Get it?

ADDY (*hesistantly*): Yet hir?   EVA (*marveling*): Oooooh?

BOB: Naturally, you may put your hands on me, Eva.

    (EVA *giggles / door squeaking / steps approaching*)

MICHEL: Follow me, Comrade Loucembert. We are to explore the immediate area, collect stones, and so on. The robots are not schooled enough yet.

    (*Steps moving away / in the distance a tiger roars*)

ADDY (*tenderly*): Hommefamme womannear

    (EVA *giggles*)

ADDY: Hammehamme

    Odarumme

    Otutarumm

    Dada Dada

    Dielemiel

    (EVA *giggles*)

ADDY: Lammeduda

    Odarumme

    Otutaramm?

    Tome!

EVA: Ohoch. Dada? Ziziwizi

    (*Steps moving away, quick and light / clumsy steps follow /*

                                door squeaking)

EVA (*breathing behind*): Hommeyouda

                      dada!

                      Takehim?

ADDY: Yehein

EVA (*tenderly*):   Hannemannemulenau

                      Shrrrrr . . .

ADDY (*energetically*): Yes sir!!!

    (*Glasses clinking / corks popping / swallowing*)

EVA: Man.

ADDY: Woman.

EVA: Child?

ADDY: Yes sir!

EVA: Youuu . . .

    O, you . . .   ADDY: Ah, youuu . . .

    (*Tender and excited breathing / small and then larger kisses /*

                              steps approaching /

                door squeaks!)

EVA: Bob!

I'm naked!

ADDY: You'll get a fur from me.

> (*In the distance a tiger roars*)

MICHEL: They've drunk of the Knowledge Ampules.

> Addy! What have you been up to?

ADDY: Beat it. Or I'll smash you ! ! !

MICHEL: Quick, get the tool box, Bob.

> These are miscreations.

ADDY: Step aside, Eva.

> He wants to slaughter us, pluck, broil, roast, grill us, unscrew us, depolarize, overhaul, overturn, dismantle us.
>
> He really has a thing about ribs, that I know.
>
> Let's split, split . . .
>
> (*Steps / pattering and trampling / panting / in the distance a tiger roars /*
>
> > *shuffling*)

MICHEL: It's pointless.

> Come back to the stars.
>
> We have to start now.
>
> Misconnected models can destroy everything.
>
> I've been part of Project Luna.
>
> Once again we've failed, Bob. The earth will become waste and void.
>
> (*Steps /door squeaks and bangs shut / clatter*)

MICHEL (*dully*): Count-down, Bob.

BOB (*distorted over the loud speaker, and with echo*): Ace,

> king, queen, jack, ten, nine, eight, seven, zero, fire!
>
> (*Rocket fires / into the roar—*)

ADDY: Here, look.

> 'N actual flaming sword.

EVA: Flaming sword, flaming sword!

> Why don't you come across with the fur you promised me?

ADDY: In the sweat of my brow . . .

> (*A tiger roars / monkeys shriek / a baby cries /* ADDY's *hunting call fades away*)

AFFAIR OF HONOR
A Radio Play

GÜNTER KUNERT
translated by A. Leslie Willson

(*Voices: Commentator, Steege, Traxel, Müllner, Bergen, Notary, Bornstedt, Mathilde, Mignet, Heine 1 & Heine 2, not two different voices but only one that is split acoustically. A music box is playing the "Marseillaise."*)

1

COMMENTATOR: From the "Foreword" to the book *French Conditions* by Heinrich Heine: Those who can read will automatically notice in my book that its greatest defects cannot be blamed on me, and those who cannot read —will notice nothing. I can also preface these pages with these simple syllogisms. If we succeed in making the broad public understand the present, then peoples will no longer be goaded into hate and war by the literary hacks of the aristocracy—the great convenant of peoples, the holy alliance of nations, will come into being. We will no longer have to feed standing armies of many hundreds of thousands of murderers because of mutual distrust. We will use their swords and horses for plowing, and we will achieve peace and prosperity and freedom. To this effect my life remains dedicated; it is my charge. The hate of my enemies can bear witness that till now I have conducted this charge faithfully and honorably. I will always show myself worthy of that hate.

2

HEINE 2: Herrn Julius Campe, Hamburg.

Paris, 12 May

Dear Campe: I have heard that the police have already interrogated you
three times because of my "Foreword" to *French Conditions*: The gendarmes
show an astonishing interest in literature, and so as a publisher you find new
readers even in circles like those, and you can thank me for it all! I have the
suspicion that the size of my printings is a result of the guardians of thought
in thirty-six German provinces devouring my works: May they belch bitterly.
My official readers even travel here to Paris to study me on the spot. While
England produces cotton and France cognac, people are busy in German
provinces with the manufacture of informers—not a very profitable business.
In the reading room where every morning I scan the German gazettes in
order to delectate myself with the latest slanders against my person instead
of with brunch, certain gentlemen take a seat near me and act as though
they were reading, while not taking their eyes off of yours truly—a pretense,
for a total ignorance of the alphabet is branded onto these characters where
other people usually have a face. They are simply disguised cattle from the
meadows of the North German lowlands, and often I am tempted to hold
out a handful of hay to them to see whether they'll eat it. Admittedly, they
aren't the only nuisances: Every German who travels to Paris wants to see
Heine, and I fancy myself a museum piece, with the difference that mu-
seums close at evening and the displays are left in peace till the next morning, whereas I may be observed evenings, too. Many succeed in surreptiti-
ously obtaining a letter of introduction somewhere, that is then presented to
me. Often they are refugees, emigrants, or such who claim to be. *En passant*
I'd like to describe for you one of the funnier cases, almost like a Molière
comedy. The incident took place in my apartment in the Cité Bergére. I was
entertaining a female visitor at the time, Mademoiselle Augustine, a slight
acquaintance from the Palais Royal, where I generally make such and similar acquaintances: I am damned to love only the basest women. In any
case I opened the door unsuspectingly in response to a knock.

STEEGE: Good day—Herr Heinrich Heine? My name is Steege, Ludwig, and
I have just arrived in Paris and have the honor of handing you this
letter from a mutual acquaintance.

HEINE 2: And before I knew what was happening, he had pressed the letter
into my hand with a staggering but later on completely logically appearing
mixture of servility and impudence, passed by me cringingly, was already in
the entry hall and on his way to the little parlor, where I followed him as
though I were the intruder and he the legitimate occupant of the apartment.
I arrived just in time to see him greet Augustine with disgusting familiarity.
I wanted to dismiss her, but she suddenly seemed to be no longer in a hurry.

(*Voices talking in the background; Augustine is noticeable only by
giggles, sighs, exclamations; she accompanies the dialogue of the
two men vocally.*)

STEEGE (*to* AUGUSTINE): It's a great honor for me to be permitted to greet
you, a muse of Heine. Thou art like a blossom, so tender, fair, and
pure. My name is Steege, Ludwig. Louis—compris?

HEINE 1: The sender of this note that introduces you, Herr—Herr Steege,
is absolutely unknown to me, a pity! Weren't you about to leave,
Augustine?

STEEGE: But let the charming young lady stay, you're upsetting her . . .

HEINE 1: Please don't give me any advice about my behavior. Very different
quarters are trying that. There's your note back. Inform the sender
that he erred in the address, that he never met me, even in a dream!
I don't make friends in my dreams. I'm a realist. And you, Augustine,
don't roll your eyes like a grazing calf that has eaten a rose by mistake.

STEEGE: Sir! The treatment to which you are subjecting this lady is outrageous!

HEINE 1: Monsieur! You amuse me. Only someone from the Lüneberg
Heath or from out in the sticks can consider this lady a lady, either
because he never saw a lady in his life or never saw a whore!

STEEGE: That word, that last word, that unspeakable word, which no decent
German man would utter, you take back that word at once, Herr
Heine!

HEINE 2: He deported himself as though he were shaken by a sudden on-slaught of Teutonic chivalry, an infectious illness from the house of Schlegel & Tieck, made worse by the earlier reception of Romantic poems that Je-hovah or some other relative sympathetic to me—and there aren't many in any case—prevented me from writing.

STEEGE: I won't stand for you to insult this young woman, this lady!

HEINE 1: It isn't libelous to call a master baker a master baker! It would be something else, if with this word that, as a German man, you choke on, I intended to designate my professional colleagues who have remained at home. With that I would demean the designation of an ancient and excellent trade by applying it to those figures who *have* sold themselves to tyrants, however, without thereby giving pleasure to anyone, for which the *lady* here is in a position to do in *any* position!

STEEGE: You take that back, you take that back at once! Before I forget myself.

HEINE 1: The latter would be the best thing you could do. I'll do the same at once after your departure!

STEEGE: Herr Heine!

HEINE 2: Herr Steege, Ludwig, the obligatory personification of German humorlessness, balled his fists and, lacking a better idea, conjured the Old Testament descent of my ancestors, called me an unpatriotic Itzig and a born ragpicker, and I retorted, saying I couldn't have earned anything with such a scoundrel as he was. One friendly word led to another. The invective flew through the air like filth, till I got tired of it and showed this odd visitor the door, in sure certainty that I had saved myself the price of a ticket for today for a loge seat in the Comédie Française. It's regrettable that my talent isn't trained for the comic stage: What money I could rake in if I wrote farces like this. Therefore I exhort you, noble Campe, to be more mindful of the latest royalty check. I'm broke, as usual. Farewell and go to the Devil.

Your Heine

3

HEINE 2: Herr Maximilian Heine, Russian Imperial Physician, St. Petersburg.

Paris, 14 May

Dearest Brother, in answer to your question: The palsy of my left hand is making "progress," which admittedly doesn't mean more progress for me myself. It's progress in the wrong direction, something it has in common with other political developments. My vision is also declining more and more, and at times I'm not sure whether I regret that because what you get to see is mostly not worth it anyway, such as the parliament's decrees, as a result of which the poets of Young Germany are outlawed like murderers and thieves, whereby the ringleader is none other than your loving brother! I am the Karl Moor of recent times. God knows, I'm happy to be sitting here in Paris instead of in a German prison, with which they propose to cure writing and poetizing at home, even though I'm often torn from my work by some nuisance or other. As an example, two days ago something insignificant, but so you can see what impedes me—a tall, pale man appears at my door. His lips compressed as though he begrudged every word, he burdens me with a letter of introduction by an unknown hand, picks a fight, imagine, because of a female! Cherchez la femme! He fell into a terrible rage. We said a few civilities to one another that would have shaken up a Berlin coachman.

STEEGE: Garlic eater! Haggling Jew! Despoiler of women! Ragpicker!

HEINE 1: I would be ashamed to haggle with such a scoundrel as you! Be glad that Jesus Christ can't see your Christianity. He'd knock your ears off properly with His Cross.

STEEGE: Here, my card! I demand satisfaction for the ghastly affront that has been done me in this house.

HEINE 1: You're surely not calling me out? Because of a grisette? Do you want us to be the laughing stock of Paris?

STEEGE: Don't evade the issue! I demand satisfaction for the insult to my honor!

HEINE 1: I'm afraid our conceptions of honor don't coincide. Mine is of a

somewhat impersonal nature, I must admit. Not private property.
STEEGE: What? You have no personal honor at all?

HEINE 2: I tried to explain to him that mine was mine only insofar as it belonged to everyone with whom I was of a like mind, but like a Vaucanson automaton he kept repeating the same thing—duel, duel, duel!

STEEGE: You're no German at all anymore. You've become a lackey of Louis-Philippe. Otherwise you'd know what Germany needs today. I have the honor to take my leave.

HEINE 2: There it was again, that creature frequently conjured up but invisible, that seemed to dwell in Herr Steege (Ludwig) like a worm in the apple. How often have I been insulted, humiliated by anthropomorphic burglar-proof safes like our Uncle Solomon; but I've really been struck and hurt. My mission was placed in doubt.

(*The voice of* STEEGE *in the background*: My dear young woman, I bid you farewell, farewell, adieu, au revoir . . .)
HEINE 1: My honor is no slighter, no less susceptible to hurt than that of someone else. It's just not a sensitive eczema, a moral hemorrhoid, produced by sitting around in the taverns of German fraternities. My honor befits all who, as soon as they have need for the unpretentious plural, mean not only their persons but the host of those who are like-minded: Our honor is identical with our convictions, Herr Steege, and it appears to me that you lack the latter, to my honest regret!
STEEGE: You may expect my seconds shortly! Since I'm the insulted party, I have the choice of weapons! Adieu, Monsieur Heine!

HEINE 2: You see, dear brother, that my life in Paris is fairly lively. My beloved homeland is sending me enough fools so that I won't die of boredom. An embrace from your

Harry.

4

COMMENTATOR: From the "Foreword" of *French Conditions*: I will not ever return to my homeland as long as even one of those noble refugees who, because of an all too great enthusiasm, could give no head to reason, must tarry in foreign parts, in misery. Never was a people more cruelly mocked by its rulers. A handful of junkers who learned nothing but a bit of horse-trading, with which you can at most dupe farmers at fairs. These men presume thus to be able to fool a whole people, and a people at that who discovered gunpowder and book-printing and the critique of pure reason. This undeserved insult, that you think we are even more stupid than you are yourselves, and that you imagine you can delude us, this is the worst insult that you inflict upon us in the presence of surrounding peoples, who wait still with astonishment to see what we will do. It is no longer a matter, they say, of freedom, but of honor.

5

HEINE 2: To Moses Moser,

Paris, 20 May

Dear Moser: Will the letter you receive from me today be pleasing to you, although the occasion is anything but pleasant? You can perform an important service for me by a loan of 400 Thaler in a time of the most grievous passion of my life. My affairs are at this moment so bad that only a fool or a friend would lend me money now. I have been at odds most bitterly recently with my uncle, the millionaire. With their amiable frivolity my French friends have caused me great financial losses; in Germany I am allowed to print nothing but tame poems and innocent fairy tales, but I have different things altogether lying in my desk. In addition, things are happening around me that occur as though behind a veil, threatening, but intangible. For this reason I am sorely troubled. Today at noon our good Traxel fetched me for lunch, distressed and silent, and when we were sitting over our bouillabaisse—you know what good food means to me—he began to explain to me the reason for his distress by asking me whether I already knew of the Ghent affair. He had just that minute heard about it.

HEINE I: The Ghent affair? Has the famous altarpiece by Grünewald been stolen?

TRAXEL: Well, in Ghent three Belgian officers challenged a journalist to a duel because of his utterances about King Leopold—that's what I was talking about...

HEINE I: I've envied monarchs more than anyone because they have a really inexhaustible reservoir from which they can take imbeciles for any mischief.

TRAXEL: That's not what I mean at all, rather...

HEINE I: Rather?

TRAXEL: Let's eat our soup first, before we spoil our appetite with the story.

HEINE I: No, my dear fellow, once you start, you've got to go all the way. Well—what's going on?

TRAXEL: I've received a warning. About a plot by Prussian officers.

HEINE I: Coup d'état in Prussia? Unthinkable! The army not only hacks others to pieces, it lets itself be hacked to pieces, assuming that they are furnished a great draught from the bottle that contains a high patriotic content! Prost, my dear fellow!

TRAXEL: I mean that these officers, after reading your famous-infamous foreword to the *French Conditions*, are said to have sworn to involve its famous-infamous author in an affair of honor in order to rid the world of him unobtrusively in that manner. So for the immediate future I recommend the greatest caution! Your frivolity, my dear Heine, in your attitude toward duels is sufficiently well known. That thing with the Frenchman recently—madness!

HEINE I: You know about that?

TRAXEL: Heine, Heine, that you would get involved in duels because of Germanomania, who would have suspected that? Just because some petit bourgeois says: Nous Allemands! You, the cosmopolite. You, the European. You, the citizen of the world!

HEINE 1: That's why. I can be all that only because I'm so very much a German. Dear Traxel, I can't escape this skin even through circumcision. My behavior was ridiculous, I know, but I know, too, that Germany will lose all that's pathologically aggressive, its fancies and crazy notions, only when it's like all other nations, neither better nor worse. To that extent have I submitted to this idiocy, not for the sake of a national supremacy but for that of equal rights, also for my own in this country.

TRAXEL: Nevertheless, for the immediate future you ought to forgo such dangerous childishness. Avoid provocations. What's the matter with you, anyway? Your soup is getting cold. Or don't you like it?

HEINE 1: I do, I do—it's excellent.

TRAXEL: Naturally, you don't have to be so very greatly concerned. You've been warned now. And besides, I already told you: It's a rumor! You're simply a European celebrity, and the gossips need big shots for their nourishment so that they can stay alive. Try the Beaujolais, Heine, it's the very best vintage!

HEINE 2: While we were drinking, the visit of Herr Steege appeared in an entirely different light to me. The letter of introduction? Presumably forged. His loathsome familiarity with Augustine? Perhaps he prepared her in advance with a few Louis d'or? And the way *he* started the argument, without subterfuge or hesitation, leading straight to the challenge to a duel—all that suddenly seemed completely clear to me. It had been a trap, and I already had one foot in it. Am I to let myself be riddled by Prussian officers for a few pages of prose, even if it was effectively written? Am I to play the hero once more, the role that till now has always ended happily for me, but that this time could be bound to absolutely certain death? A precarious position, adapted to my general situation, as a result of which I wonder whether it wouldn't be best and simplest to fall in a duel. For my miseries that would be the perfect solution, from which a marvelous Heine legend could climb like a bush of blood-red roses: beside me Goethe's Werther, an anemic figure anyway, would turn pale in comparison. If you have any advice to give me, along with the loan, give it to me without delay. But quickly.

Your Heinrich Heine

6

COMMENTATOR: From the "Foreword": It is true, only a short time ago many friends of the Fatherland wished for the enlargement of Prussia, and in its king hoped to see the sovereign of a united Germany. And they were able to entice love of country. And there was a Prussian liberalism, and the friends of freedom already were looking trustingly at the linden trees of Berlin. As far as I'm concerned, I never wanted to condescend to such a trust. Rather, I look with apprehension at this Prussian eagle, and while others boasted about how daringly it looked into the sun, I was all the more attentive to its claws. I did not trust this Prussian, this tall, hypocritical hero wearing leggings, with his expansive belly and his great maw and his swagger stick that he dips in holy water only before he hits out with it. I didn't like this philosophically Christian soldiery, this hodgepodge of light ale, lies, and sand. Repugnant, deeply repugnant to me, was this Prussia, this stiff, hypocritical, sanctimonious Prussia, this Tartuffe among states.

7

BORNSTEDT: Secret Report to His Excellency Prince Metternich in Vienna.

Paris, 27 May

Your Excellency: Yesterday I met the aforementioned Heine again in the reading room, where, somewhat stout, untidily dressed, his left arm hanging motionlessly at his side, he recognized me only after a little while and greeted me.

HEINE I: Ah, Bornstedt. How are you? What's new in the gazettes?

BORNSTEDT: He acted conceited, mimicking the French, full of boundless vanity, speaking loudly enough for those present to find out who he was. I replied I had just read in the *Revue des Deux Mondes* that he had prophesied a German revolution. He grinned in his cynically insolent way and replied:

HEINE I: That's the only thing that a man inclined to monarchy as I am can hope for. I bet my essay struck like a bombshell among the revolutionary canaille in Paris.

BORNSTEDT: Saying this, he shook with laughter, and I strove to agree, in order to keep his trust. Heine is not only a completely dishonorable fellow, he is just as great a hypocrite, without dignity and faith, cowardly and mendacious and totally unsuspecting of me, in spite of the instinct for people that he thinks he has. I said to him:

My dear Heine, with articles like that you will hardly succeed in ever lifting the ban on your writings in Germany!

He became serious and with the clear note of the utmost conviction he declared:

HEINE I: Do you really know, Bornstedt, how much Metternich esteems me? I have precise information that he reads and thinks highly of my books. I am pondering turning to His Excellency in a letter and of interceding with him because of the suppressions! I am certain he will be open to my arguments!

BORNSTEDT: I tried very hard to remain serious, since I do know the viewpoint of Your Excellency precisely. It's absolutely appropriate, since you consider Heine to be the real ringleader and head of Young Germany, whom one has to guard against the most. By the way, the prohibition of Heine's works has made a bad impression in Paris, and lends him an importance that should be avoided. Instead of putting the writer in a moderate mood, such a thing on the contrary is incitatory and will drive him more and more into the party of the revolutionaries, or at least into the opposition. Courteously, I demanded to know what there was to the rumors of an impending duel on his part. But hardly had I made the allusion than he lost all affability and courtesy of which he otherwise is master:

HEINE I: Well, what do you know about it? Gossip! Disgusting gossip! My enemies are again spreading new fictions abroad about me!

BORNSTEDT: Saying this, though, he did not give the impression that this rumor was of indifference to him. He became agitated, almost apprehensive, and he glanced about as though he were looking for someone or as though he were only searching for a quick way out because the topic of conversation was unnerving to him. I pursued the subject immediately:

> In the salons there's wide talk, honored maestro, that you are collecting all your friends in Paris about you because of a perilous infamy...?

And as though I had stuck him with a darning needle, he addressed me angrily:

HEINE I: Herr von Bornstedt! I always thought you were a cavalier, a man of taste and tact! And now you snatch up such monstrosities! All right—just go on spreading it, go ahead. I even authorize you to blab everywhere that Heine is gathering his troops for an attack from ambush! Whoever wants to believe it, can!

BORNSTEDT: Hurriedly he touched the rim of his hat, in a gesture of farewell, and before I could ask him whether he was actually serious that he had sought and found support from like-minded people and whether it suited him if I announced this news so he could in this way ward off the aforementioned attack, or whether he were ironically admitting everything solely out of an injured vanity in order to dupe me, as he liked to do with his acquaintances—thus before I could attain certainty, he had already vanished. Anyway, there must be something to this rumor about Heine's impending duel, otherwise he would not have reacted so violently. Also, his outburst and the reference he let slip out about an attack from ambush lend the matter more weight than I at first assumed. I will give Your Excellency a fresh report as soon as anything should happen to the aforementioned Heine. Until then I beg you most humbly to remit the next payment sooner than usual to the account in the Banque Munizipale to

Your Excellency's most obedient servant,
Adalbert von Bornstedt

8

HEINE 2: Herrn Ludwig Steege, Hotel of Three Lilies

Paris, 22 May

Dear Herr Steege: Yesterday two gentlemen sought me out, identifying themselves as your seconds, and to prevent your receiving false information about our conversation and its outcome, I am informing you faithfully of what transpired. The gentleman who introduced himself as Alfred Müllner...

MÜLLNER: Müllner, Alfred, and my companion here is Herr von Bergen!

HEINE 2: ... went straight to the heart of the matter.

MÜLLNER: Herr Steege has requested us to look after his interests in the affair of honor that concerns you both, and we readily agreed to his request, since we totally and completely approve of Herr Steege's conduct.

HEINE 1: Pardon my interruption, gentlemen: Are you traveling through Paris?

BERGEN: That has nothing to do with it!

MÜLLNER: Yes, traveling through, you could say.

HEINE 1: From Prussia to Prussia?

BERGEN: We have not come to you for conversation about the geographical aspects of our local sojourn, Herr Heine! To come to the point: Our client, as the injured party, has chosen the weapons, pistols, and we suggest a distance of fifteen paces. Exchange of fire until the elimination of one of the opponents. Date: next Sunday at five a.m. Place: Bois de Boulogne, behind the old plane trees—you know the place from your last affair!

HEINE 1: You seem to be well informed about my "affairs."

MÜLLNER: Name your seconds for us, so that the matter can, shall we say, be disposed of as quickly as possible.

HEINE 1: Gentlemen, I'm afraid you're getting into something that could be extremely deleterious for your reputation, or for all I care, also for your honor as gentlemen. I would be ready at any time for a duel, if it actually concerned an injury that could not otherwise be made up for.

BERGEN: We will oblige you to the extent that as the superintending physician we propose Dr. Koreff, your personal physician.

HEINE I: How do you know Dr. Koreff? Your knowledge about my private life is quite extraordinary. Too extraordinary for my taste. So you must also know then what a middling marksman I am. My previous duels were conducted with the saber. I once received a thrust in the kidney, something you must likewise know.

BERGEN: Just name your seconds, so that we can get in contact with the gentlemen.

HEINE 2: Thereupon I expressed the conjecture that you, dear Herr Steege, in your justifiable agitation, could have described the unpleasant incident unconsciously, not at all the way it actually took place, Without intending to affront you anew, I decided to give both gentlemen a calm depiction of the distressing event, purely and simply concerned that you, my dear Herr Steege, might thereby forfeit your good name and your seconds as well. I am inclined to assume that both hail from a city of muses that I treasure dearly, since it seemed to me as though one of the gentlemen commented to the other: "In Berlin we settle this sort of thing more quickly. . ." So I told both of those men how you handed me the letter of introduction, whereupon you said:

STEEGE: My name is Steege. I have just arrived in Paris and have the great honor of handing you the letter of a mutual friend. . .

HEINE 2: I took the letter, while you were courteously greeting the lady tarrying in my apartment.

STEEGE: It's a pleasure for me, mein Fräulein, to be able to greet you, a muse of the great poet Heine.

HEINE I: Weren't you about to leave, Augustine?

STEEGE: Do let this enchanting young woman stay, maitre. You would distress me, if you took this charming sight away from me.

HEINE 2: With that, I do admit, you stirred my jealously. You, the paragon of a young German, I an elderly, ailing man who could not restrain himself from voicing his sensitivity.

HEINE 1: I renounce your advice. Here, you have the letter retour. I don't know the sender. Augustine, don't roll your eyes as though you had never before seen an elegant young man!

HEINE 2: And then you said:

STEEGE: How can the creator of the lines "Thou art like a blossom, so tender, fair, and pure . . ." harm such a blossom with a coarse nand?

HEINE 2: You made me ashamed of myself. And from this shame, that I didn't want to confess, resulted my further behavior, and I said:

HEINE 1: I suppose you never ever saw a whore?
STEEGE: It wasn't for this purpose that I hurried to Paris, but to see that poet of poets, who with his songs and romances filled our hearts with a new image of womanhood and imbued us with a new feminine ideal.

HEINE 2: This formulation, which could not have occurred to me more brilliantly, deepened my unjustified ill temper, and I shouted:

HEINE 1: You take that right back! You take that back or something awful will happen.

HEINE 2: And you said, with understandable rage:

STEEGE: Are you threatening me? Are you challenging me to a duel, me, who has approached you with the noblest of intentions? Do you intend to exemplify in me what your enemies are saying about you, Herr Heine? And even if this blossoming creature here next to us lacks bourgeois virtues, virginal purity, you personally have done nothing to restore them, and as the object of a duel she would be definitely dishonored and deprived of her ultimate honor.

HEINE 2: You turned to the door, and over your shoulder you called out with cutting sharpness:

STEEGE: Heine, you belong among those scoundrels to whom the ancestors of ragpickers still cling.

HEINE 1: That's the way it happened in reality, gentlemen, and now please tell me where the reason for a duel might lie, and who the offended party is? Your client conducted himself irreproachably, possibly he used a few coarse words, but in facto he dealt me a lesson in chivalrous behavior. I wouldn't know why he should destroy his triumph over Heine by putting my admitted moral defeat itself into question, even raise it by a completely foundless challenge to a duel.

HEINE 2: In so far, dear Herr Steege, my communication with your seconds whom you, if you correctly reflect, have sent to me not only precipitously, but even in error.

With best wishes,
Your Heinrich Heine

9

COMMENTATOR: From the "Foreword": You need not be afraid, because you are all mighty and wise. You have gold and guns, and what is for sale you can buy, and what is mortal you can kill. And you also have iron pots in which you can imprison those who give you riddles on things you want to know not of. And you can seal them up and sink them into the ocean of forgetfulness—all like King Solomon. Like him you also understand the language of the birds. You know everything that is twittered and piped in the land, and if the song of a bird displeases you, you have a great scissors with which you can cut his bill into shape.

10

HEINE 2: To Heinrich Laube.

Paris, 25 May

Dear Laube: You must hear of an important occurrence of today's date because it also concerns you, and because perhaps very soon the case may
happen that I will need you, though not in a material way. Without wasting
breath: Today I set down my last will and testament. The notary just left,
shaking his head, a first-class factotum, of whom I fear I overexerted his
powers of comprehension. Not least, best Laube, do I write to you out of
precautionary reasons, so that from my hand you will learn what my mouth
whispered a few minutes ago into the waxen-pale ear of the notary, things
that I am not certain completely reached the brain that belongs to that ear.

NOTARY: So, Monsieur Heine, you are leaving all your personal goods and
    real estate to your wife Natalie.
HEINE I: Mathilde!
NOTARY: That's what I said. As well as the legal title to your works. What
    are the works involved? You see, that must be specified in order to
    avoid the possibility of subsequent controversy. Iron works? Or what?
HEINE I: Monsieur—I am a poet, a writer, my name is Heinrich Heine!
NOTARY: I *have* heard the name before—Heine? Heine? You're a Swiss,
    aren't you?
HEINE I: No, I'm German, born in Düsseldorf.
NOTARY: Oh, I love the mountains.
HEINE I: I ask you, please pay more attention! So, write this down: Heinrich
    Laube, my friend in Germany, is to be appointed as the editor of my
    collected works. He must take care that I come unmutilated to pos-
    terity. I would turn over in my grave. . .
NOTARY: Forgive me, but that is scientifically untenable. Nobody turns
    there anymore!
HEINE I: . . . turn over! if I appeared as a meek Heinrich to my beloved
    Germans, as a kind of sedative brewed from the dried petals of the
    blue flower of Romanticism. I want the scandal not to end with me
    at my death. My countrymen must choke on me, so that the gall will
    rise up in them even after a hundred years.
NOTARY: I have no idea how I'm supposed to translate all of that into legal
    terminology.

HEINE 1: Please give me the name and address of your keenest competitor! He'll be glad to find out that you turned down Heine's will!

NOTARY: I'm writing, writing down everything! But I tell you one thing: It would have been easier with iron works.

HEINE 1: To Herr Gutzkow and the other poets of Young Germany I leave something that is fully unknown to them, although they act as if they had it in abundance: I mean, talent. To the German emigrants in Paris I bestow with my best wishes two left shoes, since that's the way they behave to one another.

NOTARY: My God—and I'm supposed to disclose this some day. The things these Swiss think of! I hope you live to a ripe old age, Herr Heine.

HEINE 1: In my homeland, where quotations are loved because they replace the effort of thought, there is a recitation about the uncertainty of the personal final act: On proud horses yesterday, shot through the breast today, tomorrow in the icy grave! Not my own, but still very impressive. And you have no inkling, Sir, of how close I am to lending these lines literal reality. Except for the horse, of course, on which I have sat only metaphorically. But you can fall off a horse like that, too, and break your neck. Mine is named "Pride"!

NOTARY: You have a philosophical bent, Monsieur. May I conclude my notation?

HEINE 1: In a minute. In conclusion I want to provide for my Fatherland. This is a land that not only destroys your sleep but can destroy your life, because through its fervor and its morality, through its diligence and its faith it awakens the impression that it is a task that could be resolved. As if to humanize it entirely, you only needed to multiply its good qualities and subtract its bad ones, and this could happen easily by prior drill in books and gazettes! But only a fool believes such a thing.

HEINE 2: At this last statement the notary looked at me, my dear Laube, as though I were really crazy and had just escaped from the Charenton Asylum. Our German problems will probably eternally remain a book with seven seals for normal people. But anyway, now you know what to do, in case something happens to me, and what I request of you in perhaps the last days of my life. Guard this document well. It is conceived to refute any doubt in your legitimacy as the executor of my spiritual testament.

                                                                      Very sincerely,
                                                                      Heinrich Heine

11

COMMENTATOR: From the "Foreword": I would like to warn you of one thing, however, namely of the *Monitor* of 1793. That is a book of black magic that you can't put in chains, and it contains words of conjuration that are much mightier than gold and guns, words with which one can call the dead forth from their graves and dispatch the living into death, words with which one can make giants of dwarfs and can smash giants, words that cut all your might into shreds like the blade a royal neck. I will confess the truth to you. There are people who possess courage enough to pronounce those words.

12

COMMENTATOR: From the "Foreword": There are people who possess courage enough to pronounce those words and who would not have feared the most dreadful apparitions. But don't rely on powerlessness and fear on our part. The disguised man of the age, who has a bold heart as well as a skillful tongue, and who knows the great magic word and is able to utter it, perhaps he is already standing next to you.

13

HEINE 2: To Julius Campe, Hamburg.

Boulogne-sur-Mer, 30 May

My dear Campe: My departure from Paris to Boulogne, where I am at the moment, turned out to be simply necessary in order for me to be able to finish in peace the work of which I advised you, a recent, magnificent book that you as always will earn more from than I will. In this connection may I remind you of the monetary remittance that is due. But quickly, my dear Campe, life is expensive, and a dead author will be of no use to you. Here, with the beloved sea before me, my disposition is brightening. What a marvelous peace Nature has!

MATHILDE: How much longer are we going to stay here, Henri? When are we ever going to travel back to Paris? Nothing is as desolate as all this water? It makes me yawn constantly, horrible.

HEINE 2: Significant projects are ripening here in my isolation. As a counterpiece to my North Sea poem I am planning one about the Atlantic. . .

MATHILDE: You're trying to kill me with boredom, Henri. I'm despairing in this hole here. Shall I throw myself into the surf? And we don't know anyone here. What a miserable solitude! I can't endure it! I can't stand it, Henri!

HEINE 2: I pressed ten extra francs into the greedy claws of my concierge in Paris so that she would not betray my place of sojourn and my present residential address to anyone, not even to my best friend. Being alone with my work, with my cheerful Mathilde, is such a rare fortune that I am enjoying it profoundly.

MATHILDE: Let's play cards at least, Henri. Put your pen down! Do you intend to sit the whole, live-long day at your desk and not do anything else? What's to come of it! Come on, we'll go for a stroll. Possibly we'll come on a café chantant, where things are happening. . .

HEINE 2: This divine quiet! The ocean, hardly in motion, pours out a peace that does my tormented nerves good. If this peace surrounded me constantly, what I could accomplish!

MATHILDE: Henri! You brought me to this barren place, now pay some attention to me, too.

HEINE 2: In any case I will demand one thing of you: that you do not give this new book to the Prussian censor! I forbid you to do that! I will not sell my honor for book royalties, however bitterly I am in need of them. And I will also not let the least blemish adhere to my good name. I will not submit to the Prussian censor. I have done what a man could do, if he has a clear conscience. More I cannot do. I will retain my pure conscience. How would I otherwise be able to write in the future? I did not desert my homeland just to commit literary suicide in exile!

MATHILDE: We haven't contrived a wrestling match yet today. I want to vanquish you again, or you vanquish me, Henri. Let's start right away. . .

HEINE 2: If I were to give in only a little, I would be lost. It begins with a small concession: leave out a word here, diminish a formulation there, and the result would be to renounce specific subjects entirely, and at the same time renounce fundamentals, principles, the very essence of art, which is not an unprincipled ghost. In the end one has drawn the noose so tightly oneself, caught oneself in a circle where one poetizes flowers and bees to the full satisfaction of the censor and to the painful horror of readers, who are to be enlightened, summoned, shaken awake, shocked, and strengthened, in order to demand the Kingdom of Heaven here and now, not to be lulled and comforted till kingdom-come.

(*knocking*)
MATHILDE: Henri, someone's knocking. It looks like we're going to have visitors!

HEINE 2: Someone is knocking at the door this moment. I must break off, my dear Campe. Don't forget the transmittal of money.

(*Renewed knocking, hard*)
HEINE I: Come in, come on in!
STEEGE: Good morning, here I am, Steege, Ludwig, to have a word with you, Herr Heine! But in private!

14

(*Knocking on a door*)

STEEGE: My name is Steege, Ludwig, Herr Mignet. I've just come from your friend Heinrich Heine, who's relaxing on the seashore. He gave me this note for you: To Monsieur François-August-Marie Mignet.

MIGNET: Please take a seat, I'll be right back.

(*A door is closed. Mignet reads aloud to himself.*)

My dear friend: Today I am turning to you with a hardly usual request, that must be preceded by another, namely, one of forbearance. Since I am at the moment sojourning in Boulogne, I am unable to explain the aforementioned request in person, the extreme importance of which for me I expressly emphasize. Force of circumstances has involved me in a political struggle, and the force of petty intrigues causes me, if I wish to conduct the struggle further, to capitulate in other areas.

HEINE 2: Don't deny me your sympathy or your trust, since I need both more than ever. Act without questioning, and accept the bearer of this letter like a long-missed friend. Herr Ludwig Steege, and he is the one concerned, is one of those valiant German men from whom we must expect much in the future. The future belongs to such as him, that I emphasize most sincerely. Introduce him into the high society of Paris, so that he can make his fortune there. He has earned it. His ability is distinguished, his instinct excellent, his talents, though not unique, nevertheless developed to a degree that I would not have considered possible.

MIGNET (*reading*): I hope you do understand me. Under an average constitution is hidden an extraordinary spirit, of which an appropriate example was given me.

In friendship as ever,
Your Heine

15

COMMENTATOR: From the "Foreword": Don't you sometimes shudder when servile figures fawn about you with almost ironic humility, and suddenly you think: Maybe that's a trick. This miserable man, who conducted himself with such stupid absolutism, such bestial obedience, maybe he's a cryptic Brutus. Don't you sometimes at night have dreams that warn you of the smallest, wriggly worms that by chance you saw crawling by day? Don't be afraid! I'm only joking, you're quite safe. Don't worry in regard to the little fools who at times flit about you with questionable pranks. The big fool protects you from the little one. The big fool is a very big fool, gigantic, and it calls itself the German people. On his hat, instead of little bells hang nothing but enormously heavy church bells, and in his hand he carries a gigantic iron sword. Whenever a good friend comes to him, wanting to talk to him compassionately about his pains or even to suggest a home remedy to him, then he becomes absolutely furious and strikes at him with the iron sword. He is furious in general at anyone who means well. He is the worst enemy to his friends and a friend of his enemies.

16

HEINE 2: To Maximilian Heine, Imperial Russian Physician, St. Petersburg.

Paris, 3 June

Dear Brother: My state of health, already meager, underwent a questionable improvement in the Cité Bergére after my return. For two days I have been the possessor of such a case of jaundice that I could march through Peking without being noticed. Of course, in the medical reference books, which I consulted with greater zeal than with the real doctors, I found nothing about the reciprocity of disposition and the gall bladder, but I am firmly convinced of their indissoluble connection. My hepatitis is the direct result of an incident of which I can speak to no one but you. Just imagine, in Boulogne that fellow of whom I wrote to you before, who insisted that he intended to duel

with me, appears and demands to speak to me privately. Hardly has Mathilde left the room than he asks sarcastically why I had fled away from
Paris from him!

STEEGE: Or will you deny that, my dear sir?

HEINE I: You are mistaken, sir! The necessity of having to finish a book in
the shortest time, for which I lacked the tranquillity in Paris, forced
me to withdraw here. In case you intend to renew your challenge to
a duel. . .

STEEGE: You made use of a dastardly trick, Herr Heine, by which you are
trying to evade my challenge! You spread the rumor that Prussian
officers were planning to kill you in an affair of honor! But this ruse
will avail you naught!

HEINE I: Is it really a rumor? Anway, it isn't my idea! Your two seconds,
my dear Herr Steege, and you as well, in your approach and your
appearance, correspond entirely to this "rumor." I have credible
grounds to assume that it's a matter of actual fact. My "Foreword"
to French Conditions scared up all the reactionaries in Prussia. A
mood of pogrom prevails as in 1819 when Sand, the student, murdered the worst dramatist in the world, Kotzebue, who was by the
way a Russian agent, murdered him because in the fraternities the
national virus led its fresh fleet fervent and free life and the unfor-
tunate Sand had become infected with it. For ever and an age the
Germans have sought in others the blame for their self-inflicted
miseries. Now it's the Pope, now Napoleon, now Heinrich Heine!

STEEGE: Thanks for the informative lecture. But I'm not concerned with
the verification of a rumor. I'm concerned with something entirely
different. Mademoiselle Augustine can attest to your insult to me,
and both my seconds will swear that you lack the courage to accept
the consequences of your own behavior. I'm already in contact with
the Independent Hamburg Correspondent and will reveal in that
newspaper how it is with the valor of the bard of the Revolution!
Every gazette in Germany will reprint that with a compliment to me!

HEINE I: You have a talent for dramatics! You staged that splendidly, didn't
you? Is that the way it is?

STEEGE: I'm a physician, Herr Heine, just beginning, or even better: an
adept disillusioned by forensic medical science.

HEINE I: And it seems completely conceivable to me now that you yourself
and your accomplices spread the rumors about the officers in order
to frighten me, in order to put pressure on me—but why?

STEEGE: Heine, Heine! I'm afraid you've destroyed your reputation in Germany! As soon as your name is mentioned even faintly henceforth, your readers will renounce your books because the abyss between the ideal Heine and the real Heine has become too great for them! Your credibility, your fame as the admonisher of the nation, as the harbinger of a new, higher ethos is passé. At every line from you they'll say: It's easy to be heroic on paper, but paper is patient. . .

HEINE I: That certainly didn't grow on your provincial manure, Steege. Someone thought that out for you! Even my Prussians can't think that far!

HEINE 2: And in the moment I said that I realized: Such an intrigue could occur to only one man—to Metternich! As a result of his plan he would be rid of me in any case. He arranged this so-called duel through which, if I accepted it, I would depart this life, or in the case of a refusal I would fade away as a dishonorable coward. The latter might even be more pleasing to him, because simultaneously it would imply rendering my work harmless, my writings ineffective, whereas in a duelling death a legend would assist in the wider distribution of my books; admittedly also would complete them with finality. And the high point of the Metternich raffinesse consisted also of the fact that my physical or moral liquidation would be blamed on his Prussian allies, and he himself would remain free of any suspicion! What progress as opposed to earlier epochs, where they sent the disagreeable scrivener a cup of hemlock or a rope, so that he would know he had to do himself in.

STEEGE: My dear Heine, you have been away from your homeland for too long! The oafish German has lost his clumsiness in regard to a lot. Think of that, in case you ever again write something about Germany. Anyway, I'm not here to repeat my challenge. On the contrary, I'm prepared to renounce our duel.

HEINE 2: He withdrew his gaze from the ceiling and stared at me expectantly. I fell silent, since I hadn't even a glimmer of what he had in mind. I imagined that I had never stood so clearly and so closely to the brink of disaster, into which I would pull down not only my existing creations but with them also the greater and more general endeavors that lay at the root of my works

and for which those very works of mine in return form the foundation. The
Berlin corporal, the Hamburg moneybags, the Rhenish pastor, they would
be jubilant since there would be confirmation of what they believed they
always already knew about Heine. I could already hear their wolfish howl
of triumph, already could feel them assailing me, and I became very miserable, dear Brother. Steege, Ludwig, who was looking at me so mutely,
finally explained himself:

STEEGE: I'd require a letter of introduction from you to a really important
        personage in Paris society, in which I have determined to seek my
        fortune! I'm thinking of remaining in Paris and becoming a rich
        man. You must open up the door to the haute volée for me, Heine!
        That would be my wish! If you were to fulfill this small favor, I'd
        forget our trivial quarrel with all my heart. I'd also be grateful for
        a modest sum. I had heavy expenses, engaging three extras for a
        small comedy that I had the *honor* of presenting for the most famous
        poet of the day . . .

HEINE 2: Again that ominous word, a concept of which nobody has a correct
concept. An empty vessel into which every epoch pours a different soup
that the following epoch has to spoon up. It's something eternally incompar-
able. The honor of a virgin is different from that of a soldier: If he falls,
his is recognized—not hers, in the same situation! In addition, there are
two qualities to every honor: one smaller and one larger, and the heart-
rending thing consists of the fact that you cannot possess both at the same
time. To keep the larger you must frequently give up the smaller. To decide
between them both means a decision between two entirely different forms
of existence, and even he who is not aware of that chooses anyway. I also
have done it. And I know how posterity will judge my choice. Greetings and
an embrace

                                        from your brother, Heinrich

17

COMMENTATOR: We need not out of a mutual mistrust provide fodder for a standing army of many hundreds of thousands of murderers. We will achieve peace and prosperity and freedom. My life remains dedicated to this end. It is my charge. The hate of my enemies can bear witness that I have till now conducted this charge faithfully and honorably. I will always show myself to be worthy of that hate.

AFTERWORD

WHEN THE TEXTS THAT APPEAR ON THE PRECEDING PAGES WERE WRITTEN, translated, and published for the first time in the magazine DIMENSION, neither their authors nor the editor, A. Leslie Willson, had any idea of collecting them one day and presenting them to students—and also to other readers in the United States—as selections in a *Reader*. That is an advantage at the very start. Behind this *Reader* there is no official position, much less critical censure. The editor did not knit his brow deliberating about how these poems might be utilized for instruction, or about which stories might have a classical quality that would outlast the day. This *Reader* does not put literature on a pedestal inscribed "Do not touch!" No, with a profusion of exciting texts it meets halfway those who are learning the German language and those who want to become acquainted with its authors and with the places where they live and receive their inspiration.

The texts have the advantage of immediacy. It shows in the poems, stories, novel chapters, and radio plays: Most came directly from the desks of the authors to the desk of the editor. They establish the temperaments of their authors, the times when they were written, and much information about the countries in which German is spoken and where there exist comparable but also completely individual difficulties concerning life and its commonplace qualities. Even more, the chosen texts say something about what—to use a catchword—we might call the "political" and "cultural" situation. In addition these are texts from four different geographic and ethnographic European areas: from Austria and German-speaking Switzerland and from the two countries that "Germany" is still divided into and in which opposite social orders and governments prevail.

The selection begins with the year 1968—a year that in retrospect we recognize as a cutoff point, where something old came to an end and something new began. The magazine DIMENSION began in 1968, too, and the authors of the "Letters from Germany"—with which each issue begins—recorded it historically. "No time for esthetics," Hanspeter Krüger wrote in volume 1, number 1, 1968. Literature had doubts about itself at the time. It defended itself against "pretty writing." It expressed opposition, not just against the the war in Vietnam but against traditional, middle-class, petrified ideals. It chanced upon opportunities; it proposed utopias; it pleaded for "changes." It also brought a concession of more attention and more influence to writers in the estimation of the public.

In literature—and not only in German literature—such cutoff points have been repeated many times. Tendencies, fashions, and new thrusts alternated with one another. The "literature of the seventies," which defines this selection, differs from the previous decades; and in retrospect today we can discern its accomplishments and peculiarities. To begin with, lyric poetry played an important role. Never was its effect so immediate, its language so clear, its testimony so transferable to the life and behavior of people of all classes. In East Germany lyric poetry disengaged itself from the program prescribed by cultural functionaries. Hence it came in conflict with censorship. True, because of the poems authors in East Germany were imprisoned, reprimanded, or expelled from the country. The lyric poetry of Austria carried on with experimental poetry—which had elsewhere become silent in the middle of the sixties—in a playful way, often even in a cabaret style.

It became evident in the middle of the decade how prose, above all the novel, acquired a broader and broader scope. Young storytellers—an extraordinary number in Switzerland—caused astonishment because of the perfection of their first novels and the additional newly won representation of previously hidden realities. Authors of all generations vied with one another in the construction of themes drawn from life that had previously scarcely been noticed: for example, life in a factory or in an office, life in skyscrapers or in suburban developments, and—again and again—age, sickness, and death. Women described their situations and publicized their newly defined roles and their independence in a masculine-oriented environment. Authors of both sexes and of all generations occupied themselves (and occupy themselves still) with the search for the past, going back to the beginning of the century. Those in their forties, who were still children in the Nazi years and the years of World War II, scrutinized in true detective fashion the behavior of their fathers during the Third Reich. On the other hand drama and radio plays stagnated. Thus there were no new plays presented on the stage that could have surpassed the effectiveness of pieces by Rolf Hochhuth, Peter Weiss, Tankred Dorst, Thomas Bernhard, Martin Walser, Heiner Müller, and Peter Hacks, who were already on the scene.

A quick sketch of the background of the times and its literature could be used as a frame for the collected texts that have appeared during these twelve years in the magazine DIMENSION. Authors of all generations have participated. Hermann Kesten still represents the literature of the twenties and thirties, as well as exile literature. After him comes the much larger flock of authors who began to write after 1945 and who laid a foundation for a new beginning, who consciously meant to be contrasted with a literature that had served the system of government and remained indifferent to its inhumanity. Ilse Aichinger, Martin Walser, Siegfried Lenz, Stephan Hermlin are numbered among them. H.C. Artmann, Horst Bienek, Gisela Elsner, Walter Helmut Fritz, Hugo Loetscher, Angelika Mechtel, Gabriele Wohmann, among others, came on the literary scene for the first time in the fifties. Among the youngest authors who made their first appearances in the climate of the year 1968 special attention should be given to Wolf Wondratschek, Rolf Dieter Brinkmann, and Jürgen Theobaldy, the latter two primarily also because, in their frankly hostile attacks on previous literature, they not only carried on a controversy but also knew how to prove their "subjectivity" and "sensibility" poetically and theoretically. Their models were American authors of the post-beat generation. They—the great American authors—beginning with Ernest

Hemingway, William Faulkner, and William Carlos Williams through Jack Kerouac, Allen Ginsberg, and Gregory Corso to Frank O'Hara, Charles Bukowski, Ted Berrigan, and others, were models for a democratic literature rich in form and theme, more for authors in the Federal Republic of Germany than in the other German-speaking areas.

This *Reader* would be imperfectly characterized if events that occurred in its background and resulted in a new chapter of German-American literary exchange were not mentioned here. The meeting of the Group 47 at Princeton University in 1966 gave A. Leslie Willson, who was present as a member of the audience, the impetus to establish the magazine DIMENSION and also to arrange for the unique visiting lectureship for German-language authors at The University of Texas at Austin. Year after year since 1967 German authors have come to the Department of Germanic Languages there—and come still—in order to teach seminars and colloquia in literature; better yet, to embody and to champion literature. And this very presence is incorporated into the *Reader*. Not even in the literature of the four German-speaking countries themselves is there a comparable volume.

Cologne, 20 January 1981   HANS BENDER
                                                   translated by Jeanne R. Willson

AUTHORS AND TRANSLATORS

ILSE AICHINGER (1921–) was born in Vienna and studied medicine. In 1953 she married the late German poet Günter Eich. Best known as a storyteller, as in the collection *The Bound Man* (1956), she is also a novelist, *Herod's Children* (1963), and the author of radio plays and poems. *Ilse Aichinger*, with a selection in English translation by J.C. Alldridge, appeared in 1969.

H(ANS) C(ARL) ARTMANN (1921–) lives in Salzburg. He is known as a polyglot and, an irrepressible experimentalist, he is a choreographer of style and literary modes. A best-selling author of poetry and extravagant prose, and a translator from English, Spanish, French, and Swedish into German, he has yet to have one of his own books published in English.

GUIDO BACHMANN (1940–) was born in Lucerne and lives in Bern. He is the author of novels, two volumes of poetry, and several shorter prose pieces but no volume has appeared in English.

THOMAS I. BACON, who has a Ph.D. from The University of Texas at Austin, taught at Furman and now is on the faculty of Texas Tech University in Lubbock.

JUREK BECKER (1937–) was born in Poland. After surviving concentration camp incarceration he studied philosophy in East Berlin after World War II and received international acclaim for his novel *Jacob the Liar* (1975), which also became a remarkable film. An uncompromising literary artist and a born raconteur, he is the author of other novels and a recent collection of stories. He was visiting writer at Oberlin College in the spring term of 1978. He now lives in West Berlin.

HANS BENDER (1919–) was co-founder (with Walter Höllerer) and editor from 1954 to 1981 of the most distinguished literary magazine in Germany, *Akzente*. Bender is acclaimed as a master of the short story and as an anthologist of unerring taste. As an arbiter of the German literary scene, always independent and selective, his first publications of a host of contemporary German-language authors make *Akzente* a who's who of German writing today. Bender was visiting lecturer in the fall of 1968 and again in the fall of 1979 at The University of Texas at Austin.

THOMAS BERNHARD (1931–) was born in Holland of Austrian parents and is a leading author of Austria, principally as a novelist, *Gargoyles* (1970), and dramatist of joyless art, as in *The Force of Habit* (1976). His characters seem obsessed with violence and death.

HORST BIENEK (1930–) was born in Silesia and spent five years after World War II interned in a prison camp in Siberia. The fantasies of a prisoner in isolation are contained in his novel (which he filmed) *The Cell* (1972, translated by Ursula Mahlendorf). In the manner of Borges he treats the Russian anarchist in *Bakunin, An Invention* (1977, translated by Ralph R. Read III). His first volume of a tetralogy describing events on the German-Polish border on the eve of World War II is *The First Polka* (1978, translated by Ralph R. Read III). Bienek is a lyric poet of rare vision and voice.

GERALD BISINGER (1936–) was born in Vienna but has long lived principally in Berlin, an associate with Walter Höllerer of the Berlin Literary Colloquium. He writes poems while traveling and is an editor.

J. JAFKOM BLAMSKAG is the pseudonym of James F. Berger, Sherry L. Fuzesy, Wendy L. Guggenheim, Herbert Johnson III, Elwynne Johnson, Robert G. Kelly, Charles Korman, Thomas W. Leonhardt, Pamela Mar, Robert J. Matthews, and Margarethe Sparing, who undertook a team translation of poems by Rudolf Helmut Reschke under the guidance of A. Leslie Willson at the University of California at Berkeley in 1971.

VOLKER BRAUN (1939–) was born in Dresden. After studies in philosophy at the Karl Marx University in Leipzig he was a dramaturgist with the Berlin Ensemble. He is a poet and dramatist.

ROLF DIETER BRINKMANN (1940–1975) was a poet and novelist, born in Vechta. He was a leading exponent and translator of American pop and underground literature, as represented in the collection *ACID* (1969). He championed confrontations with a world out of joint with his own bursts of creative and desperate fury, though underneath the eccentric veneer he was a deeply loving and singular man. The first volume of his collected poetry, *Standphotos*, was published in 1980. In the spring of 1974 he was visiting lecturer in the Department of Germanic Languages at The University of Texas at Austin.

ALLEN H. CHAPPEL is an associate professor of German at the University of New Orleans.

FRANKIE SUIT DENTON studied at The University of Texas at Austin and later taught Scandinavian studies at the University of Wisconsin, Madison.

HILDE DOMIN (1912–) was born in Cologne. Impending political events caused her to leave Germany in 1932, and she lived in Italy, England, the Dominican Republic, Spain, and the United States before returning to Heidelberg in 1954. An intrepid literary critic, she is the author of volumes of poetry and a novel, none of which have been translated into English.

GISELA ELSNER (1937–) was born in Nuremberg. She studied in Vienna and lived in London, Paris, and Hamburg before moving to Munich. A commentator on society's trivia and brutality, she is the author of stories and novels, such as *The Giant Dwarfs* (1964).

MICHAEL P. ELZAY, a New York banking executive, studied at Duke University and lives on Long Island.

JAMES FEUGE, a graduate with a Ph.D. in language pedagogy from The University of Texas at Austin, is a part-time rancher in the Texas hill country.

HUBERT FICHTE (1935–) was born in Perleberg (now East Germany) and resides in Hamburg, when not trekking around in the jungles of South America and the Caribbean islands, pursuing studies in the rites of syncretistic Afro-American religions. His novels, such as *Die Palette* (1968) and *Versuch über die Pubertät* (1974), are concerned largely with society's outsiders. None of his works has been translated into English.

ERICH FITZBAUER (1927–) was born in Vienna, near which he now lives. He is the author of stories and poems that explore creative artistic impulses and he is, at the same time, a consummate watercolorist and graphic artist.

WOLFGANG H. FLEISCHER (1940–) is an Austrian writer of stories and dramas. He has made a career in preparing literary films for television, most recently one on Joseph Roth. He publishes art criticism and is involved in the writing of film scenarios for television.

KARLHANS FRANK (1937–) is a poet, novelist, and anthologist of children's stories. His work is permeated with irrepressible wordplays and reflects a continuing preoccupation with creative efforts in new directions, as in the novel *Willi kalt und heiß* (1978).

DIETER FRINGELI (1942–) was born in Bern, where he still lives. He studied at the University of Freiburg im Breisgau and is the author of volumes of poetry and the editor of an anthology of ninety-seven Swiss-German authors, *Gut zum Druck* (1972).

MAX FRISCH (1911–) was born in Zurich and became an architect before turning to literary ventures that made his name world famous with the publication of the novel *I'm Not Stiller* (1954). A renowned diarist and essayist, with works such as *Sketchbook* (1974), Frisch is also a notable dramatist, author of *The Chinese Wall* (1951), *Count Oderland* (1962), and *Biedermann and the Firebugs* (1962). Other plays include *Don Juan or the Love of Geometry* (1969) and *Biography* (1969). Other novels include *Homo Faber: A Report* (1959) and *A Wilderness of Mirrors* (1965), the English translation of *Mein Name sei Gantenbein* (1964). The fragmentary story published here was revised and expanded into the short novel *Man in the Holocene* (1980, translated by Geoffrey Skelton), considered by some to be Frisch's best work.

WALTER HELMUT FRITZ (1929–) was born in Karlsruhe, where he teaches today and is a voluminous author of poetry and prose. He is a member of the Mainz Academy of the Sciences and of Literature.

RICHARD GERLACH (1899–1975) was born in Hanover and became a well-known naturalist author and poet. He published books on fish, reptiles, and volumes of general interest on animals. He was the author of six collections of poems, many of which contain lyric portraits of animals.

DAVID GILL, a native of England, studied German at University College, London, and at Oxford. He is well known as a translator of contemporary German poets.

MINETTA ALTGELT GOYNE holds a Ph.D. in German literature from The University of Texas at Austin and lives in Arlington, Texas.

MARTIN GREGOR-DELLIN (1926–) was born in Naumberg and lives in Munich, where he works as a literary critic. A biographer (Wagner), he is also a storyteller and novelist. One novel, *The Lamppost* (1962), has been published in English.

E.W. GUNDEL, who earned a Ph.D. in German literature from The University of Texas at Austin, teaches in Hawaii.

PETER HACKS (1928–) was born in Breslau and is known principally as a dramatist and theoretician of the theater. He studied in Munich and moved to East Germany in 1955. His play *Omphale* appeared in English translation (by André Lefevere) in DIMENSION in 1973. He has produced a number of books for children.

BRIAN L. HARRIS, who holds a Ph.D. in German literature from The University of Texas at Austin, lives in Colorado.

EDWARD HARRIS is an associate professor of Germanic languages at the University of Cincinnati.

HERBERT HECKMANN (1930–) was born in Frankfurt am Main, where he studied Baroque tragedy. A prize-winning novelist and short story writer, who also has written children's books, Heckmann has the rare ability to poke fun at his own culture with sharp but loving satire.

HUBERT HEINEN is an associate professor in the Department of Germanic Languages at The University of Texas at Austin.

HELMUT HEIßENBÜTTEL (1921–), who was born in Rüstringen near Wilhelmshaven and now lives in Stuttgart, is best known for his rejection of traditional literary modes and styles. He transforms words and syntactic units and combines and atomizes them in an effort to depict a new reality.

STEPHAN HERMLIN (1915–) was born in Chemnitz (now Karl-Marx-Stadt). From 1936 to 1945 he was in voluntary exile in Egypt, Palestine, and England, finally being interned in Switzerland after wartime involvement in Spain and France. He returned to East Germany in 1947, where he has established himself as a leading poet, storyteller, and translator of Verlaine and Neruda.

WOLFGANG HILDESHEIMER (1916–), born in Hamburg, lived in England and worked for British forces in Palestine during World War II. Since 1957 he has lived in Poschiavo, Switzerland. A storyteller, novelist, and author of plays for stage and radio, as well as an artist, Hildesheimer depicts humankind's struggle for sense in a world pervaded by anxiety. His biography of *Mozart* is the only one of his works to appear in English (1981).

EBERHARD HILSCHER (1927–) lives in East Berlin. He is the author of volumes of stories as well as of critical books on Thomas Mann, Arnold Zweig, and Gerhard Hauptmann. The four chapters taken from his novel about the medieval poet Walter von der Vogelweide (1976) emphasize the stylistic virtuosity of which Hilscher is capable. He is at work on a mammoth novel that focuses on personalities who contributed to the shaping of twentieth-century culture.

DIETER HOFFMANN (1934–) was born in Dresden, where he attended art school and worked as an editor before moving to West Germany in 1957. He lives in Frankfurt am Main and is an art critic and the author of several volumes of poetry.

ASTRID IVASK, born in Latvia, has published collections of verse in her native language. She has translated stories by Heimito von Doderer and Herbert Eisenreich, among others. She lives in Norman, Oklahoma.

ERNST JANDL (1925–) was born in Vienna, where he lives still. Now retired as a schoolteacher, Jandl is a prolific and inventive writer, known for his unremitting linguistic experimentation and flagrant wit. A superb performer of his works, he embodies nonstop energy. His play *Aus der Fremde* (1980) won widespread critical acclaim.

UWE JOHNSON (1934–) was born in Kammin, Pomerania, studied German literature under Hans Mayer in Leipzig, and in 1959 moved to West Berlin. He now lives in England. His unorthodox literary style, combined with the subject matter of his first published novel—the dilemma of East and West Germany—won him immediate recognition in 1959 with *Speculations about Jacob* (1963). That work was followed in English by the novels *Two Views* (1966) and *The Third Book about Achim* (1967). His massive, still unfinished four-volume *Jahrestage* (1970 ff.) has appeared in part in English under the title of *Anniversaries* (1975). The essay *A Part of New York* was written as a commentary for a German television documentary and furnished background text for portions of *Anniversaries*, much of which takes place in New York.

HERMANN KESTEN (1900–) was born in Nuremberg. He was forced to flee Germany in 1932 after he attacked Hitlerism in a novel, *Der Scharlatan*. He lived for a time in Amsterdam and then moved to New York, where he became an American citizen. Since 1952 he has lived in Rome. He is the author of novels, *Joseph Breaks Free* (1930) and *Happy Man!* (1935), fictionalized biographies, such as that of *Ferdinand and Isabella* (1946) and Philipp II, *I, the King* (1939), and topical works, *Children of Guernica* (1939). A novel of Germany between wars is *The Twins of Nuremberg* (1946), which was published in English translation before it appeared in German (1947), not an unusual occurrence among German exile authors. Kesten has written plays, but he indulged his talent for poetry only after he turned seventy, with *Ich bin der ich bin* (I Am Who I Am), published in 1974.

HANS KROLICZAK (1936–), born in Pomerania, is a Cologne homicide detective. He takes material for his poems from the milieu of his police work and has been widely anthologized.

GÜNTER KUNERT (1929–) was born in Berlin, where he lived in an eastern suburb until the fall of 1979, when he made an anguished move to Itzehoe near Hamburg, after a valiant but futile attempt to come to terms with the strictures placed on writers by East Germany. An adamant critic of those who indulge indignities on humankind, Kunert is a prodigious talent, author of poems, stories, novels, radio plays, and essays, as well as being an artist. Many of his works were published either only in West Germany or first there, a practice that irritated East German bureaucrats intolerably. Kunert's works have been translated into Dutch, Italian, French, and Swedish, but he has no volume in English. He guest-edited a special East German issue of DIMENSION in 1973, after spending a semester in the fall of 1972 at The University of Texas at Austin as guest-lecturer.

ANDRÉ LEFEVERE, a native of Belgium, is a professor of English literature in Antwerp. Lefevere is a theoretician of literary translation, as well as a practitioner, and is the author of *Translating Poetry* (1975) and *Translating Literature: The German Tradition from Luther to Rosenzweig* (1979).

SIEGFRIED LENZ (1926–) was born in Lyck (East Prussia) and studied at the University of Hamburg. Known principally as a novelist, Lenz is also the author of stories and radio and stage plays. His works include *The Survivor* (1965), a translation of *Stadtgespräche* (1963); *The German Lesson* (1972), a masterful novel on the subject of obsessive duty; *An Exemplary Life* (1976); and most recently, *The Heritage* (1981), the translation by Krishna Winston of *Heimatmuseum*, a novel that defends an act of arson as a means of avoiding propagandistic exploitation. *The Lightship* (1960) is a collection of stories. The story printed in the present volume was adapted by Lenz into a two-act play.

EARL N. LEWIS is a retired professor of German from Louisiana State University in Baton Rouge.

HUGO LOETSCHER (1929–) was born in Zurich. He is a novelist, playwright, and literary critic, as well as a trenchant commentator and political analyst.

ONDRA LYSOHORSKY (1905–) was born in Frydek in the Ostrava region of what is now Czechoslovakia, the ninth child of a miner. He studied in Prague and in the 1930s published volumes of poetry in his native Lachian idiom. After the German occupation of Czechoslovakia he went to Poland, was interned for a short time by the Soviet army, and after the war taught in Moscow. The Czech authorities have banned his Lachian books, although he has been translated into Czech and other languages. His *Selected Poems* appeared in 1971, in translation by several hands, among them his friend and admirer, the late W. H. Auden. Lysohorsky writes still in German and lives in retirement in Bratislava.

MAX MAETZ (a pseudonym) was born in Asten, Austria, in 1945. Formerly a farm laborer, he acquired a large farm near Linz by marriage. Now he writes for entertainment and farms as a profession.

FRIEDERIKE MAYRÖCKER (1924–) was born in Vienna, where she later taught English in Viennese schools. Best known as a laconic, imagistic poet, she is also the author of experimental prose, skeptical in tone, and radio plays. She draws her images from a bottomless reservoir of pungent awareness of life's frailties and strengths, often finding that literary collage works best to transmit her vision.

INGEBORG MCCOY, who holds a Ph.D. in German literature from The University of Texas at Austin, teaches at Southwest Texas State University in San Marcos.

SAMMY MCLEAN teaches German and comparative literature at the University of Washington in Seattle. He is himself a poet.

RUTH and MATTHEW MEAD, natives of England, have lived in Bad Godesberg for many years. They are sought-after translators of contemporary German poets. Matthew Mead is also a poet himself.

ANGELIKA MECHTEL (1943–) was born in Dresden and lives in an old farmhouse near Munich. She is a prolific poet and novelist, as well as a writer of short stories and documentaries, notably with investigations of the fate of aged and nearly forgotten writers and that of women whose men are in prison. She has not been translated into English.

CHRISTOPH MECKEL (1935–) was born in Berlin and grew up in Freiburg im Breisgau. At the age of nineteen Meckel published a remarkable book of drawings, *Moël*, which was followed by others, each with about fifty drawings and a laconic text. In later works the literary aspect overshadows the graphic, but each complements the other. Meckel is a contemporary fabulist of enormous talent, who still does not have a volume in English translation.

JOHN K. MENZIES studied at The University of Texas at Austin and at the University of California at Berkeley. He presently is a teacher and administrator at the University of California at Santa Barbara.

CHARLES MERRILL obtained a Ph.D. degree in German literature at The University of Texas at Austin and is on the faculty of the University of North Carolina at Charlotte.

CHRISTOPHER MIDDLETON is professor of German at The University of Texas at Austin, a translator of rare insight, and himself the author of volumes of poetry and short prose. He is a member of the Berlin Academy of Fine Arts.

RICHARD MILLS studied German literature and computer science at The University of Texas at Austin. He is a translator of Hubert Fichte.

HELGA M. NOVAK (1935–) was born in Berlin. She is known principally as a lyric poet, though she is also the author of fiercely critical prose that confronts today's self-indulgent society.

PAUL T. O'HEARN (1948–1971), a brilliant young translator and poet who took his own life, studied at The University of Texas at Austin and the University of Illinois.

FRITZ VON OPEL (1899–1971) headed the Adam Opel Corporation which, under his leadership, became one of the largest automobile manufacturers in the world and a pioneer of rocket-powered, manned flight (1928). Opel indulged his proclivity for writing poetry at seventy when, in 1969, he published a volume of verse to critical acclaim. The present poem was written in the spring of 1970 when Opel experienced a premonition of the approaching death of his good friend Erich Maria Remarque (1898–1970).

EWALD OSERS (1917–) was born in England, where he is a distinguished translator of over fifty books, including works by Hans Habe, Ondra Lysohorsky, Hans-Jürgen Heise, and Reiner Kunze.

JULIA PENN received a Ph.D. in German literature from The University of Texas at Austin, a city in which she lives and works as a social worker.

GEORGE F. PETERS, who holds a Ph.D. from Stanford University in German literature, teaches at the University of New Mexico and is co-founder and co-director (with Peter Pabisch) of the German Summer School near Taos.

LUTZ RATHENOW (1952–) was born in Jena and lives in East Berlin. He has published poems in various magazines and anthologies in East and West Germany, but the publication of his first book of prose, *Mit dem Schlimmsten wurde schon gerechnet* (1979), only in West Germany, got him into trouble with East German overseers of literary activity. He is one of the more talented newer writers in East Germany.

RALPH R. READ III, associate professor in the Department of Germanic Languages at The University of Texas at Austin, has translated two books by Horst Bienek, *Bakunin* (1977) and *The First Polka* (1978). Read, who lost his sight several years ago, has just published a cookbook for the blind, *When the Cook Can't Look* (1981), with Continuum. Read is a beloved prize-winning teacher and an insistent and talented translator.

ARNO REINFRANK (1934–) was born in Mannheim and lived many years in England after 1955 before returning to Germany. The author of several volumes of poetry, he calls himself a "poet of facts."

CHRISTA REINIG (1926–) was born in Berlin and lived in East Germany until 1964, when she moved to her present home in Munich. She is the author of cool, observant poems, stories for children, and recent novels that come to grips with increasing feminine consciousness. In other works she is a master of grotesque satire. None of her books has been translated into English.

RUDOLF HELMUT RESCHKE (1931–) was born in Schneidemühl, Silesia, lived in Berlin, worked in Hamburg, and now resides in Gütersloh. He is a translator from the English and is himself principally a poet.

W.E. RICHARTZ (1927–1980) was the pseudonym of Walter Richard von Bebenburg, a chemist and prolific author of prose tales, dramas, and novels. He was a translator of Ring Lardner, H.L. Mencken, F. Scott Fitzgerald, Lewis Carroll, and Thoreau. He took his own life early in 1980.

HERMAN SALINGER is emeritus professor of German at Duke University and is well known as the translator of poetry by Karl Krolow, Rudolf Hagelstange, Wolfgang Weyrauch, and Peter Henisch. He is himself an occasional poet.

HARTMUT SCHNELL studied German literature at The University of Texas at Austin.

RAINER SCHULTE is professor of comparative studies at The University of Texas at Dallas, where he edits the *Translation Review* for the members of the American Literary Translators Association.

GARY A. SMITH, a graduate of The University of Texas at Austin, is on the faculty of the College of William and Mary in Williamsburg, Virginia.

PAUL SOLYN studied English at Indiana University and teaches at Linfield College in Oregon. He is a published poet himself.

GEROLD SPÄTH (1939–) was born in Rapperswil, Switzerland. He is the author of novels, such as *A Prelude to the Long Happy Life of Maxmilian Goodman* (1975), the English translation of *Unschlecht*, and others. He also has published a volume of stories. In 1979 he was the first recipient of the Döblin Prize.

PETER SPYCHER is professor of German at Oberlin College in Ohio, the author of critical studies of Dürrenmatt and Hesse, and an indefatigable translator.

PATRICIA R. STANLEY studied at the University of Virginia and teaches on the faculty of Florida State University in Tallahassee.

GUY STERN taught for many years at the University of Cincinnati and is now the vice president and provost at Wayne State University in Detroit.

JÜRGEN THEOBALDY (1944–) was born in Straßburg and lives in Berlin. He is principally a poet, the author of several volumes of lyrics, but he also works as editor and translator.

JOHANNES VAZULIK is associate professor in the Department of Modern Languages at North Dakota State University.

FRED VIEBAHN (1947–) was born in Cologne. He is a novelist and playwright. He was a fellow in the International Writers Program at the University of Iowa in the fall of 1976 and in the spring of 1977 was visiting lecturer in the Department of Germanic Languages at The University of Texas at Austin. He subsequently taught for two years at Oberlin College in Ohio, before returning to Germany.

MARTIN WALSER (1927–) was born at Wasserberg on Lake Constance. He earned a Ph.D. degree at the University of Munich with a dissertation on Franz Kafka, whose influence is apparent in Walser's early stories. His first long prose work was *Marriage in Philippsburg* (1961). One volume of a trilogy, *The Unicorn*, appeared in England in 1971. His best-selling short novel *A Runaway Horse* appeared in 1980 in English. The play *Acting Is Our Business* was published in 1969 in DIMENSION; a play about marital strife, *Home Front*, was published in 1972. Walser was visiting lecturer in the Department of Germanic Languages at The University of Texas at Austin in the fall of 1975.

DAVID WARD is working toward a Ph.D. in German literature at The University of Texas at Austin.

STEPHEN H. WEDGWOOD was a student in graduate studies in German literature at Indiana University. He was last seen in San Francisco.

WOLFGANG WEYRAUCH (1907–1980) was born in Königsberg and studied in Frankfurt am Main. An uninhibited storyteller, Weyrauch first became widely known just after World War II as an anthologist and promoter of literature, an activity he later continued as the founder of the Leonce and Lena Prize for poetry, for which he yearly selected a young poet for recognition. Weyrauch remained ever in the forefront of experimental literature in prose, poetry, and radio play, representative always of strong moral commitment.

A. LESLIE WILLSON, founder of DIMENSION (1968), is professor of German at The University of Texas at Austin. He is a member of the Mainz Academy of the Sciences and of Literature and is the holder of the Officer's Cross, First Class, of the Federal Republic of Germany and of the Goethe Medal from the Goethe Institute, Munich. Aside from numerous translations for DIMENSION and other periodicals, he has translated two plays by Günter Grass: *The Wicked Cooks* (1969) and (with Ralph Manheim) *Max* (1971). He edited the entries for German literature for the second edition of the *Columbia Dictionary of Modern European Literature* (1980).

JEANNE R. WILLSON is a librarian in the Barker Texas History Center at The University of Texas at Austin. She translates and edits unsparingly.

GABRIELE WOHMANN (1932–) was born in Darmstadt, where she still lives. Her poems, radio plays, numerous stories, and novels focus on social and family relationships, often pointing at human isolation and the ongoing search for identity. Many readers regret that none of her books have appeared in English translation.

CHRISTA WOLF (1929–) was born in Landsberg an der Warthe and is a leading novelist in East Germany. Her short novel *The Quest for Christa T.* appeared in English translation (by Christopher Middleton) in 1970. *Divided Heaven* (written in 1963) appeared in 1976. In 1978 a collection of her critical essays appeared under the title of *The Reader and the Writer*.

WOLF WONDRATSCHEK (1943–) was born in Rudolstadt in Thuringia. He is the author of poems, stories, and radio plays. A recipient of the Leonce and Lena Prize, he is best known as a best-selling poet.